KEIGO MAKI

3

SHIKIMORI'S
not just a cutie

Contents
volume.3

SHIKIMORI'S
not just a cutie

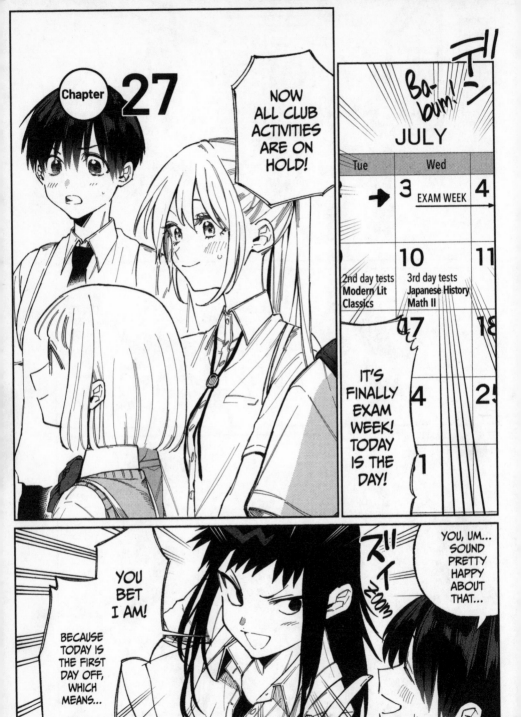

Chapter 27

NOW ALL CLUB ACTIVITIES ARE ON HOLD!

Ba-bum!

JULY

Tue	Wed	
→ **3** EXAM WEEK	**4**	
2nd day tests Modern Lit Classics	**10** 3rd day tests Japanese History Math II	**11**
17		**18**
4		**25**
1		

IT'S FINALLY EXAM WEEK! TODAY IS THE DAY!

YOU BET I AM!

BECAUSE TODAY IS THE FIRST DAY OFF, WHICH MEANS...

ZOOM

YOU, UM... SOUND PRETTY HAPPY ABOUT THAT...

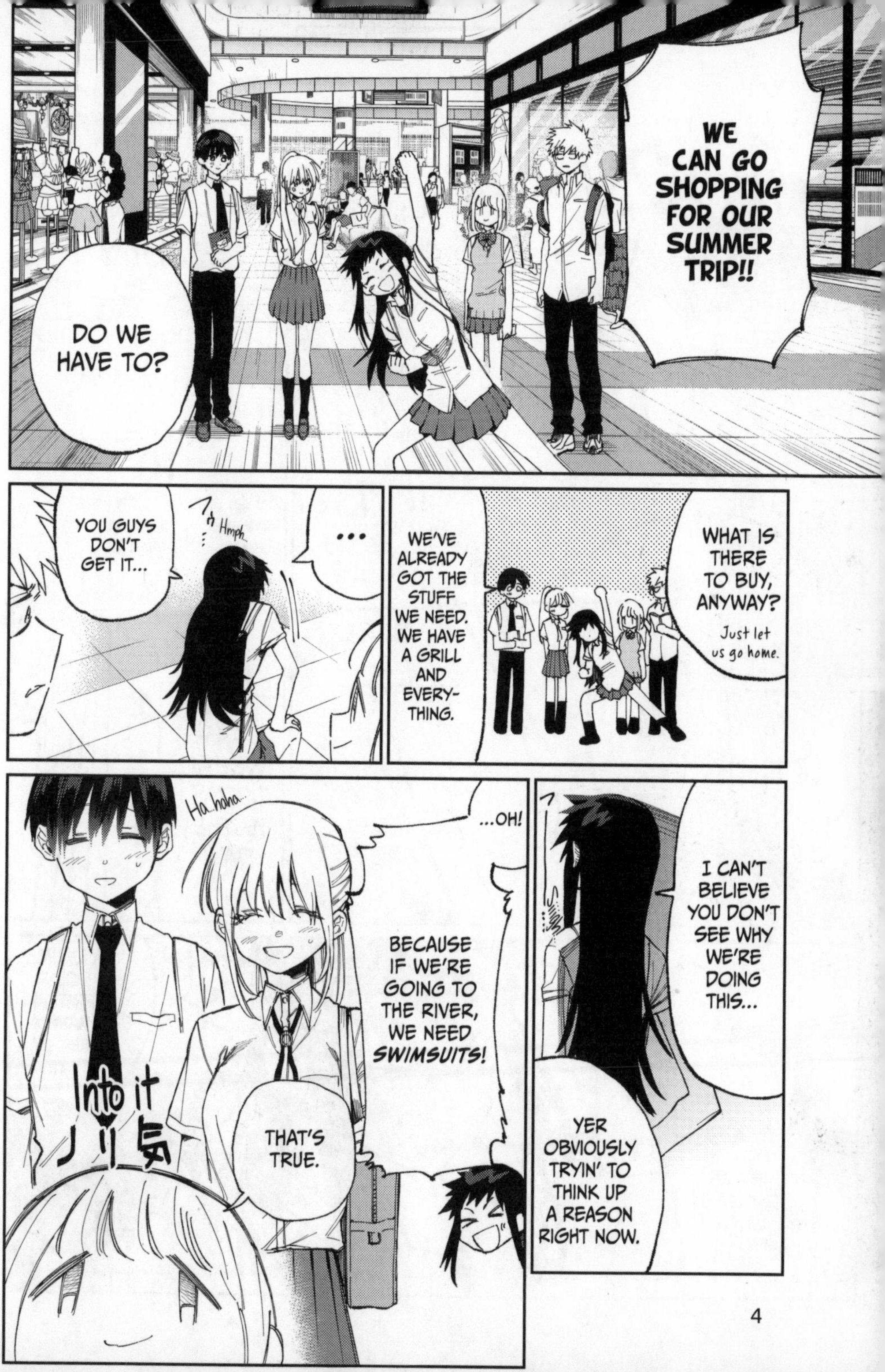
WE CAN GO SHOPPING FOR OUR SUMMER TRIP!!
DO WE HAVE TO?
WHAT IS THERE TO BUY, ANYWAY?
Just let us go home.
WE'VE ALREADY GOT THE STUFF WE NEED. WE HAVE A GRILL AND EVERY-THING.
...
Hmph...
YOU GUYS DON'T GET IT...
I CAN'T BELIEVE YOU DON'T SEE WHY WE'RE DOING THIS...
YER OBVIOUSLY TRYIN' TO THINK UP A REASON RIGHT NOW.
...OH!
BECAUSE IF WE'RE GOING TO THE RIVER, WE NEED SWIMSUITS!
Ha...haha...
THAT'S TRUE.
Into it
ノリ気

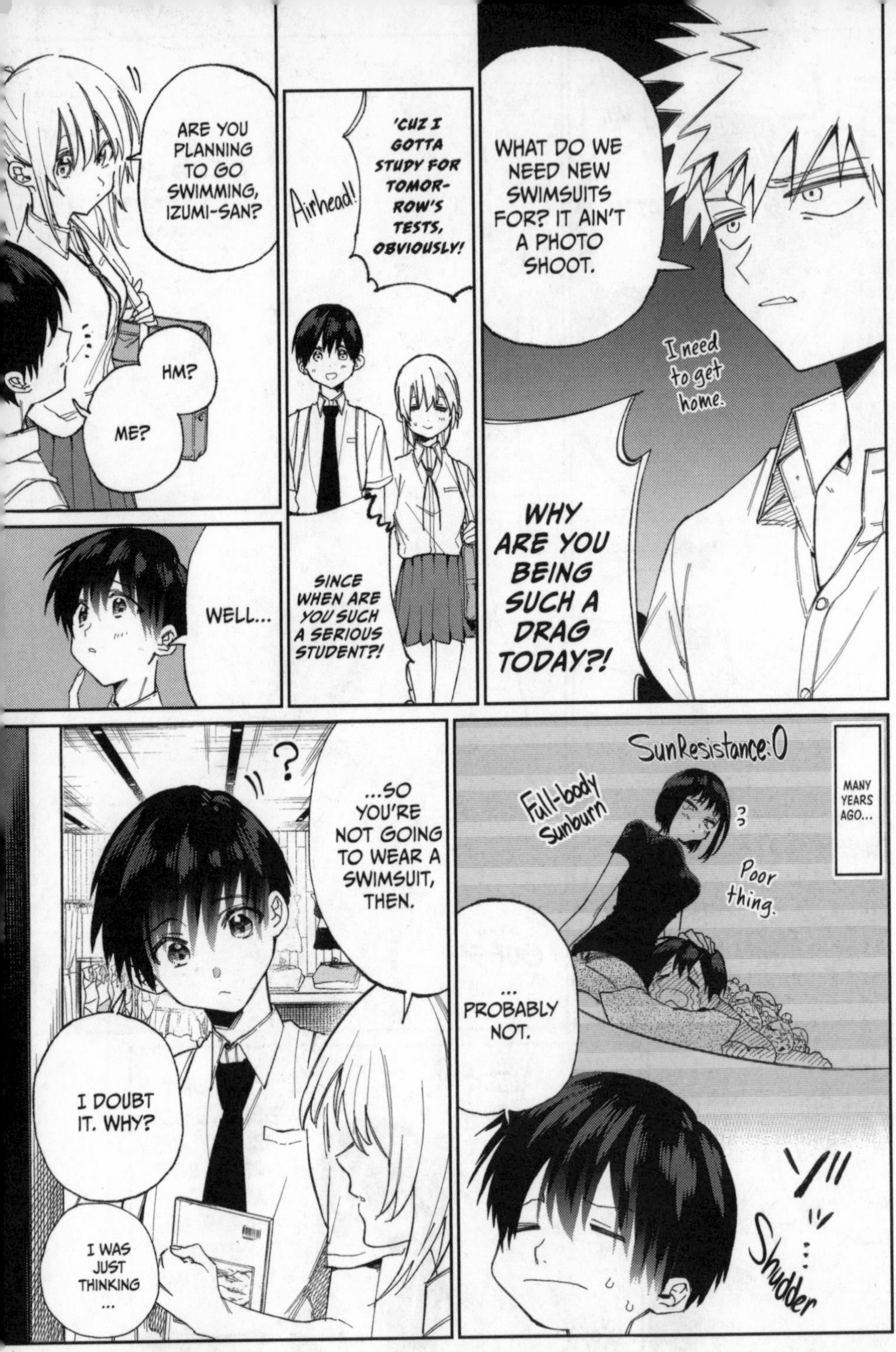

ARE YOU PLANNING TO GO SWIMMING, IZUMI-SAN?
HM?
ME?
WELL...
'CUZ I GOTTA STUDY FOR TOMORROW'S TESTS, OBVIOUSLY!
Airhead!
SINCE WHEN ARE YOU SUCH A SERIOUS STUDENT?!
WHAT DO WE NEED NEW SWIMSUITS FOR? IT AIN'T A PHOTO SHOOT.
I need to get home.
WHY ARE YOU BEING SUCH A DRAG TODAY?!
I DOUBT IT. WHY?
I WAS JUST THINKING ...
...SO YOU'RE NOT GOING TO WEAR A SWIMSUIT, THEN.
MANY YEARS AGO...
SunResistance:0
Full-body Sunburn
Poor thing.
... PROBABLY NOT.
Shudder

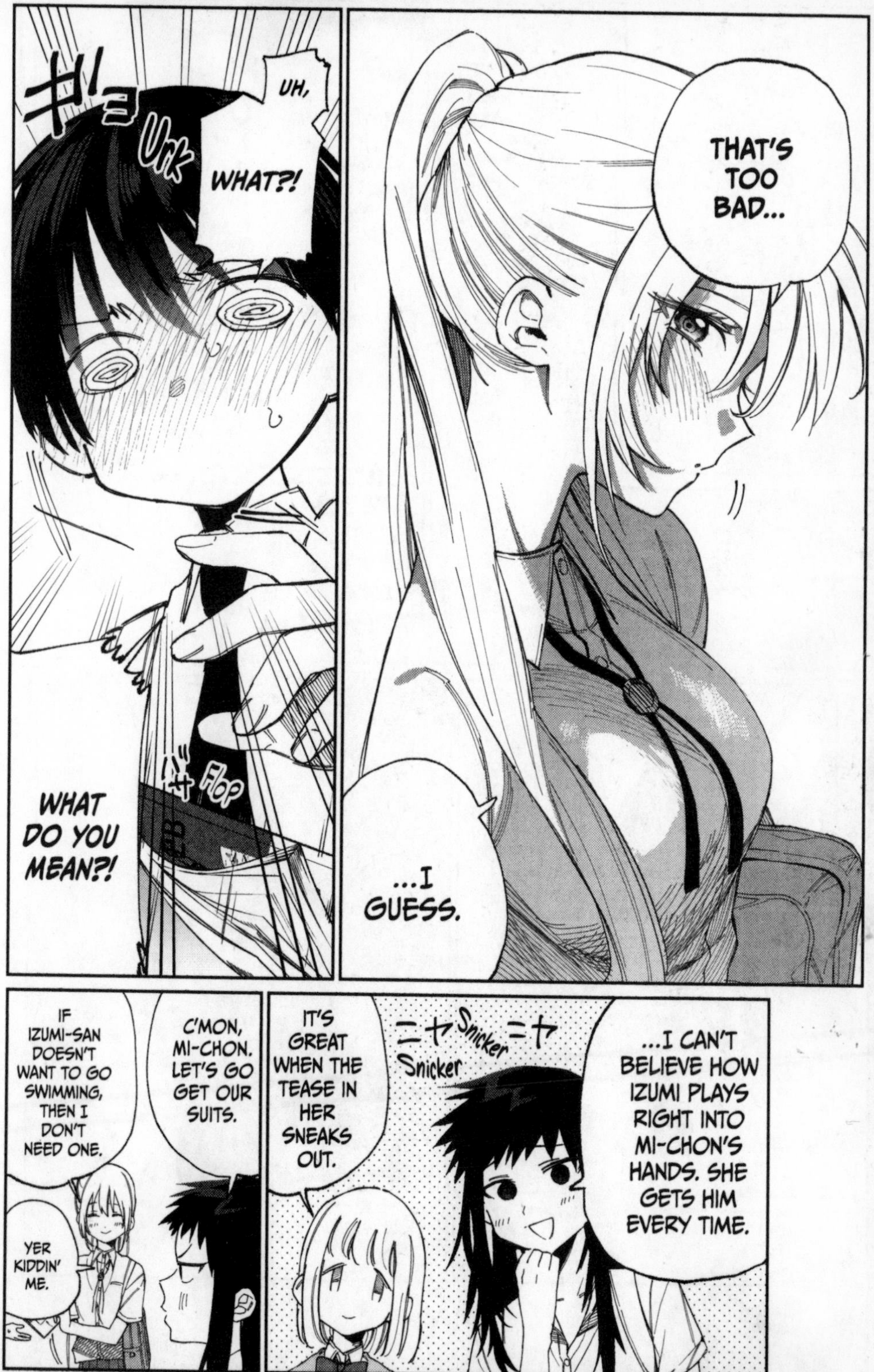
THAT'S TOO BAD...
...I GUESS.
UH, WHAT?!
Urk
ギョ
Flop
WHAT DO YOU MEAN?!
...I CAN'T BELIEVE HOW IZUMI PLAYS RIGHT INTO MI-CHON'S HANDS. SHE GETS HIM EVERY TIME.
ニヤ Snicker ニヤ Snicker
IT'S GREAT WHEN THE TEASE IN HER SNEAKS OUT.
C'MON, MI-CHON. LET'S GO GET OUR SUITS.
IF IZUMI-SAN DOESN'T WANT TO GO SWIMMING, THEN I DON'T NEED ONE.
YER KIDDIN' ME.

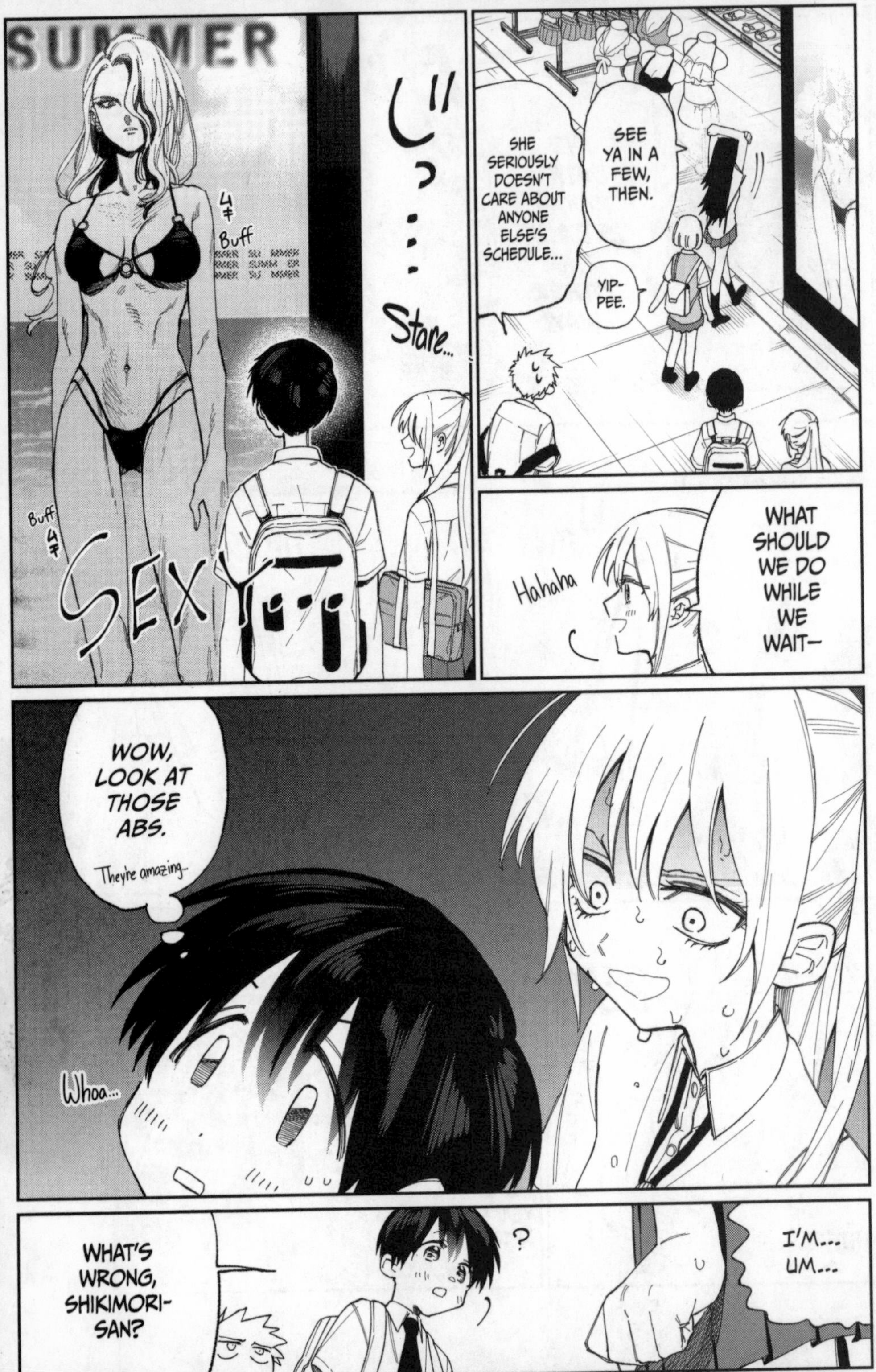
SEE YA IN A FEW, THEN.
SHE SERIOUSLY DOESN'T CARE ABOUT ANYONE ELSE'S SCHEDULE...
YIP-PEE.
WHAT SHOULD WE DO WHILE WE WAIT—
Hahaha
じっ…
Stare...
SUMMER
ムキ
Buff
Buff
ムキ
SEXY—
WOW, LOOK AT THOSE ABS.
They're amazing...
Whoa...
I'M... UM...
?
WHAT'S WRONG, SHIKIMORI-SAN?

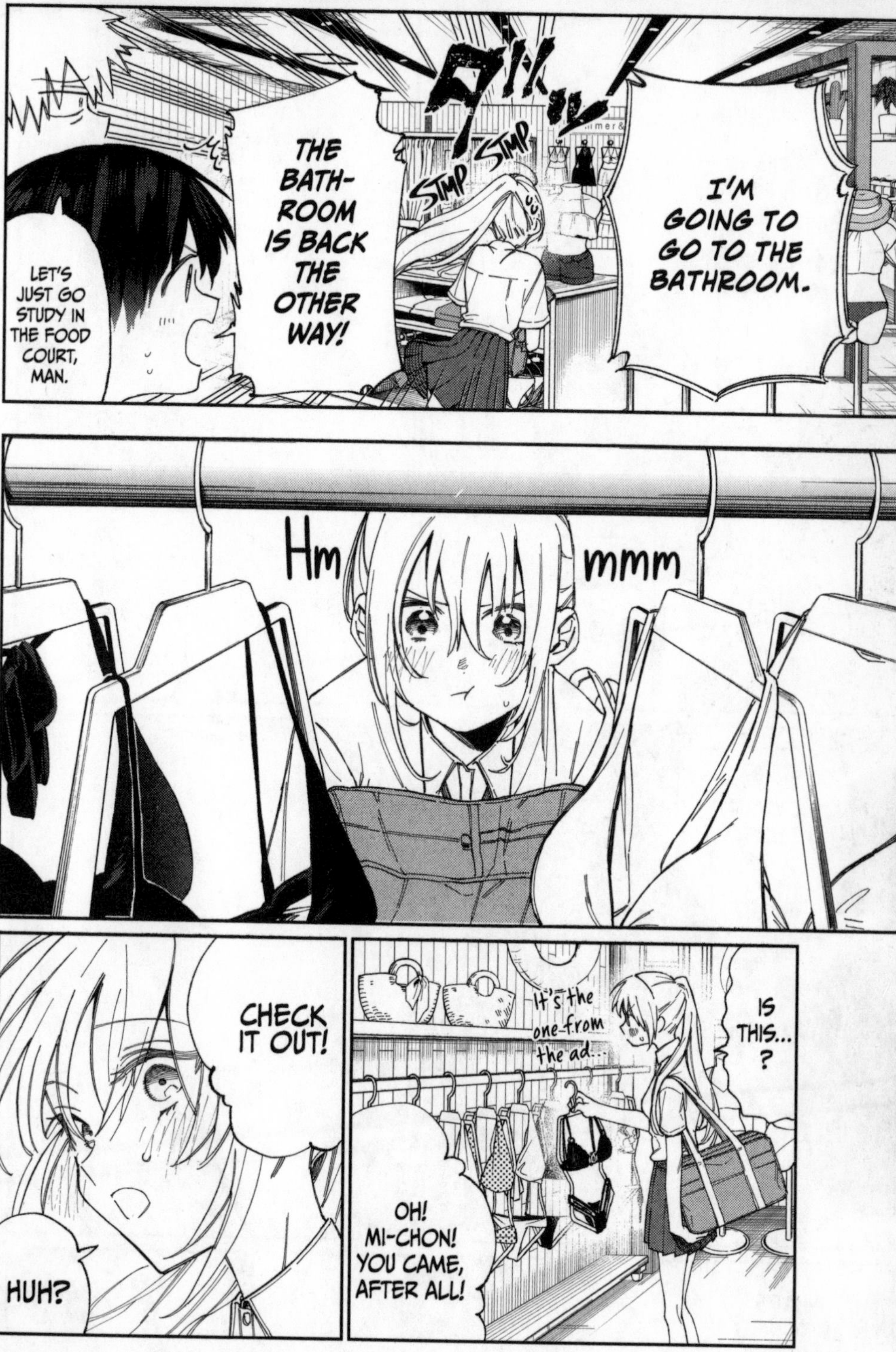
I'M GOING TO GO TO THE BATHROOM.
THE BATHROOM IS BACK THE OTHER WAY!
STMP STMP
LET'S JUST GO STUDY IN THE FOOD COURT, MAN.
Hmmmm
IS THIS...?
It's the one from the ad...
OH! MI-CHON! YOU CAME, AFTER ALL!
CHECK IT OUT!
HUH?

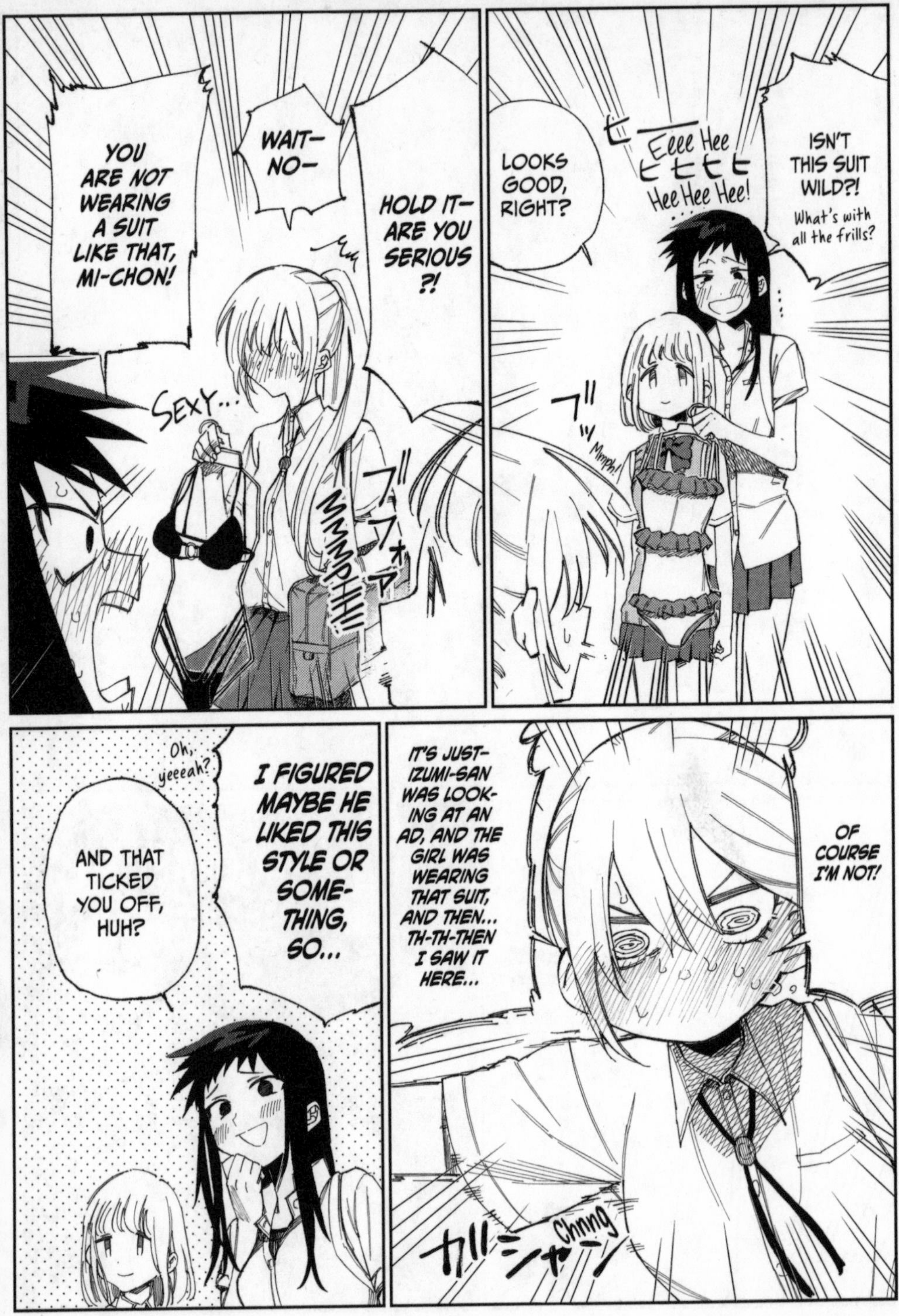
ISN'T THIS SUIT WILD?!
What's with all the frills?
Eeee Hee
Hee Hee Hee!
LOOKS GOOD, RIGHT?
Mmmph!
WAIT— NO—
HOLD IT— ARE YOU SERIOUS?!
YOU ARE NOT WEARING A SUIT LIKE THAT, MI-CHON!
SEXY...
MMMPH!!!
OF COURSE I'M NOT!
IT'S JUST— IZUMI-SAN WAS LOOKING AT AN AD, AND THE GIRL WAS WEARING THAT SUIT, AND THEN... TH-TH-THEN I SAW IT HERE...
Chnng
I FIGURED MAYBE HE LIKED THIS STYLE OR SOMETHING, SO...
Oh, yeeeah?
AND THAT TICKED YOU OFF, HUH?

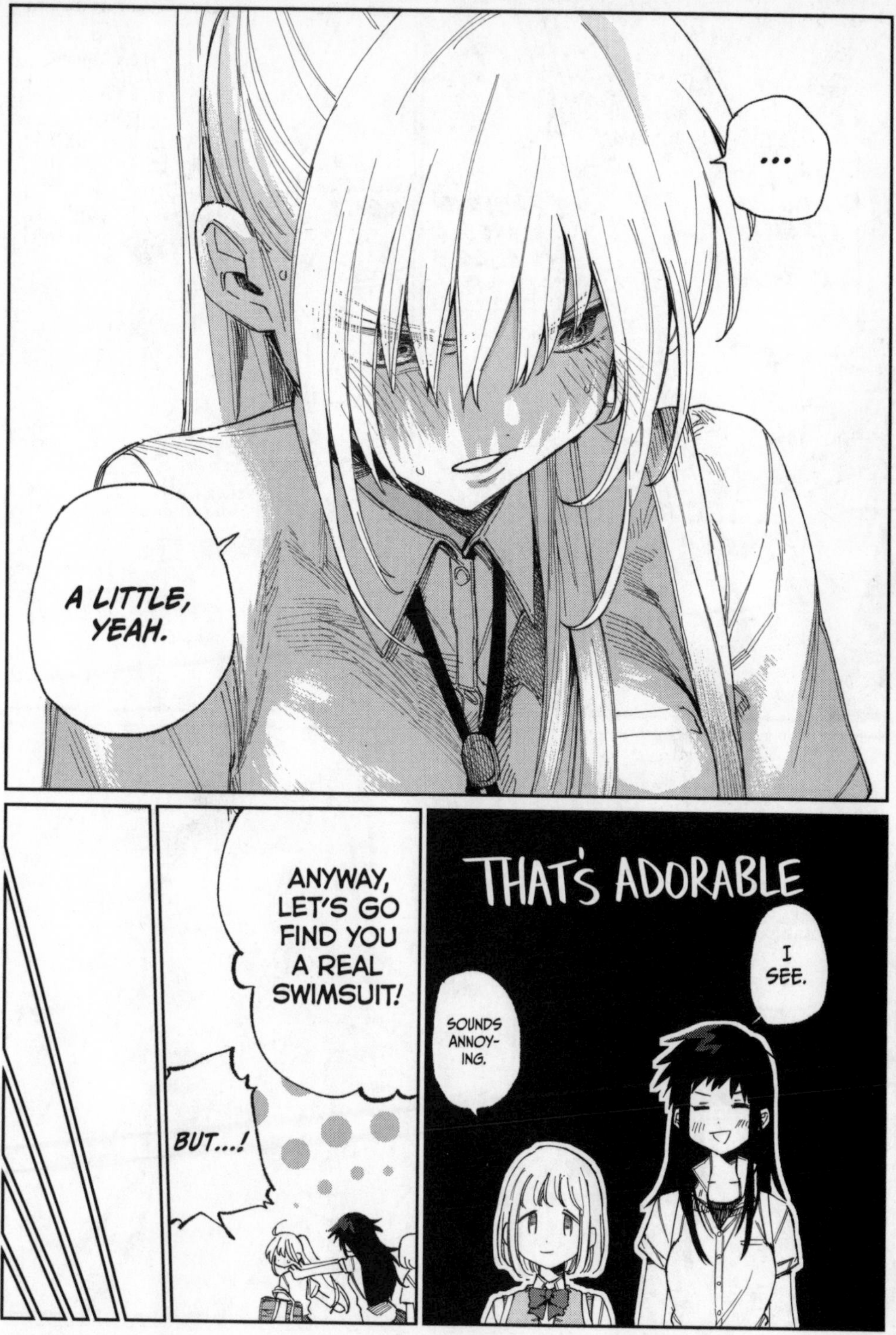
...
A LITTLE, YEAH.
THAT'S ADORABLE
I SEE.
SOUNDS ANNOY-ING.
ANYWAY, LET'S GO FIND YOU A REAL SWIMSUIT!
BUT...!

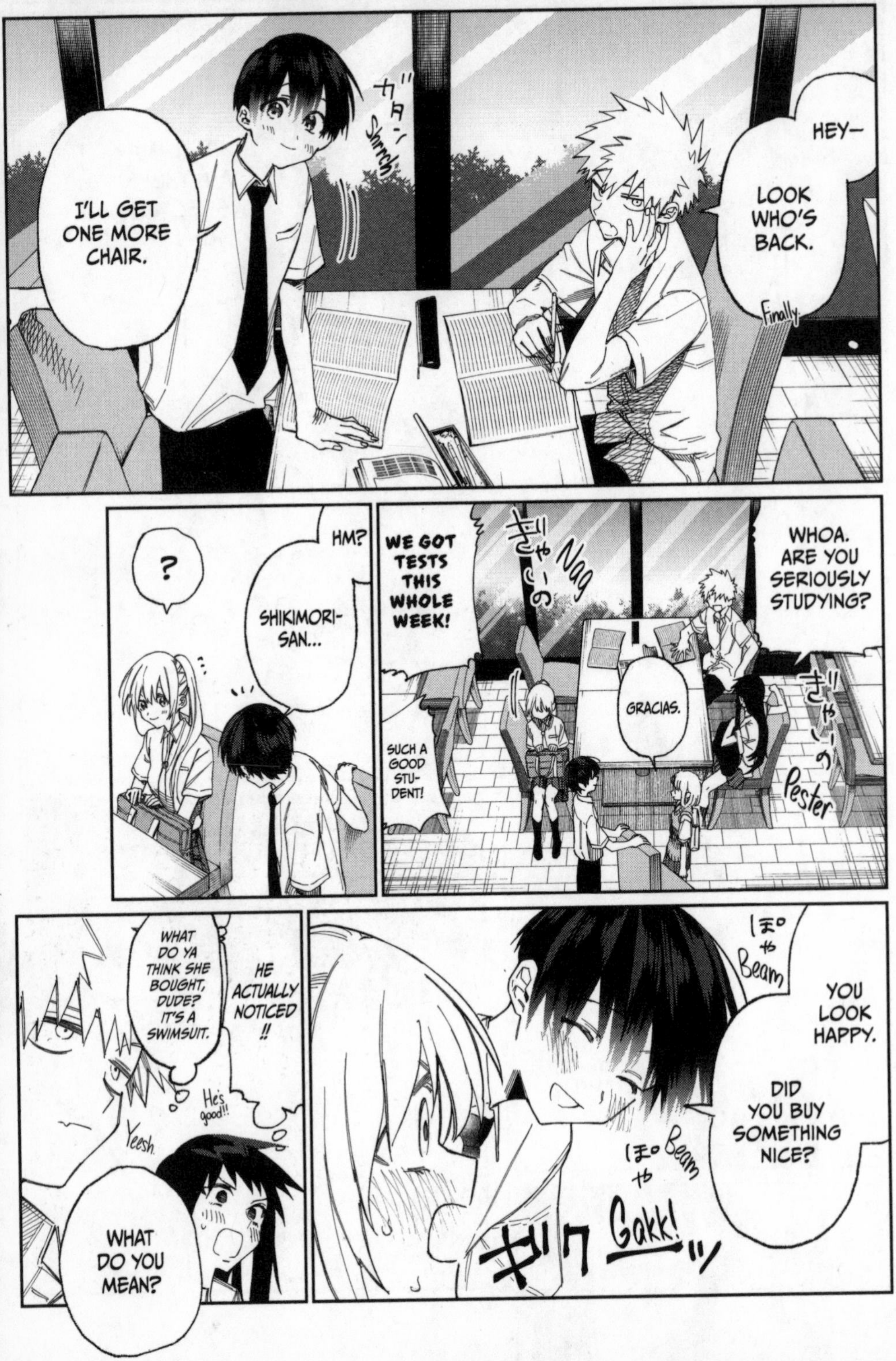
HEY—
LOOK WHO'S BACK.
Finally.
ガタン
Shrrrch
I'LL GET ONE MORE CHAIR.
WHOA. ARE YOU SERIOUSLY STUDYING?
ぎゃーの
Pester
GRACIAS.
WE GOT TESTS THIS WHOLE WEEK!
ぎゃーの
Nag
SUCH A GOOD STUDENT!
HM?
SHIKIMORI-SAN...
?
ほや
Beam
YOU LOOK HAPPY.
DID YOU BUY SOMETHING NICE?
ほや
Beam
ギク
Gakk!
HE ACTUALLY NOTICED !!
WHAT DO YA THINK SHE BOUGHT, DUDE? IT'S A SWIMSUIT.
He's good!!
Yeesh.
WHAT DO YOU MEAN?

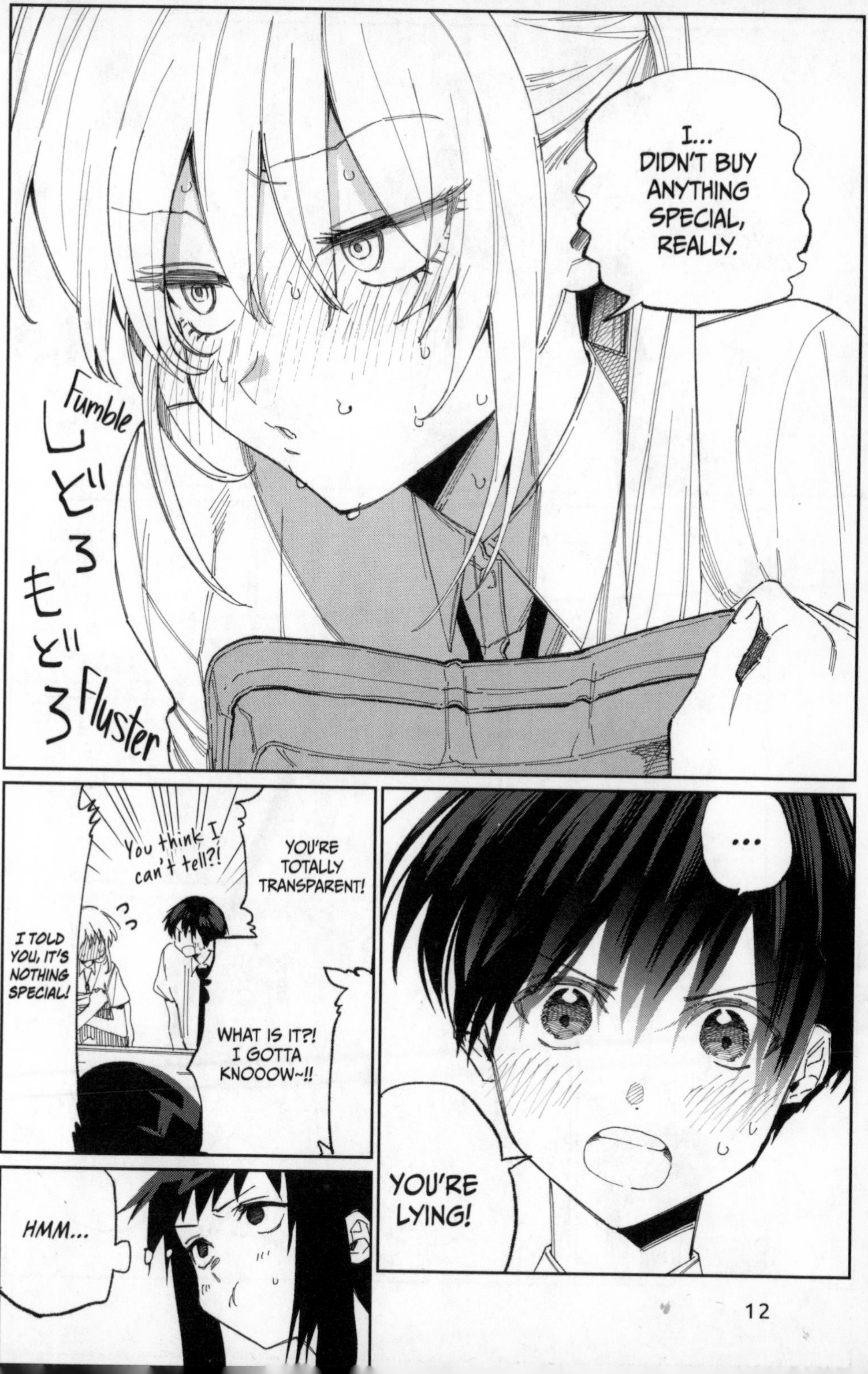
I... DIDN'T BUY ANYTHING SPECIAL, REALLY.
しどろもどろ
Fumble
Fluster
...
YOU'RE LYING!
YOU'RE TOTALLY TRANSPARENT!
You think I can't tell?!
I TOLD YOU, IT'S NOTHING SPECIAL!
WHAT IS IT?! I GOTTA KNOOOW~!!
HMM...

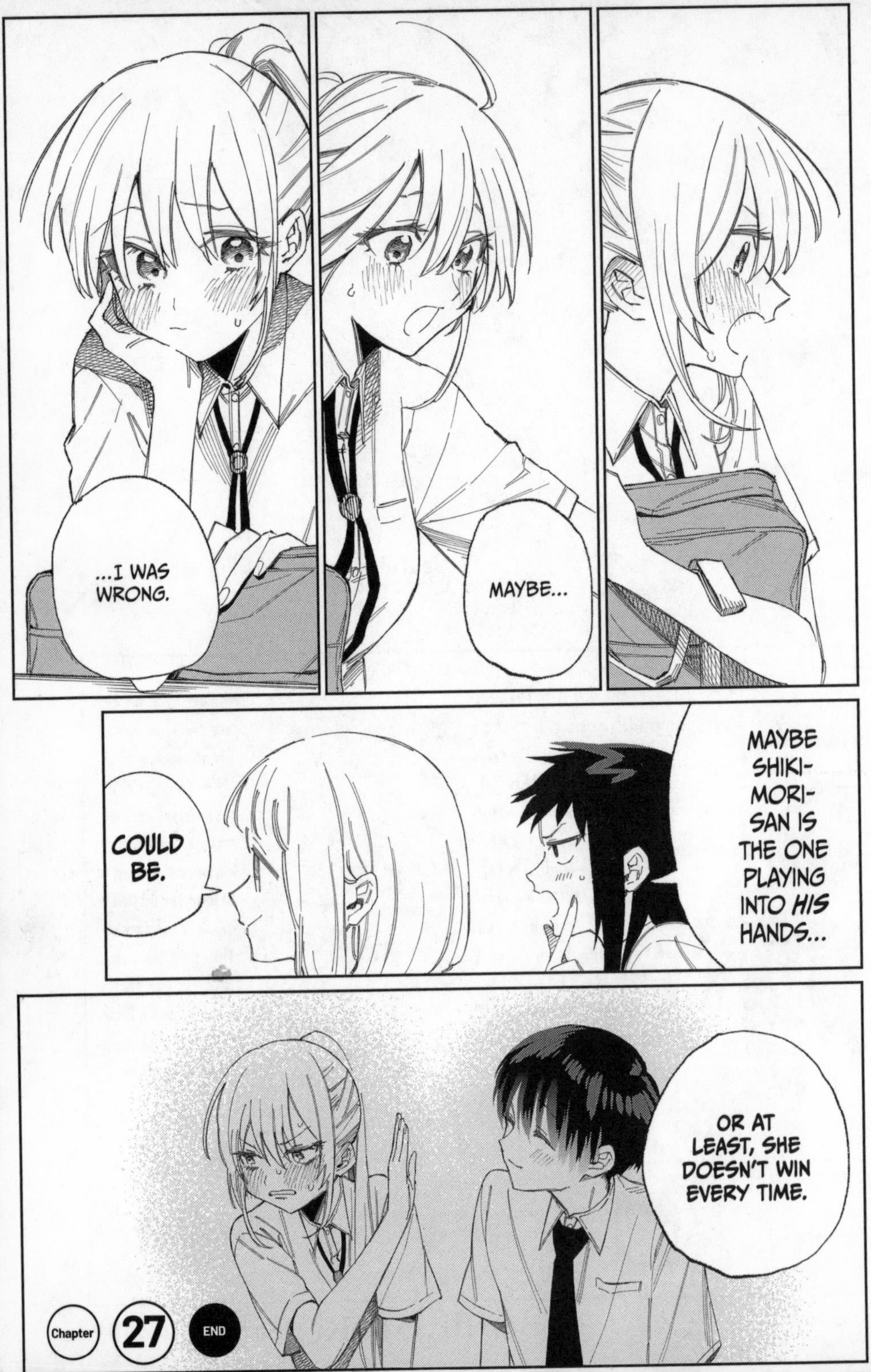
MAYBE...
...I WAS WRONG.
MAYBE SHIKI-MORI-SAN IS THE ONE PLAYING INTO HIS HANDS...
COULD BE.
OR AT LEAST, SHE DOESN'T WIN EVERY TIME.
Chapter 27 END

Inuzuka hates slacking off.

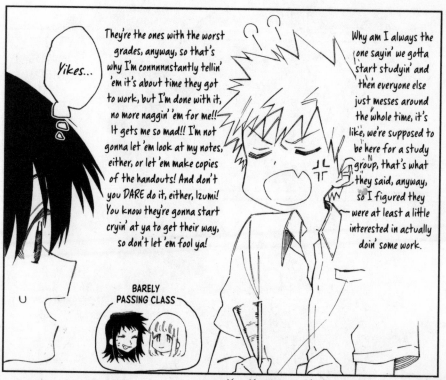

Yikes...

They're the ones with the worst grades, anyway, so that's why I'm connnnnstantly tellin' 'em it's about time they got to work, but I'm done with it, no more naggin' 'em for me!! It gets me so mad!! I'm not gonna let 'em look at my notes, either, or let 'em make copies of the handouts! And don't you DARE do it, either, Izumi! You know they're gonna start cryin' at ya to get their way, so don't let 'em fool ya!

Why am I always the one sayin' we gotta start studyin' and then everyone else just messes around the whole time, it's like, we're supposed to be here for a study group, that's what they said, anyway, so I figured they were at least a little interested in actually doin' some work.

BARELY PASSING CLASS

SHiKiMORi'S not just a cutie

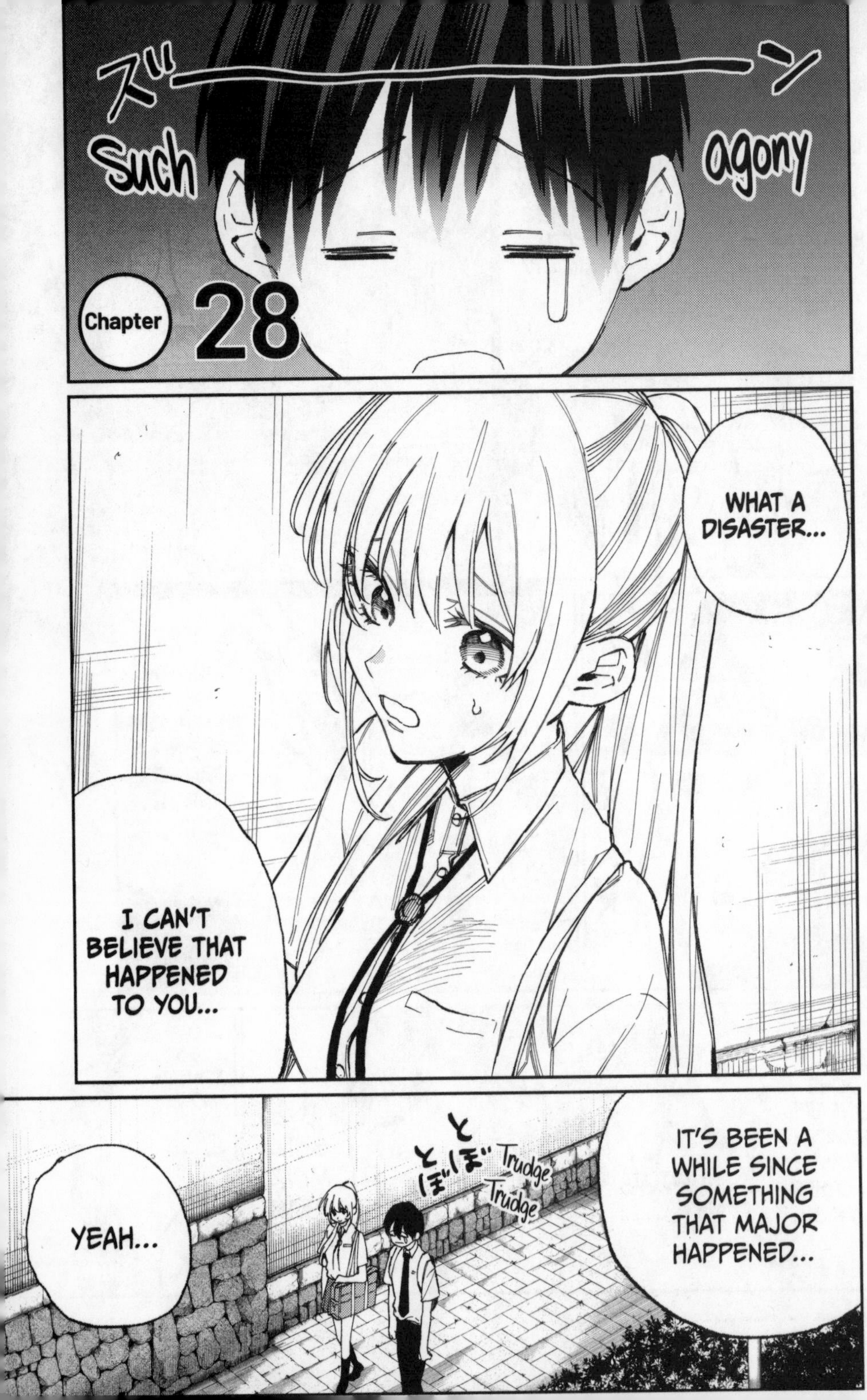
ズーーーン
Such agony
Chapter 28
WHAT A DISASTER...
I CAN'T BELIEVE THAT HAPPENED TO YOU...
IT'S BEEN A WHILE SINCE SOMETHING THAT MAJOR HAPPENED...
とぼとぼ Trudge Trudge
YEAH...

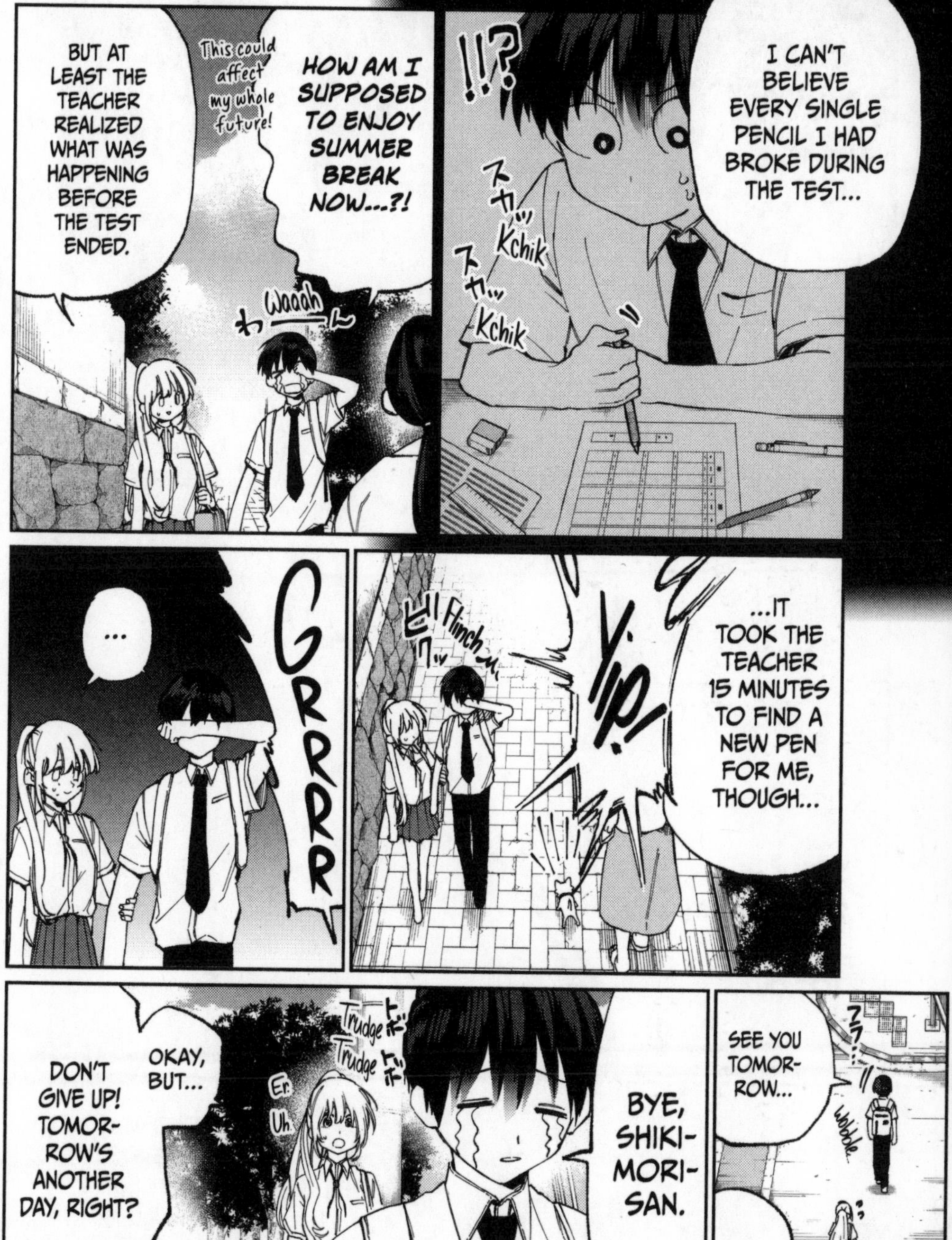

I CAN'T BELIEVE EVERY SINGLE PENCIL I HAD BROKE DURING THE TEST...
!!?
Kchik
Kchik
HOW AM I SUPPOSED TO ENJOY SUMMER BREAK NOW...?!
This could affect my whole future!
BUT AT LEAST THE TEACHER REALIZED WHAT WAS HAPPENING BEFORE THE TEST ENDED.
Waaah
...IT TOOK THE TEACHER 15 MINUTES TO FIND A NEW PEN FOR ME, THOUGH...
Yip!
Flinch
GRRRR
...
SEE YOU TOMORROW...
Wobble
HEY—
BYE, SHIKIMORI-SAN.
Trudge
Trudge
Er.
Uh.
OKAY, BUT...
DON'T GIVE UP! TOMORROW'S ANOTHER DAY, RIGHT?

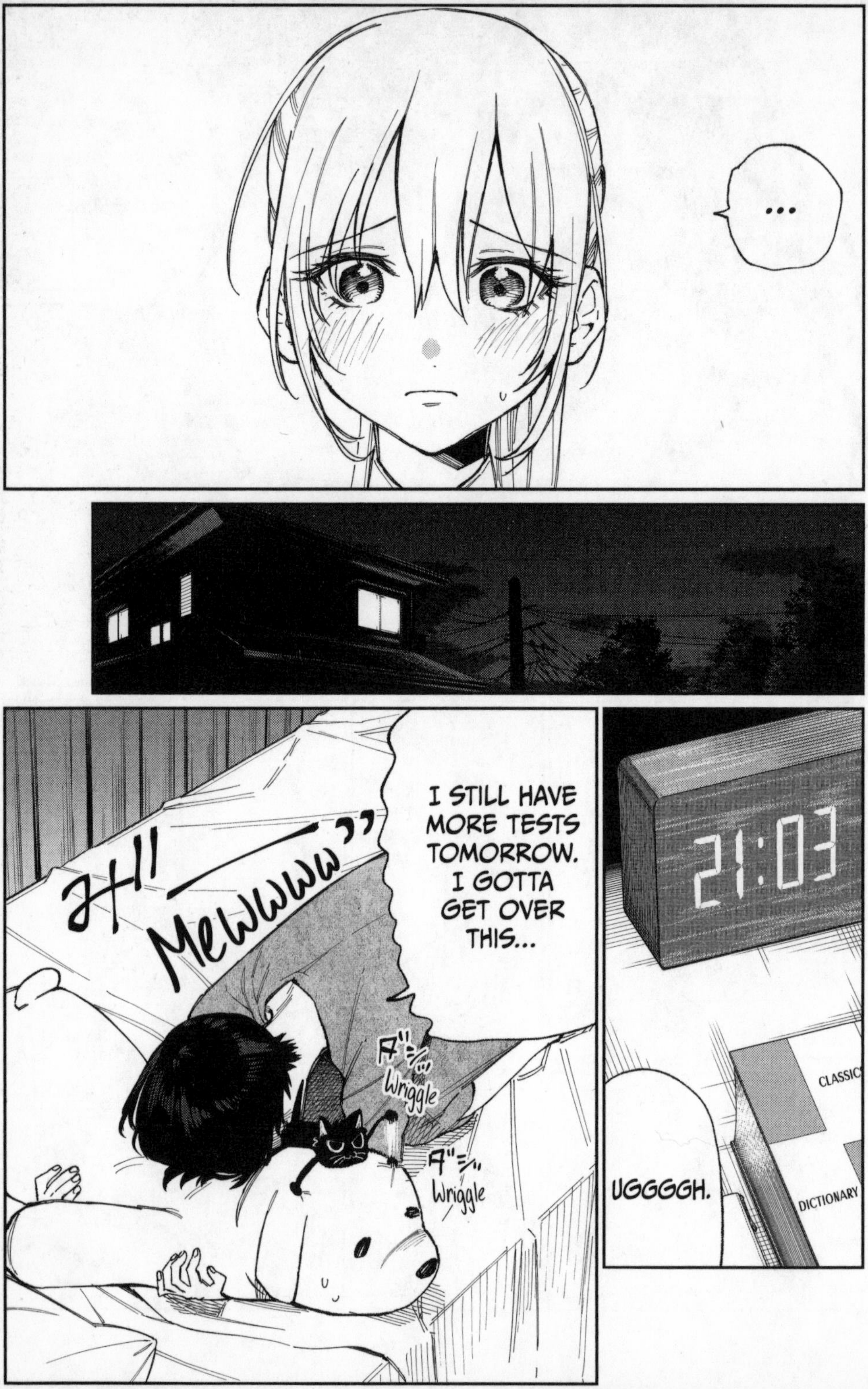
...
21:03
UGGGGH.
CLASSIC
DICTIONARY
I STILL HAVE MORE TESTS TOMORROW. I GOTTA GET OVER THIS...
Mewwww
Wriggle
Wriggle

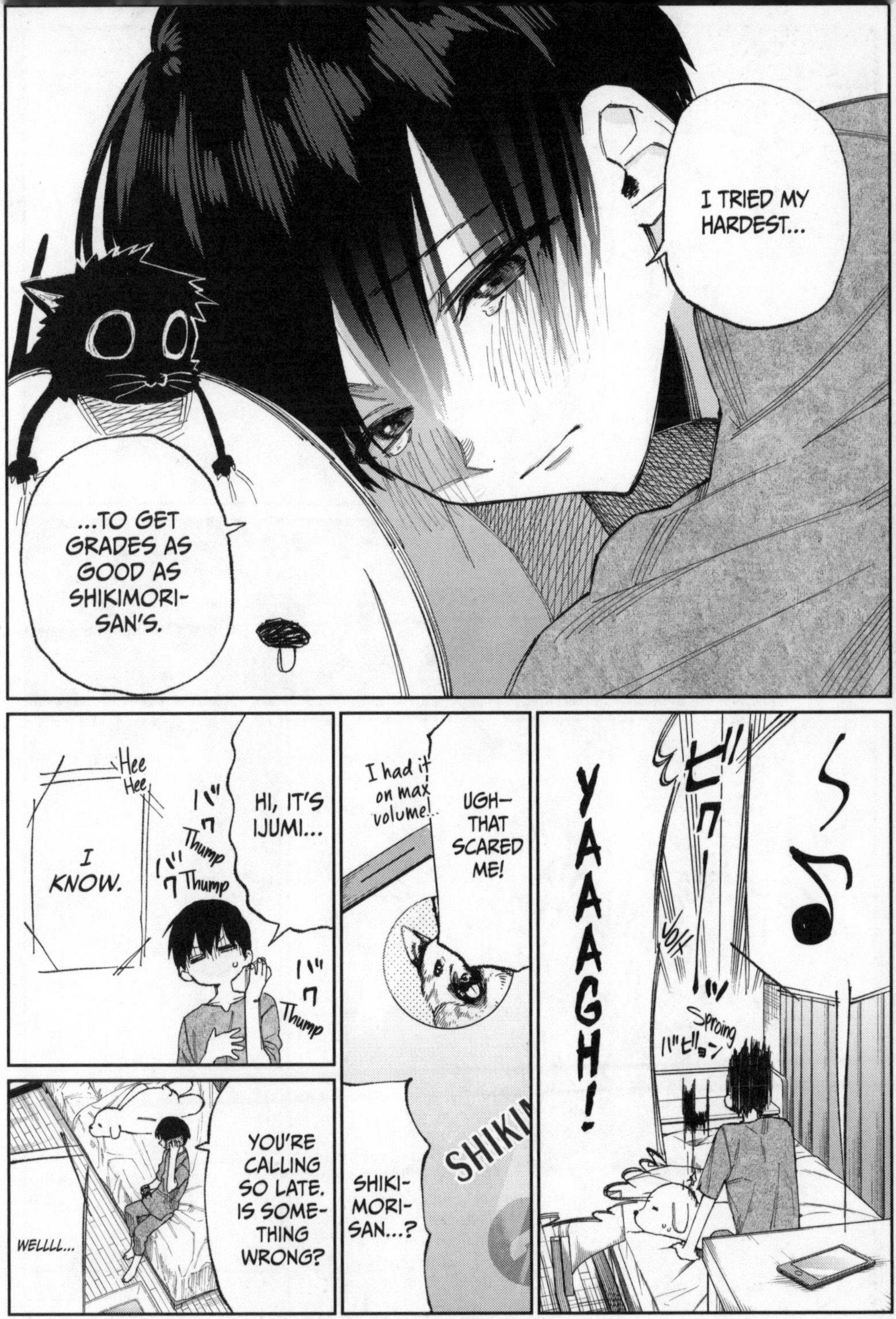
I TRIED MY HARDEST...
...TO GET GRADES AS GOOD AS SHIKIMORI-SAN'S.
ビクーッ
Jolt
YAAAGH!
Sproing
バビョン
UGH—THAT SCARED ME!
I had it on max volume!
SHIKI
SHIKI-MORI-SAN...?
HI, IT'S IJUMI...
Hee Hee
I KNOW.
バク
Thump
バク
Thump
バク
Thump
YOU'RE CALLING SO LATE. IS SOME-THING WRONG?
WELLLL...

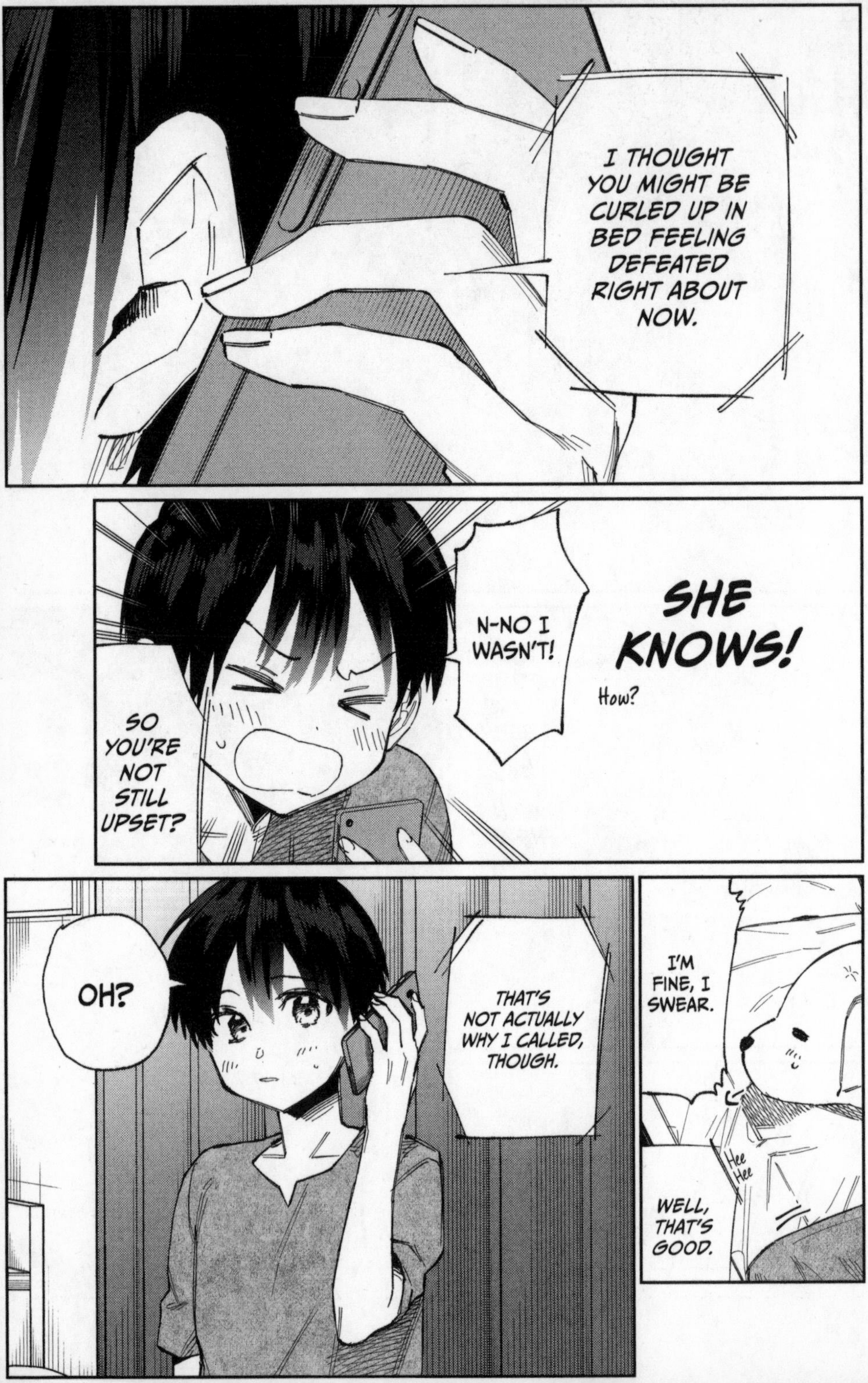
I THOUGHT YOU MIGHT BE CURLED UP IN BED FEELING DEFEATED RIGHT ABOUT NOW.
SHE KNOWS!
How?
N-NO I WASN'T!
SO YOU'RE NOT STILL UPSET?
I'M FINE, I SWEAR.
Hee Hee
WELL, THAT'S GOOD.
THAT'S NOT ACTUALLY WHY I CALLED, THOUGH.
OH?

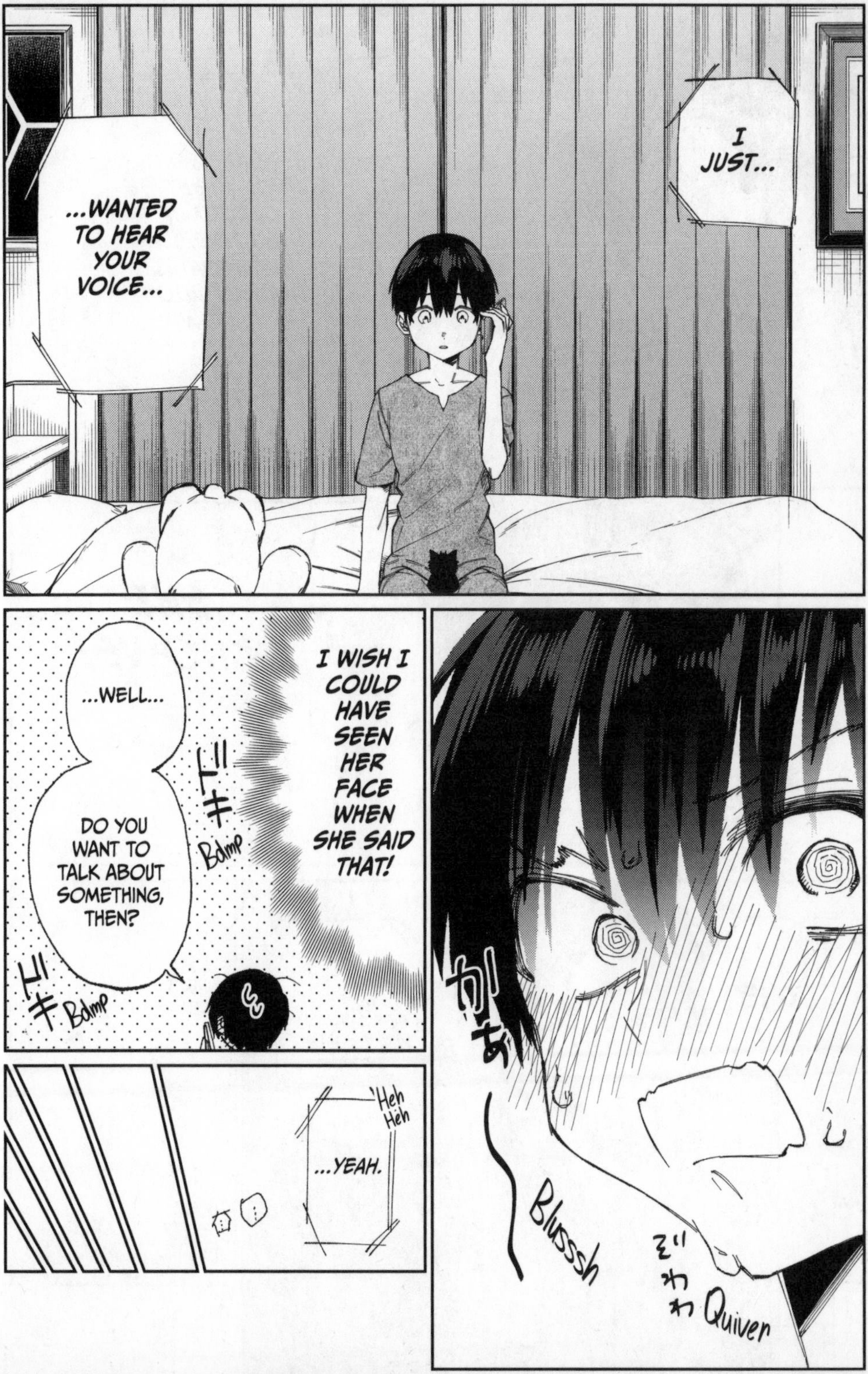
I JUST...
...WANTED TO HEAR YOUR VOICE...
Blussssh
Quiver
I WISH I COULD HAVE SEEN HER FACE WHEN SHE SAID THAT!
...WELL...
DO YOU WANT TO TALK ABOUT SOMETHING, THEN?
ドキ Bdmp
ドキ Bdmp
Heh Heh
...YEAH.

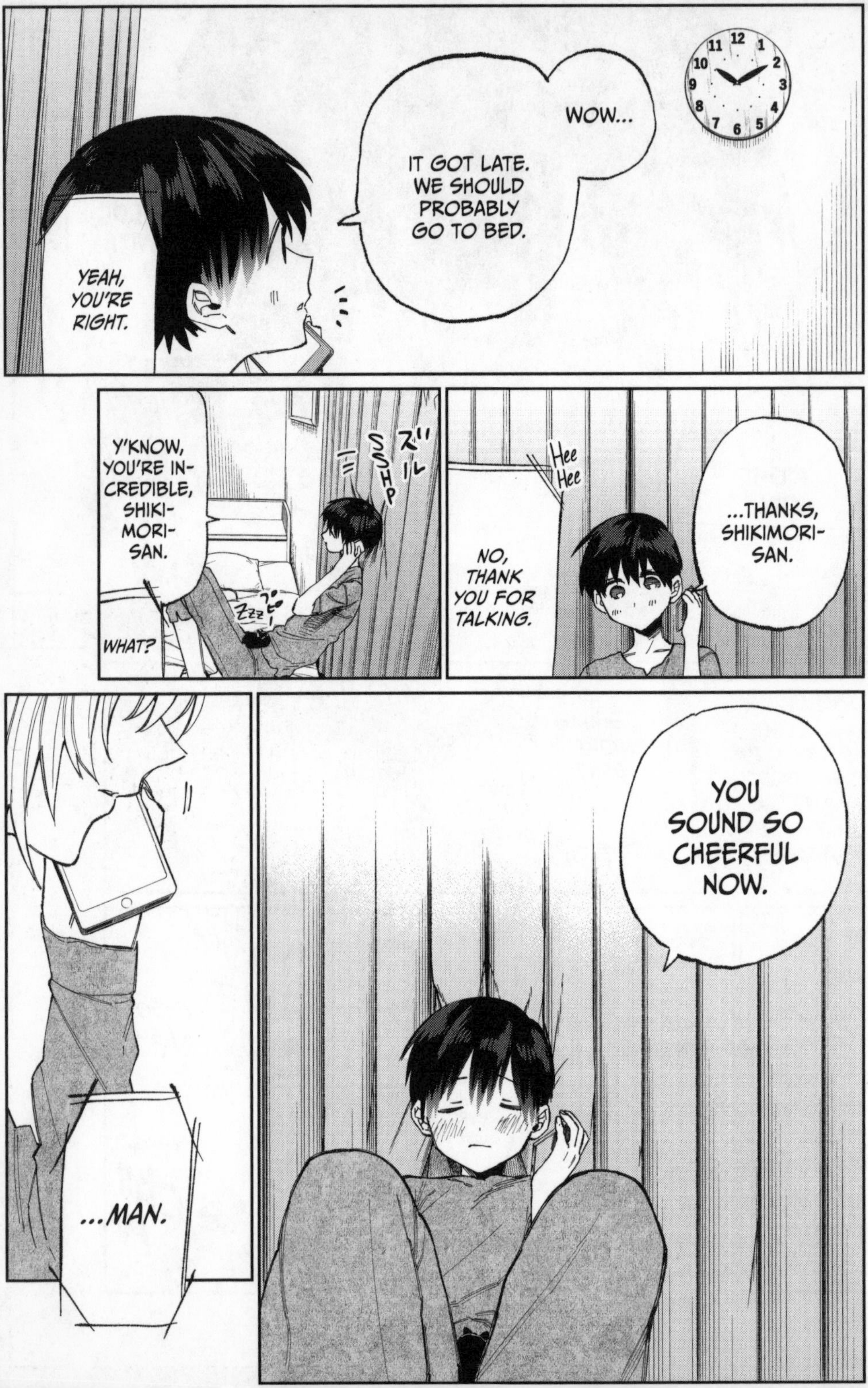

WOW...
IT GOT LATE. WE SHOULD PROBABLY GO TO BED.
YEAH, YOU'RE RIGHT.
...THANKS, SHIKIMORI-SAN.
Hee Hee
NO, THANK YOU FOR TALKING.
ズル
SSHP
Y'KNOW, YOU'RE IN-CREDIBLE, SHIKI-MORI-SAN.
Zzz
WHAT?
YOU SOUND SO CHEERFUL NOW.
...MAN.

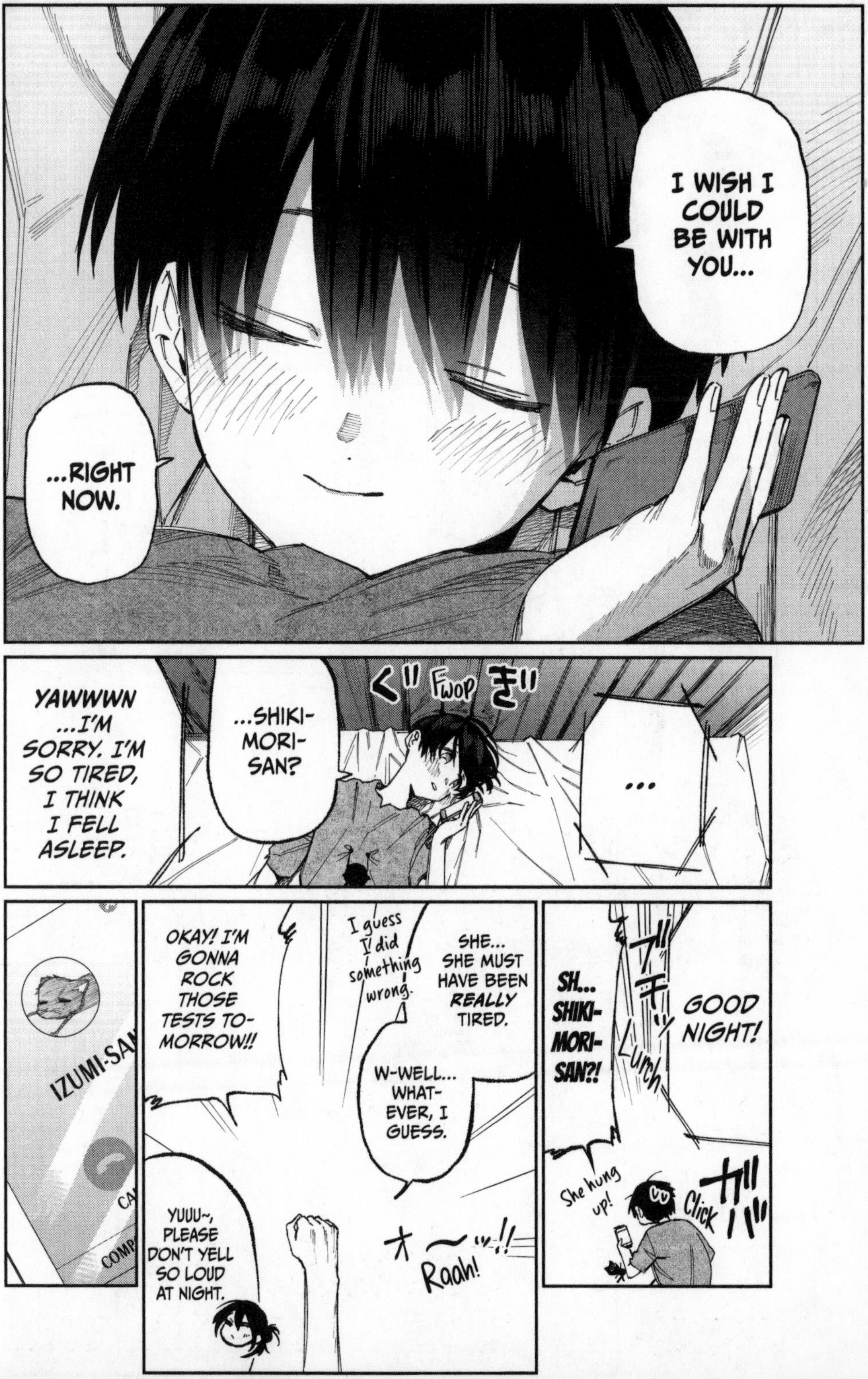
I WISH I COULD BE WITH YOU...
...RIGHT NOW.
...
Fwop
...SHIKI-MORI-SAN?
YAWWWN ...I'M SORRY. I'M SO TIRED, I THINK I FELL ASLEEP.
GOOD NIGHT!
SH... SHIKI-MORI-SAN?!
Lurch
She hung up!
Click
SHE... SHE MUST HAVE BEEN REALLY TIRED.
I guess I did something wrong.
OKAY! I'M GONNA ROCK THOSE TESTS TO-MORROW!!
W-WELL... WHAT-EVER, I GUESS.
Raah!
YUUU~, PLEASE DON'T YELL SO LOUD AT NIGHT.
IZUMI-SA

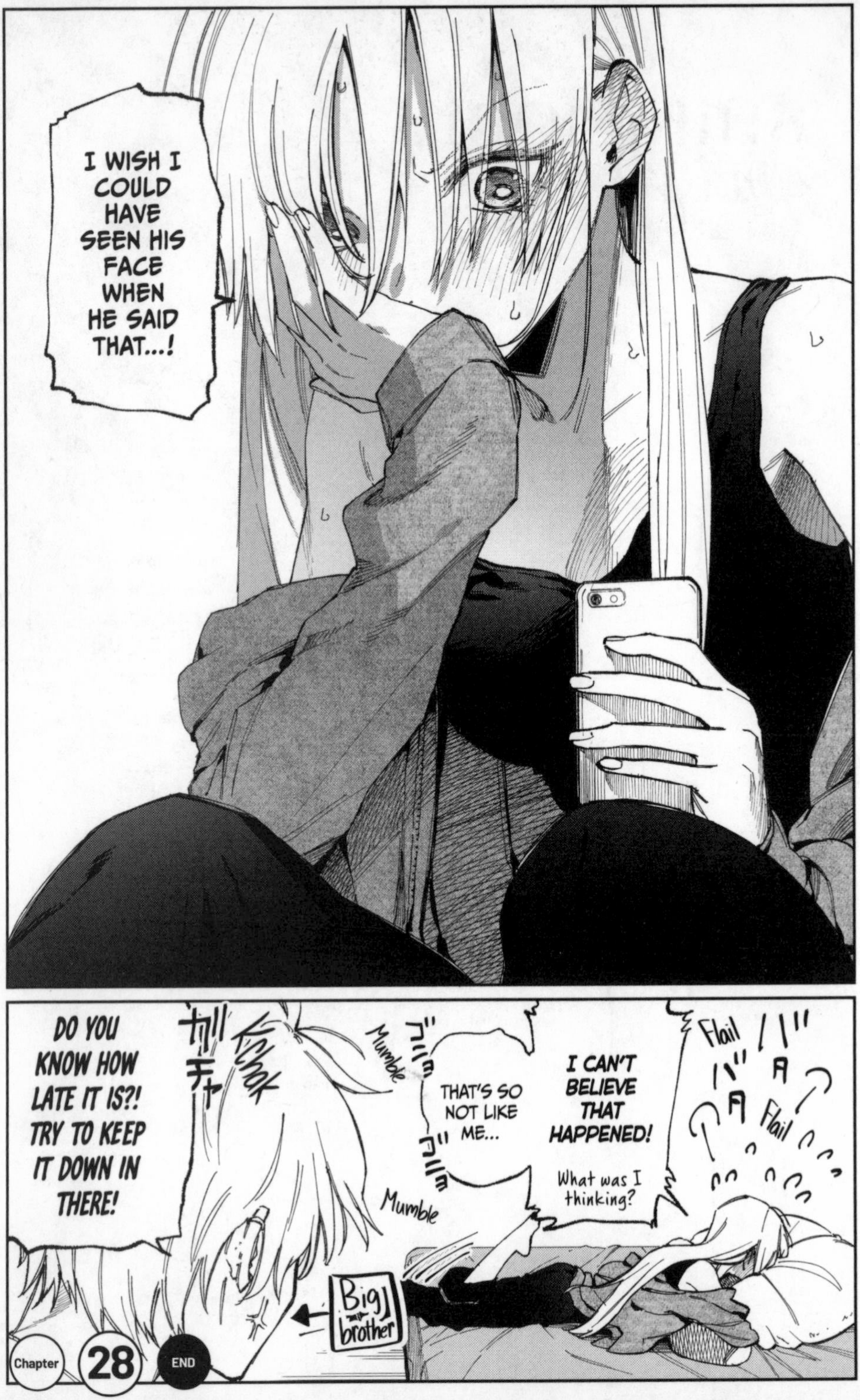
I WISH I COULD HAVE SEEN HIS FACE WHEN HE SAID THAT...!
Flail
Flail
I CAN'T BELIEVE THAT HAPPENED!
What was I thinking?
THAT'S SO NOT LIKE ME...
Mumble
Mumble
ガチャ
K-chok
DO YOU KNOW HOW LATE IT IS?! TRY TO KEEP IT DOWN IN THERE!
Big brother
Chapter 28 END

SHIKIMORI'S not just a cutie

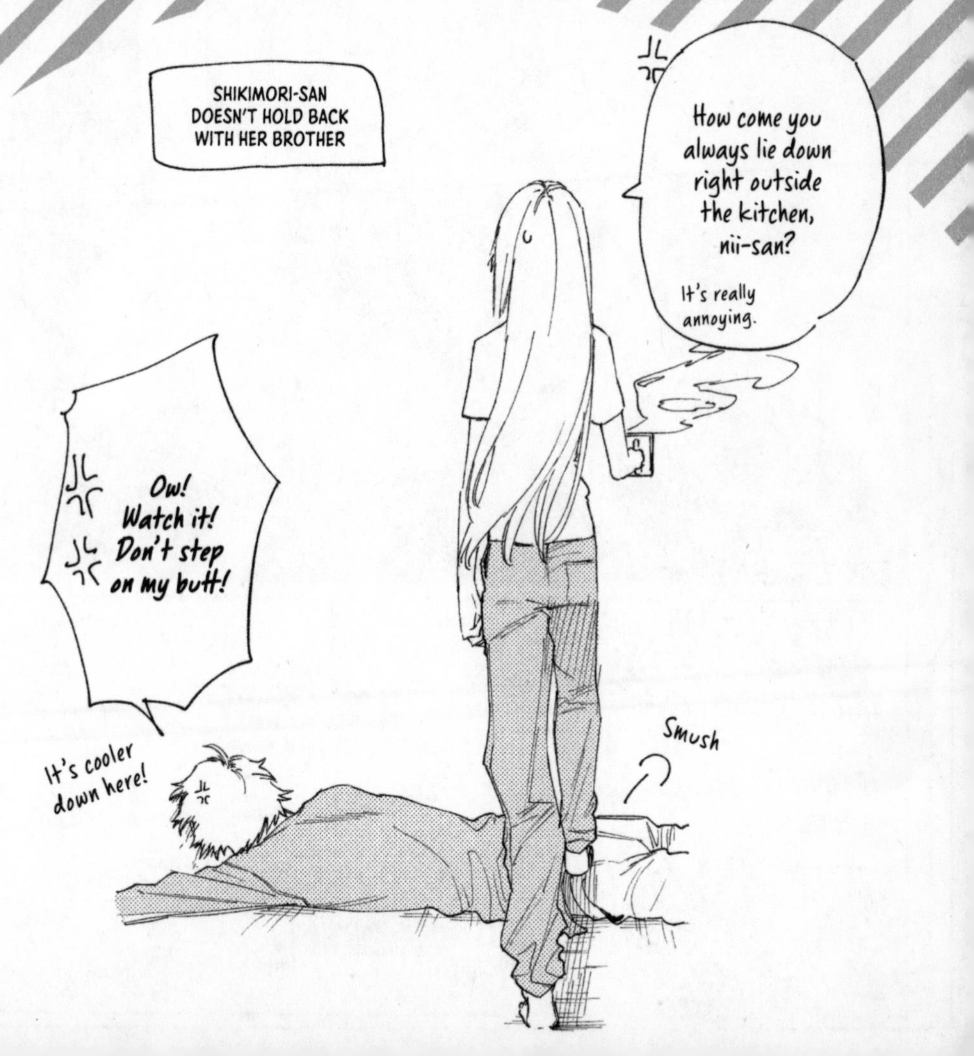
SHIKIMORI-SAN DOESN'T HOLD BACK WITH HER BROTHER
How come you always lie down right outside the kitchen, nii-san?
It's really annoying.
Smush
Ow! Watch it! Don't step on my butt!
It's cooler down here!

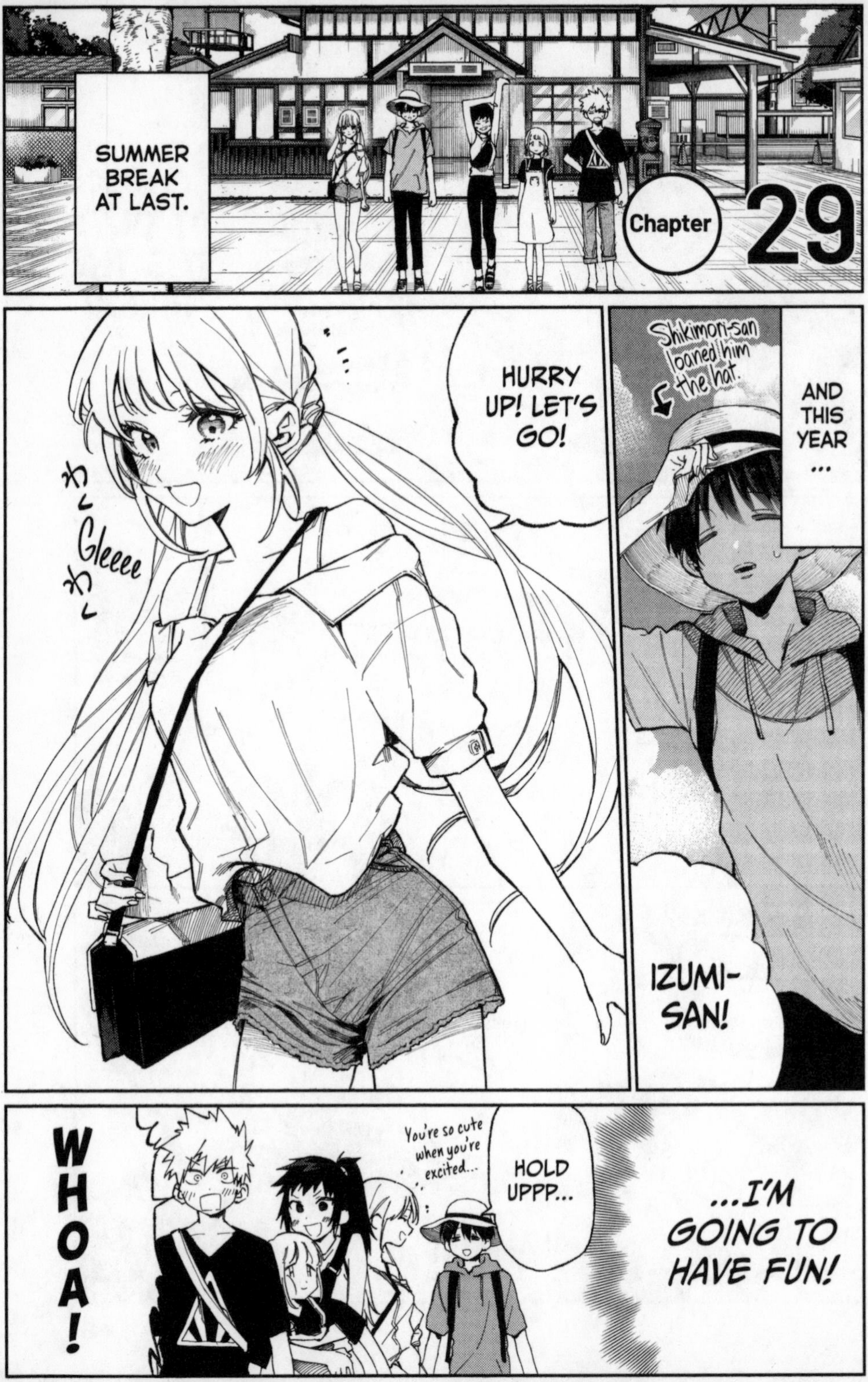
Chapter 29
SUMMER BREAK AT LAST.
AND THIS YEAR ...
Shikimori-san loaned him the hat.
IZUMI-SAN!
HURRY UP! LET'S GO!
わく Gleeee わく
...I'M GOING TO HAVE FUN!
HOLD UPPP...
You're so cute when you're excited...
WHOA!

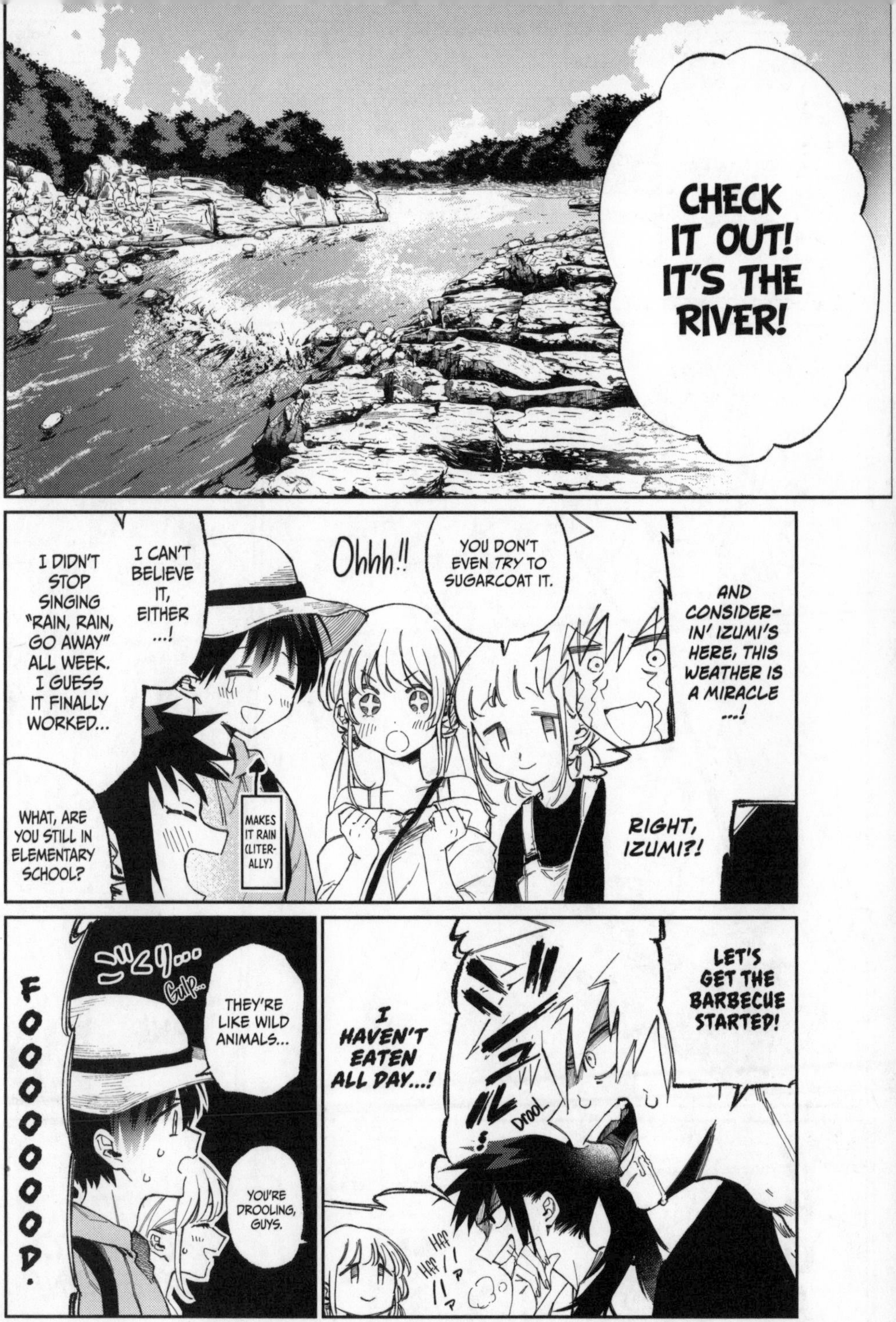
CHECK IT OUT! IT'S THE RIVER!
AND CONSIDER-IN' IZUMI'S HERE, THIS WEATHER IS A MIRACLE ...!
RIGHT, IZUMI?!
YOU DON'T EVEN TRY TO SUGARCOAT IT.
Ohhh!!
I CAN'T BELIEVE IT, EITHER ...!
I DIDN'T STOP SINGING "RAIN, RAIN, GO AWAY" ALL WEEK. I GUESS IT FINALLY WORKED...
MAKES IT RAIN (LITERALLY)
WHAT, ARE YOU STILL IN ELEMENTARY SCHOOL?
LET'S GET THE BARBECUE STARTED!
I HAVEN'T EATEN ALL DAY...!
Drool
Hff Hff
THEY'RE LIKE WILD ANIMALS...
ごくり… Gulp...
FOOOOOOOOD.
YOU'RE DROOLING, GUYS.

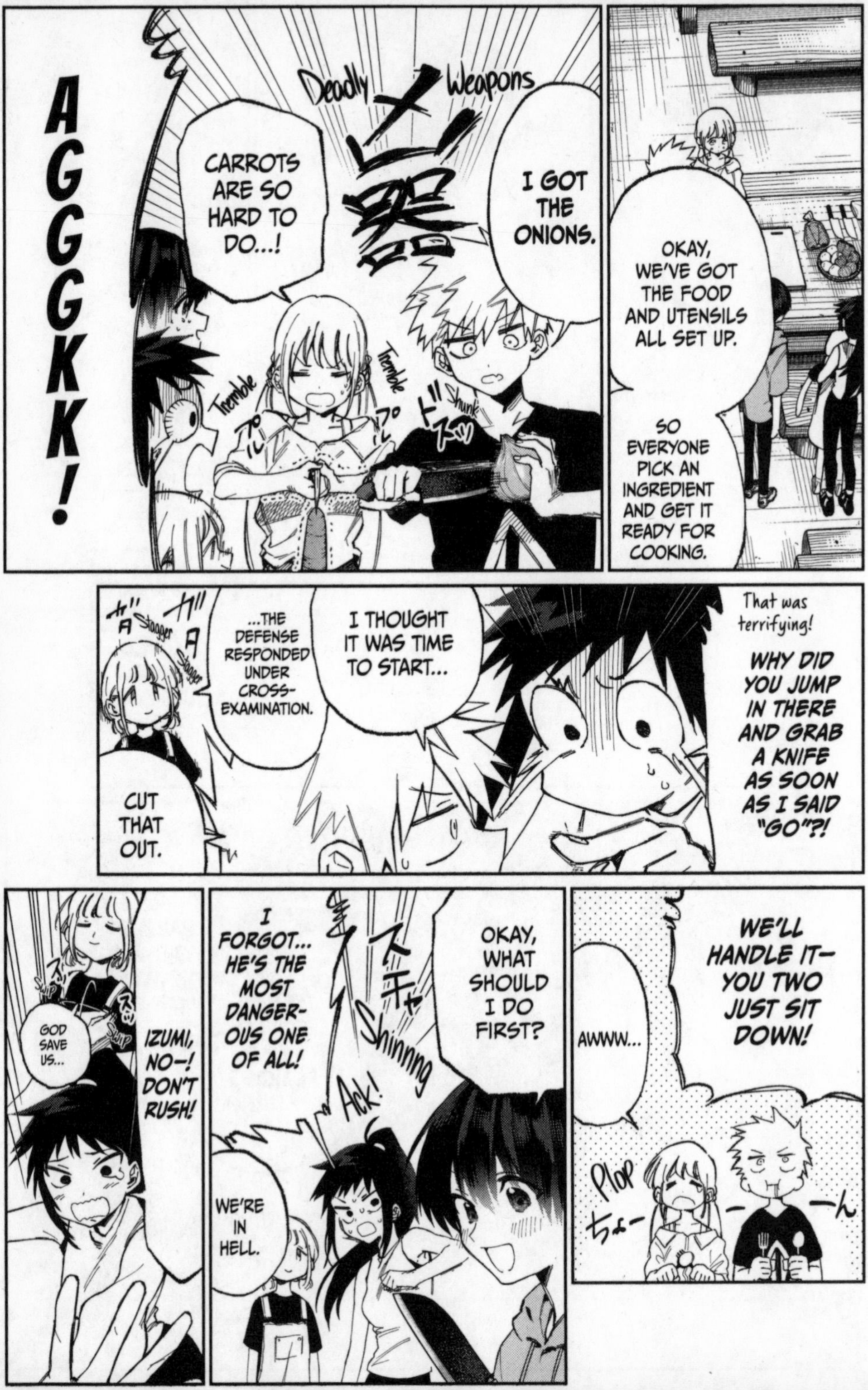
OKAY, WE'VE GOT THE FOOD AND UTENSILS ALL SET UP.
SO EVERYONE PICK AN INGREDIENT AND GET IT READY FOR COOKING.
I GOT THE ONIONS.
Deadly Weapons
Shunk
CARROTS ARE SO HARD TO DO...!
Tremble
Tremble
AGGGKK!
That was terrifying!
WHY DID YOU JUMP IN THERE AND GRAB A KNIFE AS SOON AS I SAID "GO"?!
I THOUGHT IT WAS TIME TO START...
...THE DEFENSE RESPONDED UNDER CROSS-EXAMINATION.
Stagger
Stagger
CUT THAT OUT.
WE'LL HANDLE IT— YOU TWO JUST SIT DOWN!
AWWW...
Plop
OKAY, WHAT SHOULD I DO FIRST?
Shinnng
I FORGOT... HE'S THE MOST DANGER-OUS ONE OF ALL!
Ack!
WE'RE IN HELL.
IZUMI, NO—! DON'T RUSH!
Swip
Swip
GOD SAVE US...

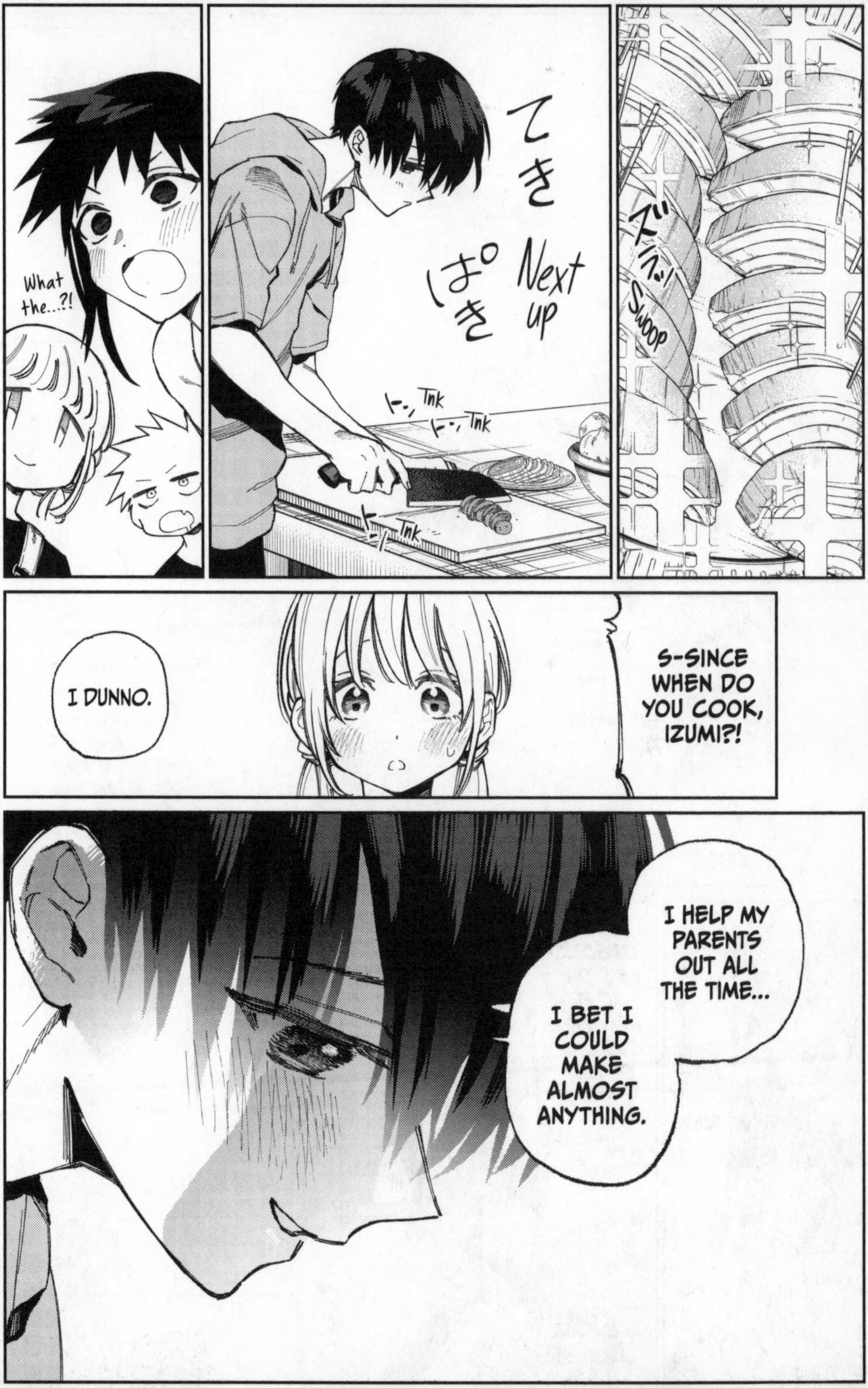
Swoop
てきぱき
Next up
トン Tnk
トン Tnk
トン Tnk
What the...?!
S-SINCE WHEN DO YOU COOK, IZUMI?!
I DUNNO.
I HELP MY PARENTS OUT ALL THE TIME...
I BET I COULD MAKE ALMOST ANYTHING.

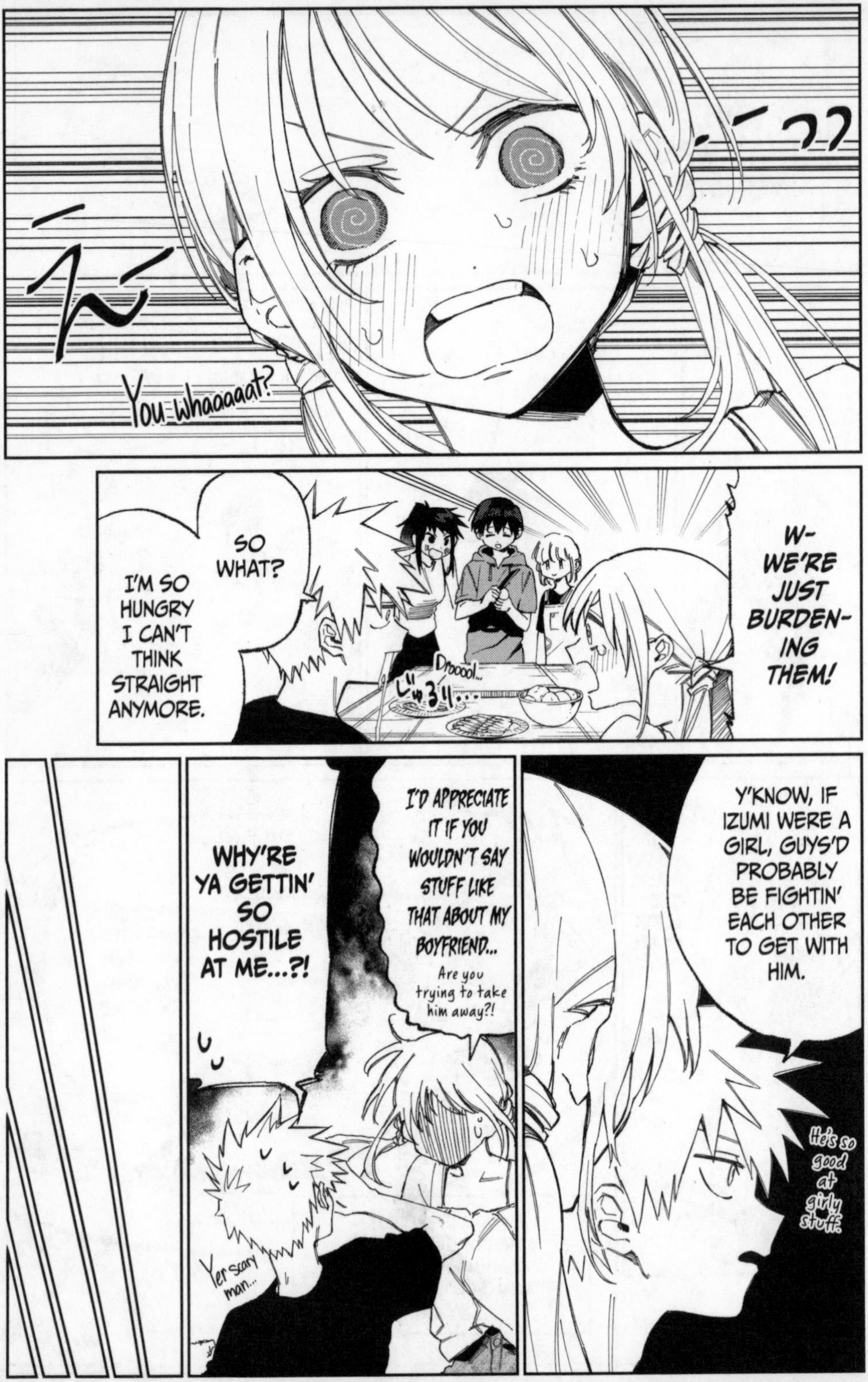
You whaaaaat?
W-WE'RE JUST BURDENING THEM!
Droooool...
SO WHAT?
I'M SO HUNGRY I CAN'T THINK STRAIGHT ANYMORE.
Y'KNOW, IF IZUMI WERE A GIRL, GUYS'D PROBABLY BE FIGHTIN' EACH OTHER TO GET WITH HIM.
He's so good at girly stuff.
I'D APPRECIATE IT IF YOU WOULDN'T SAY STUFF LIKE THAT ABOUT MY BOYFRIEND...
Are you trying to take him away?!
WHY'RE YA GETTIN' SO HOSTILE AT ME...?!
Yer scary man...

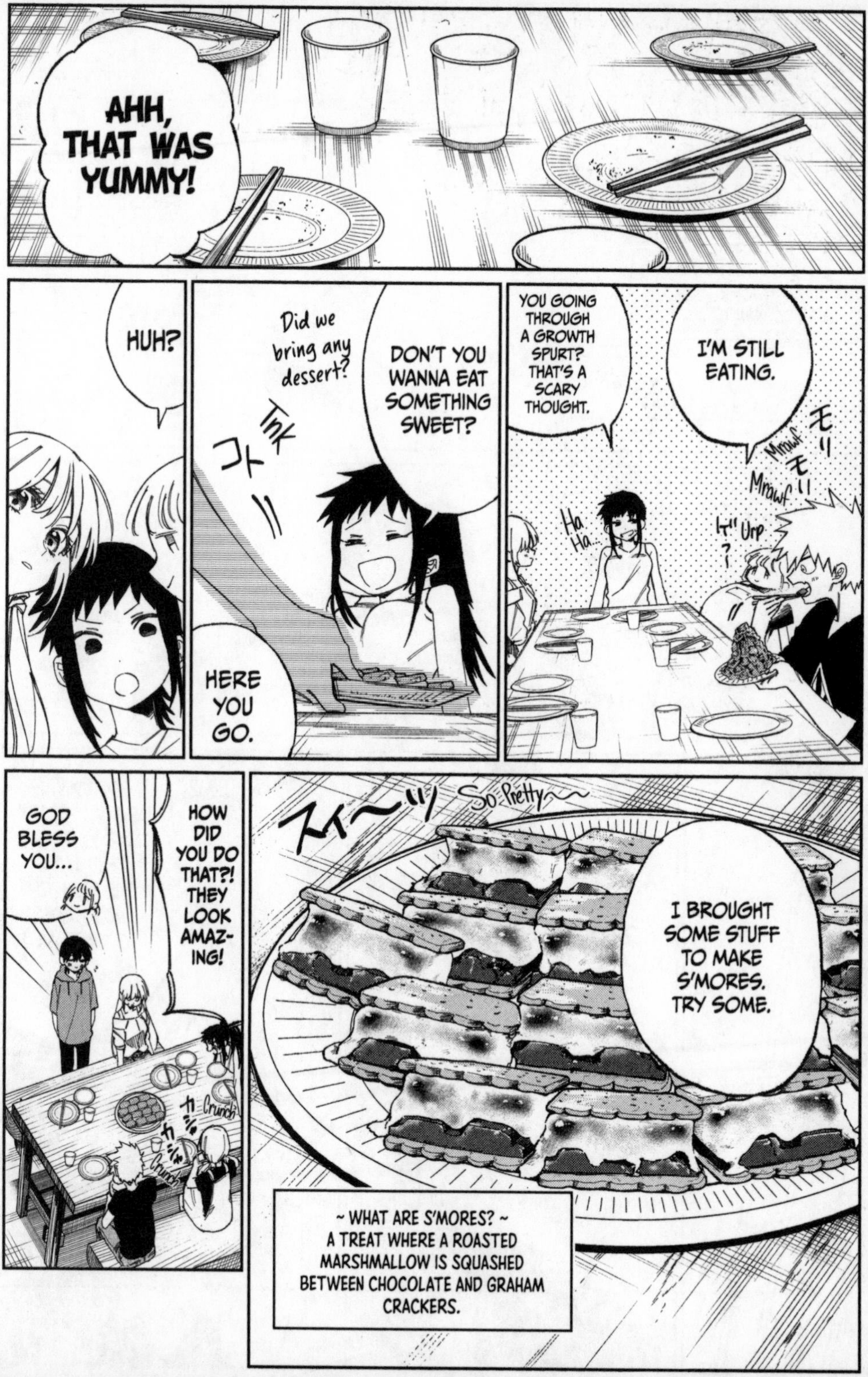
AHH, THAT WAS YUMMY!
I'M STILL EATING.
Mrawf
Mrawf
YOU GOING THROUGH A GROWTH SPURT? THAT'S A SCARY THOUGHT.
Ha Ha...
Urp
DON'T YOU WANNA EAT SOMETHING SWEET?
Did we bring any dessert?
Tnk
HERE YOU GO.
HUH?
So Pretty
I BROUGHT SOME STUFF TO MAKE S'MORES. TRY SOME.
~ WHAT ARE S'MORES? ~ A TREAT WHERE A ROASTED MARSHMALLOW IS SQUASHED BETWEEN CHOCOLATE AND GRAHAM CRACKERS.
HOW DID YOU DO THAT?! THEY LOOK AMAZ-ING!
GOD BLESS YOU...
Crunch
Crunch

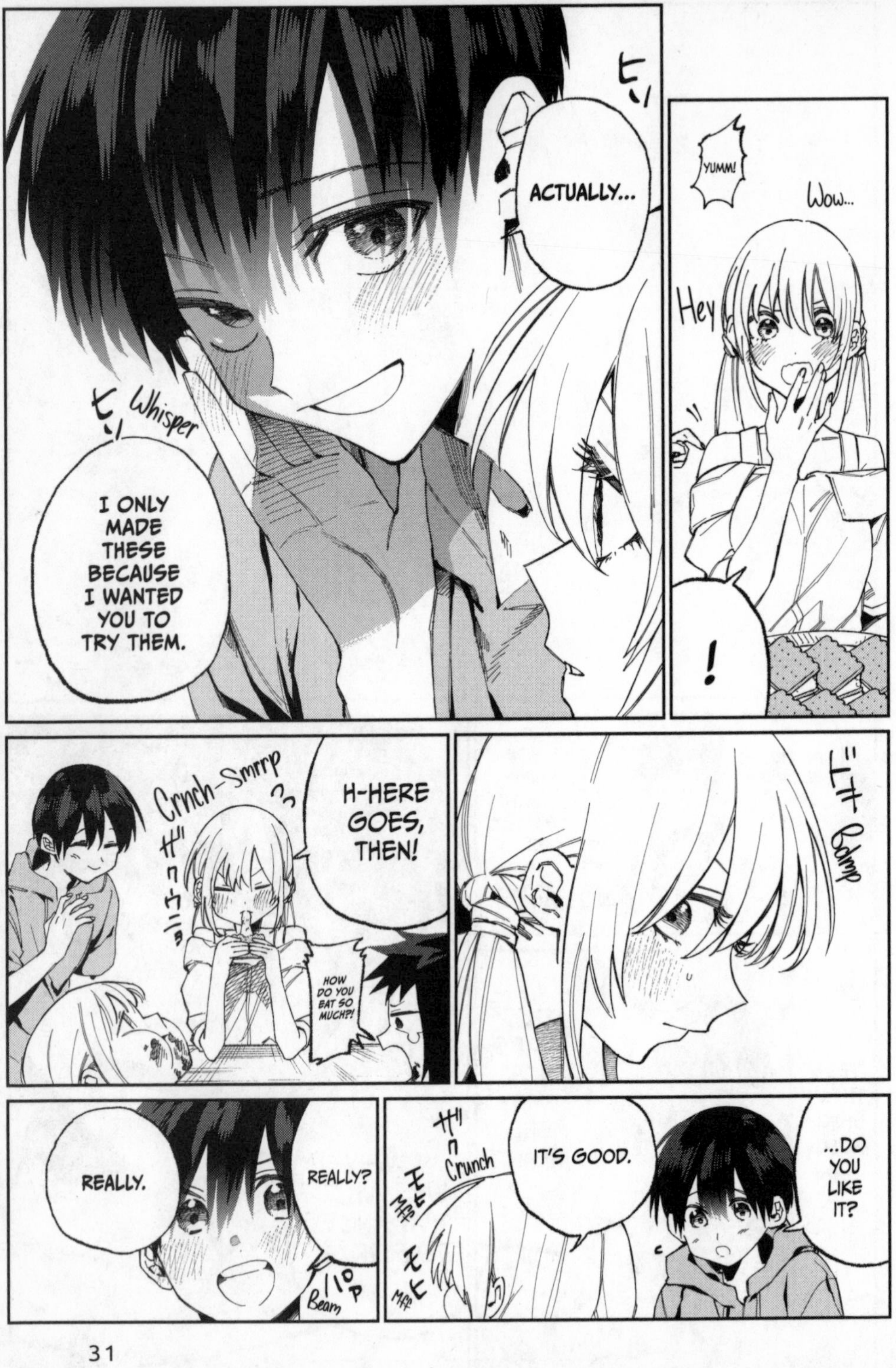
YUMM!
Wow...
Hey
!
ACTUALLY...
Whisper
I ONLY MADE THESE BECAUSE I WANTED YOU TO TRY THEM.
Bdmp
H-HERE GOES, THEN!
Crnch-Smrrp
HOW DO YOU EAT SO MUCH?!
...DO YOU LIKE IT?
IT'S GOOD.
Crunch
Mff
REALLY?
REALLY.
Beam

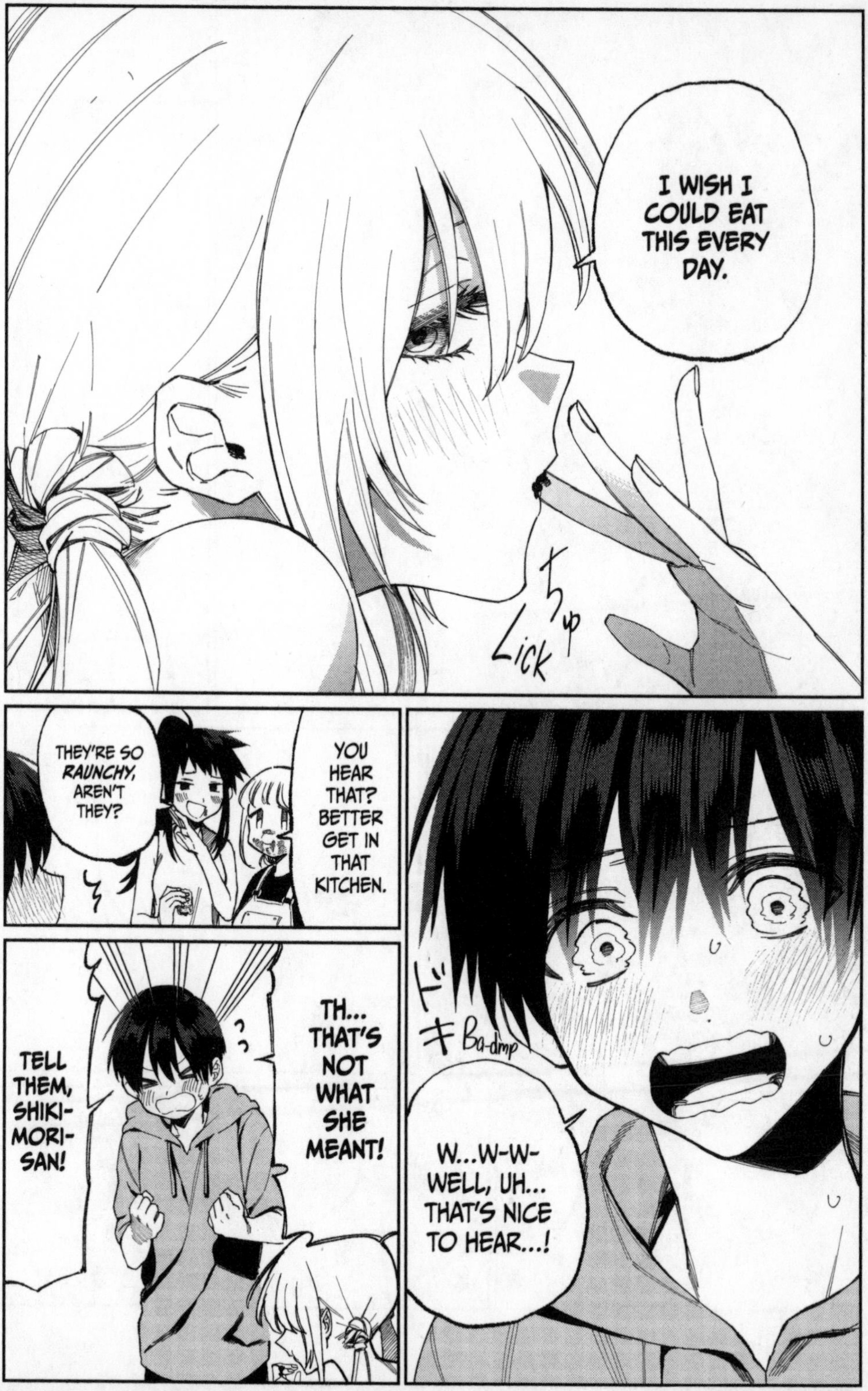
I WISH I COULD EAT THIS EVERY DAY.
ちゅ
Lick
ドキ
Ba-dmp
W...W-W-WELL, UH... THAT'S NICE TO HEAR...!
YOU HEAR THAT? BETTER GET IN THAT KITCHEN.
THEY'RE SO *RAUNCHY*, AREN'T THEY?
TH... THAT'S NOT WHAT SHE MEANT!
TELL THEM, SHIKIMORI-SAN!

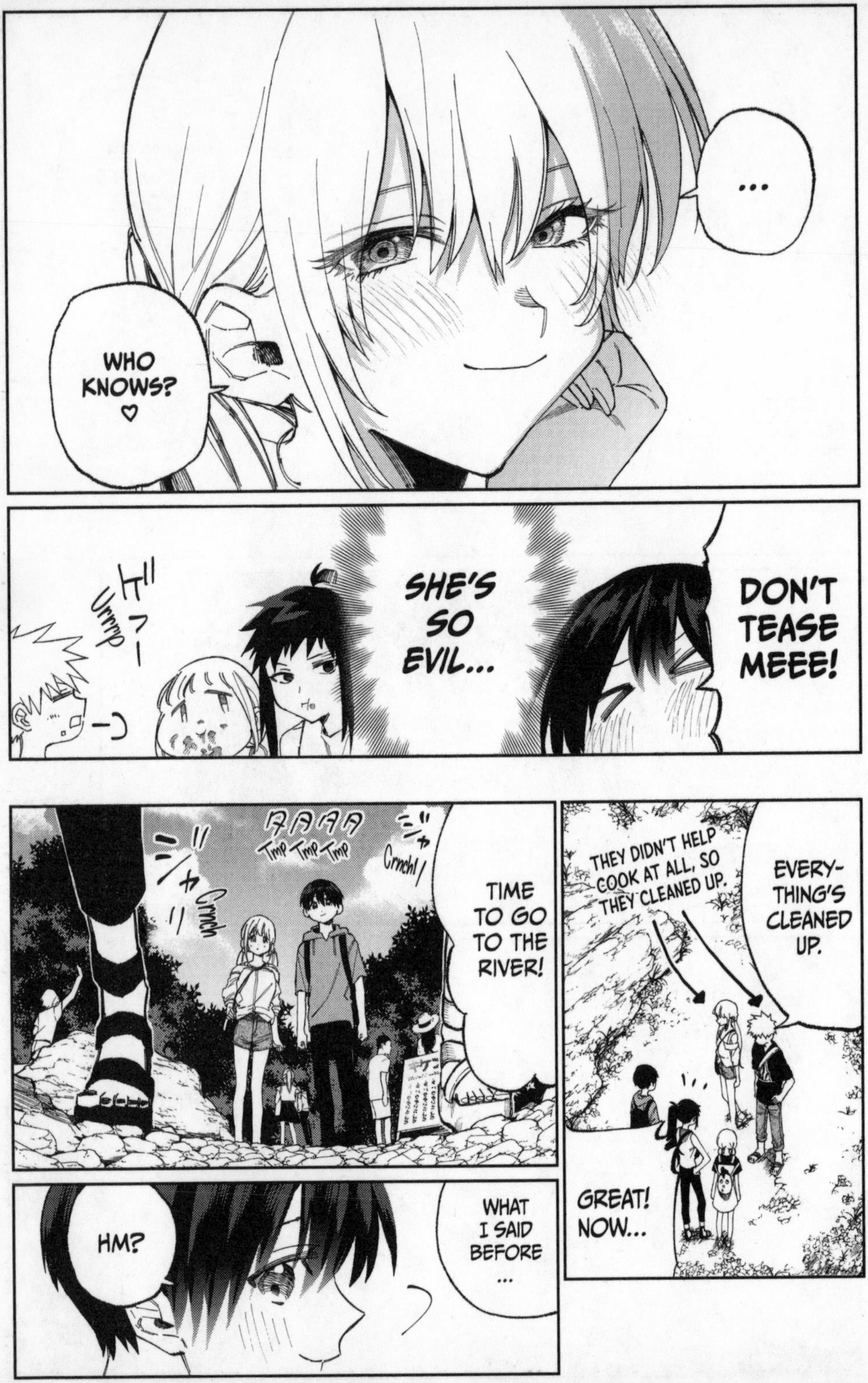

...
WHO KNOWS? ♡
DON'T TEASE MEEE!
SHE'S SO EVIL...
Urrrp
EVERY-THING'S CLEANED UP.
THEY DIDN'T HELP COOK AT ALL, SO THEY CLEANED UP.
GREAT! NOW...
TIME TO GO TO THE RIVER!
Crnch!
タタタタ Tmp Tmp Tmp
Crnch
WHAT I SAID BEFORE ...
HM?

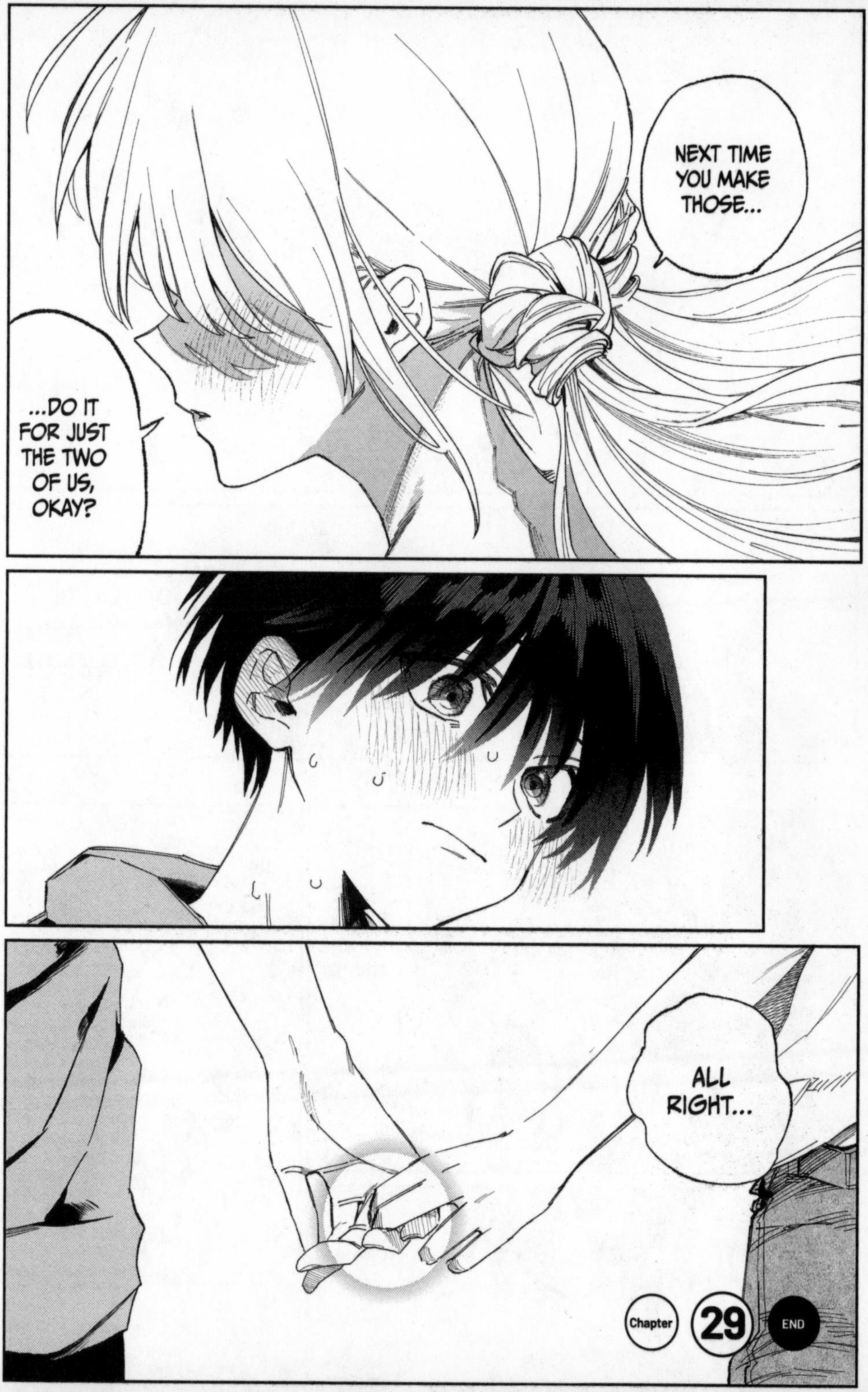
NEXT TIME YOU MAKE THOSE...
...DO IT FOR JUST THE TWO OF US, OKAY?
ALL RIGHT...
Chapter 29 END

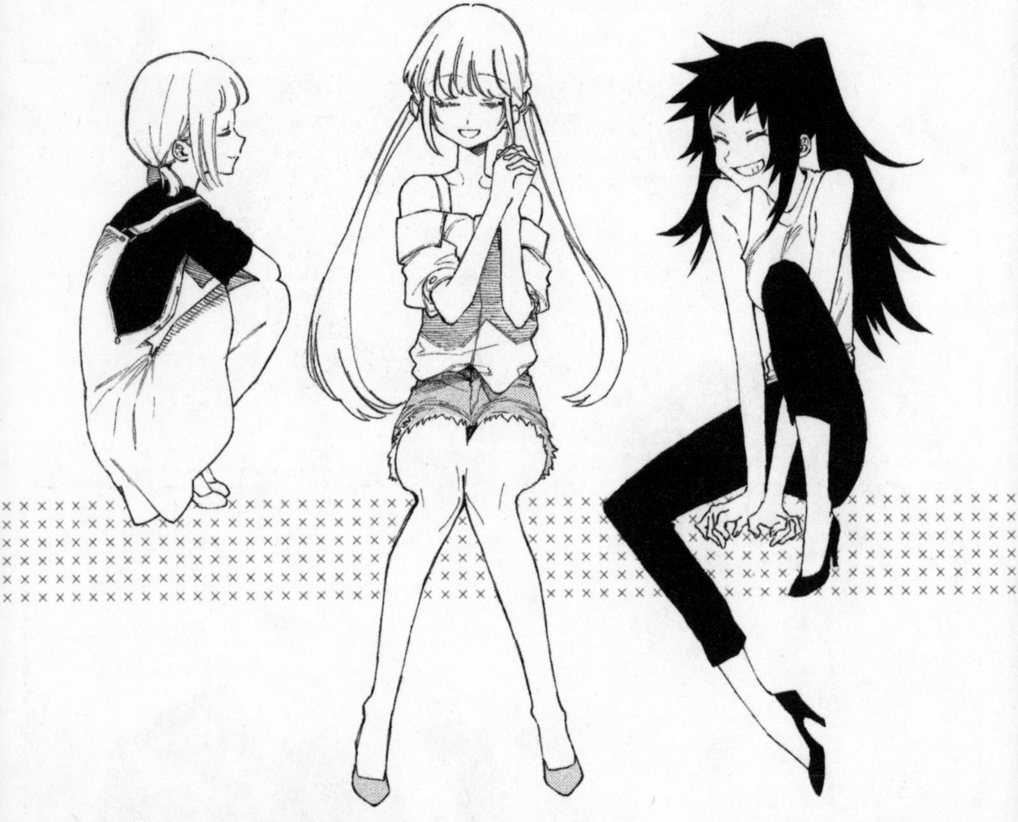

SHIKIMORI'S not just a cutie

SHIKIMORI'S
Not just a cutie

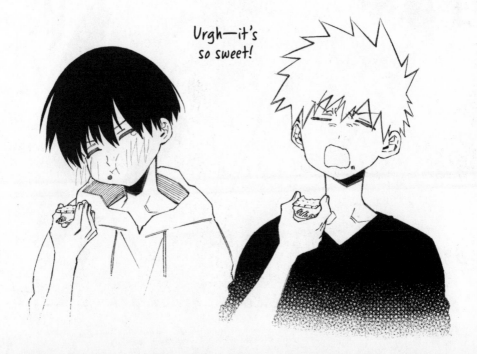

Urgh—it's
so sweet!

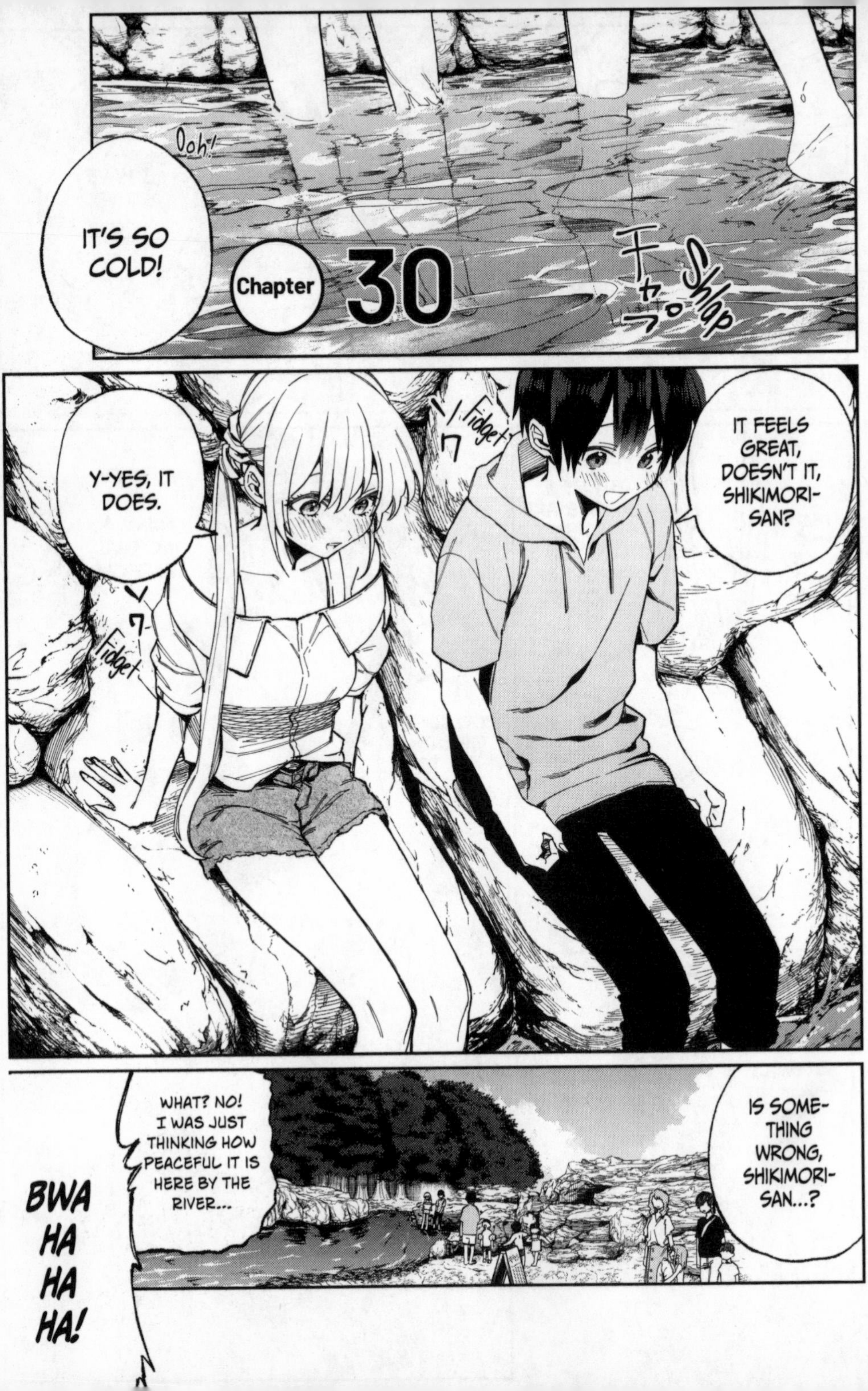
チャプ
Shlap
Chapter 30
Ooh!
IT'S SO COLD!
IT FEELS GREAT, DOESN'T IT, SHIKIMORI-SAN?
Fidget
Y-YES, IT DOES.
Fidget
IS SOMETHING WRONG, SHIKIMORI-SAN...?
WHAT? NO! I WAS JUST THINKING HOW PEACEFUL IT IS HERE BY THE RIVER...
BWA HA HA HA!

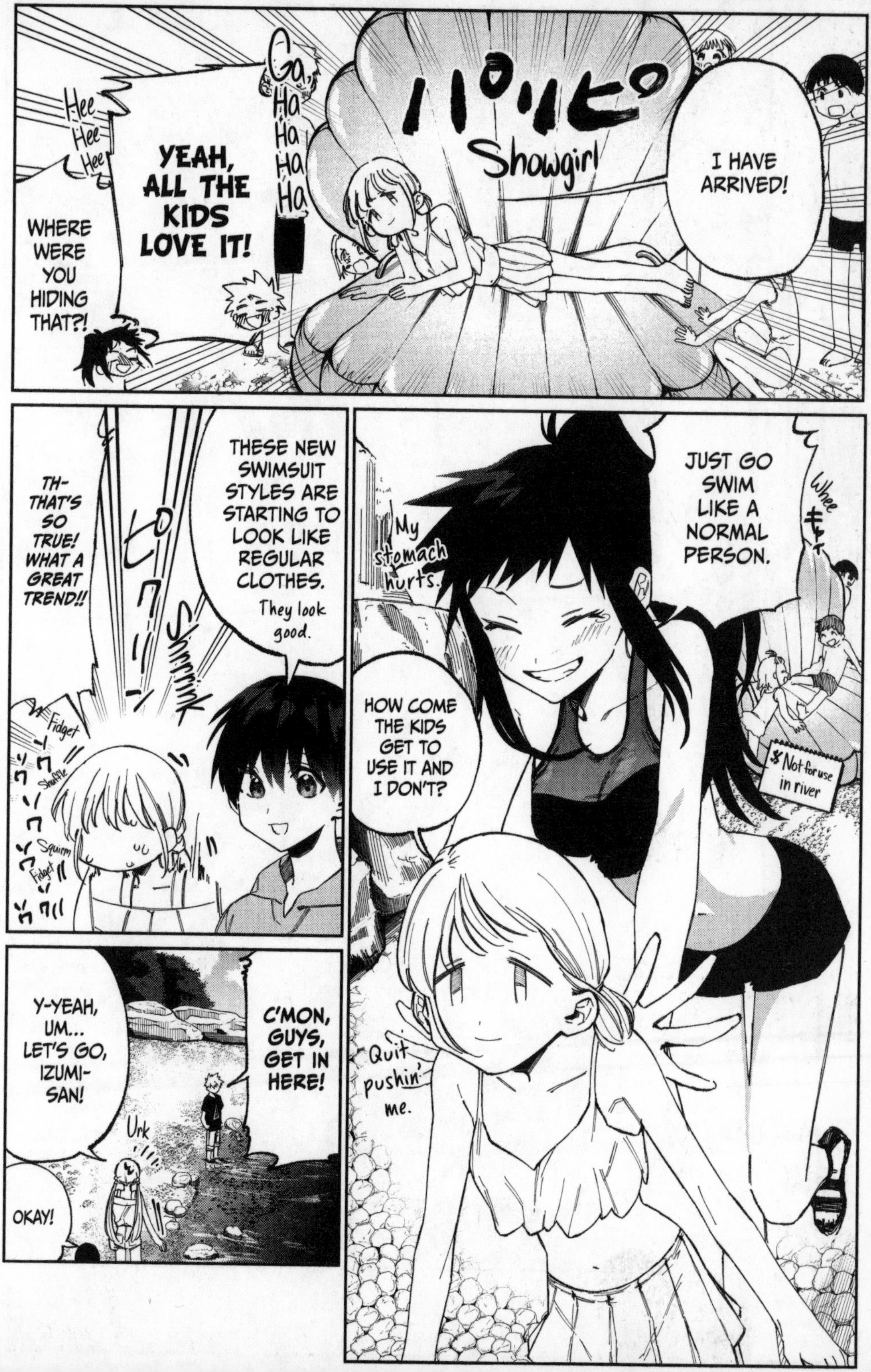
I HAVE ARRIVED!
Showgirl
Ga, Ha Ha Ha Ha
YEAH, ALL THE KIDS LOVE IT!
Hee Hee Hee
WHERE WERE YOU HIDING THAT?!
JUST GO SWIM LIKE A NORMAL PERSON.
Whee
My stomach hurts.
HOW COME THE KIDS GET TO USE IT AND I DON'T?
Not for use in river
Quit pushin' me.
THESE NEW SWIMSUIT STYLES ARE STARTING TO LOOK LIKE REGULAR CLOTHES.
They look good.
Shrrrink
TH-THAT'S SO TRUE! WHAT A GREAT TREND!!
Fidget
Shuffle
Squirm
Fidget
C'MON, GUYS, GET IN HERE!
Y-YEAH, UM... LET'S GO, IZUMI-SAN!
Urk
OKAY!

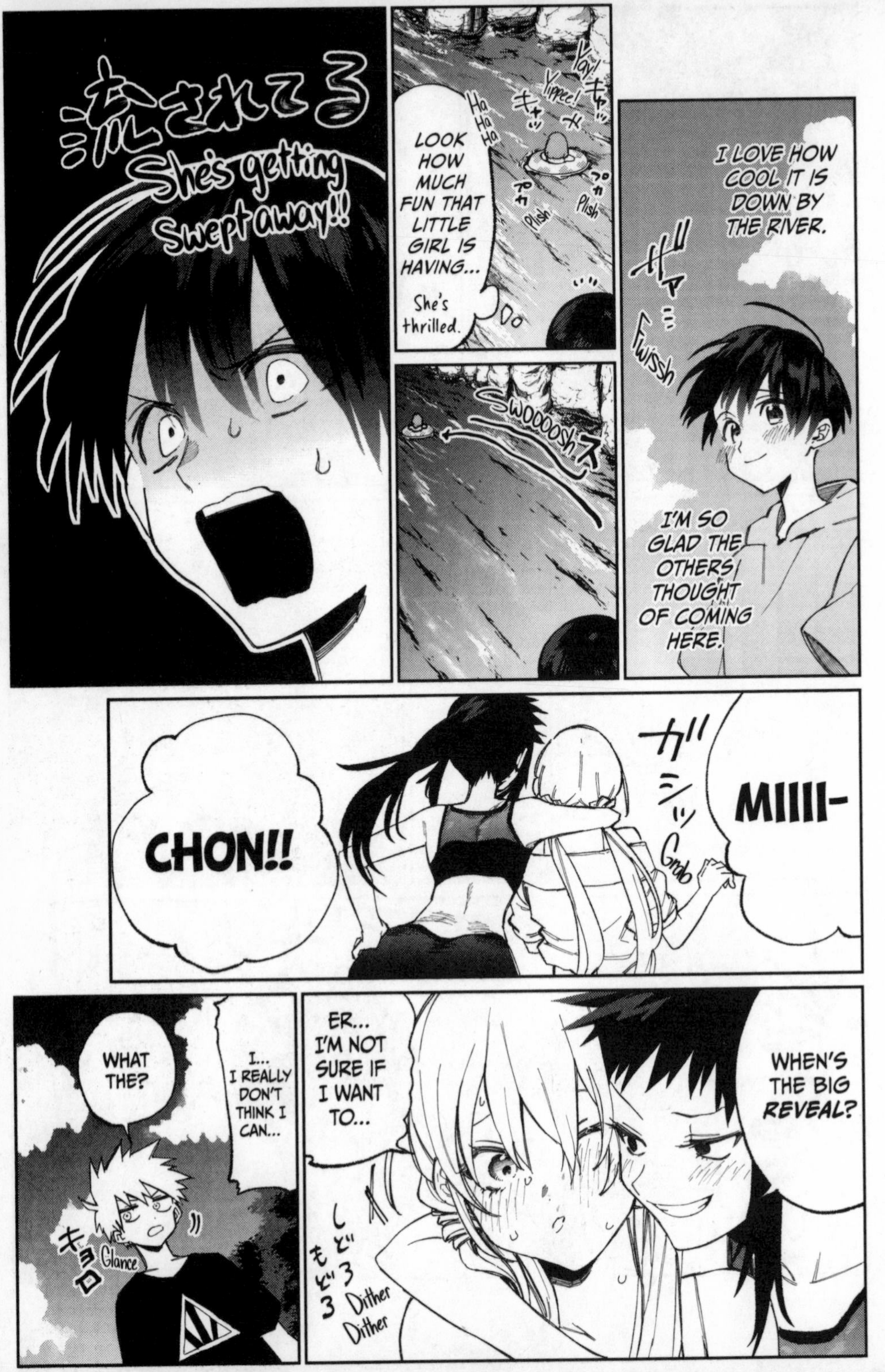
I LOVE HOW COOL IT IS DOWN BY THE RIVER.
Fwissh
I'M SO GLAD THE OTHERS THOUGHT OF COMING HERE.
Yay!
Yippee!
Ha Ha Ha
LOOK HOW MUCH FUN THAT LITTLE GIRL IS HAVING...
She's thrilled.
Plish
Plish
Do
Swoooosh
流されてる
She's getting swept away!!
MIIII-
Grab
CHON!!
WHEN'S THE BIG *REVEAL*?
ER... I'M NOT SURE IF I WANT TO...
Dither Dither
I... I REALLY DON'T THINK I CAN...
WHAT THE?
Glance

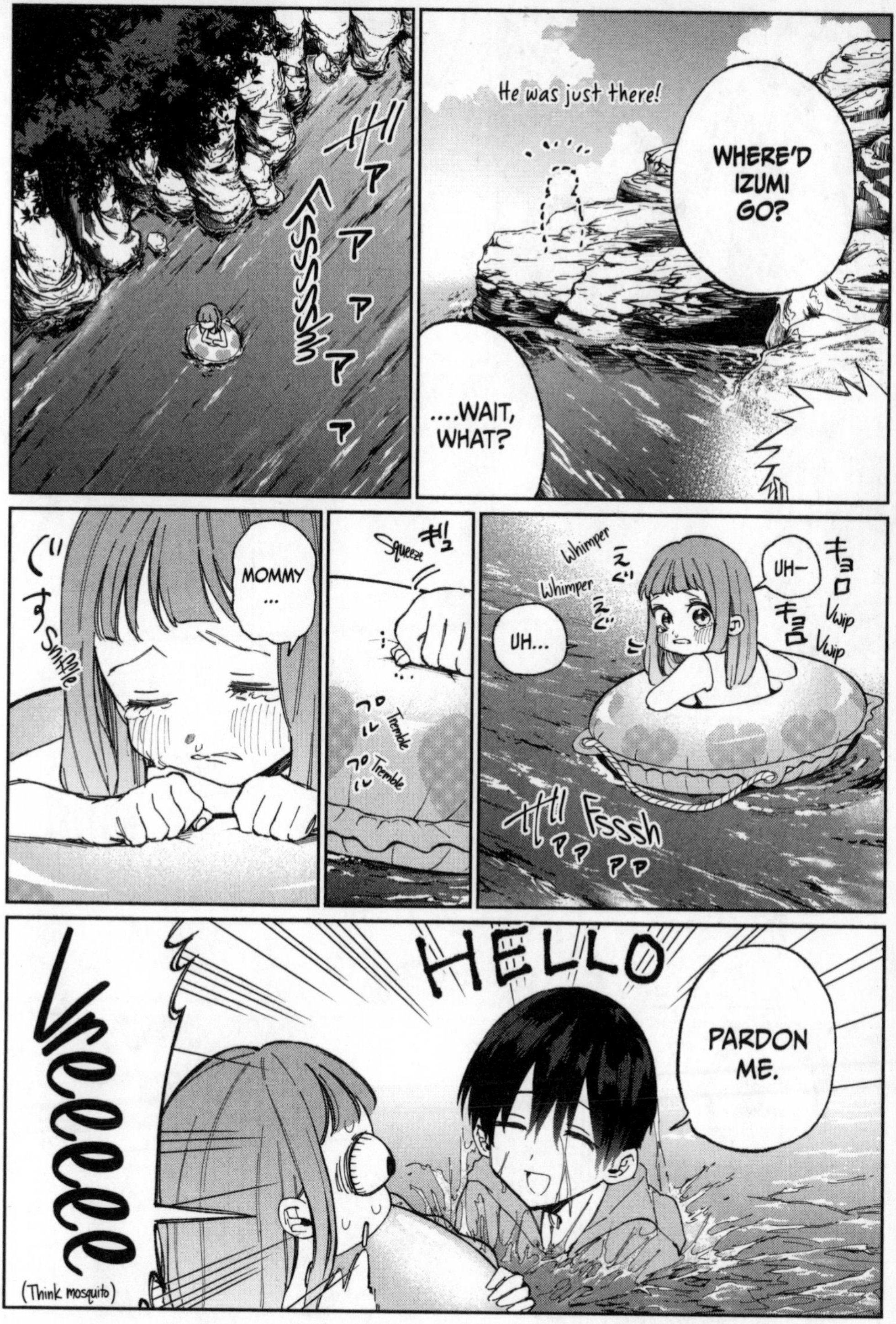
He was just there!
WHERE'D IZUMI GO?
....WAIT, WHAT?
Fssssssh
Whimper
Whimper
UH–
Vwip
Vwip
UH...
Fsssh
Squeeze
Tremble
Tremble
MOMMY ...
Sniffle
HELLO
PARDON ME.
Veeeeee
(Think mosquito)

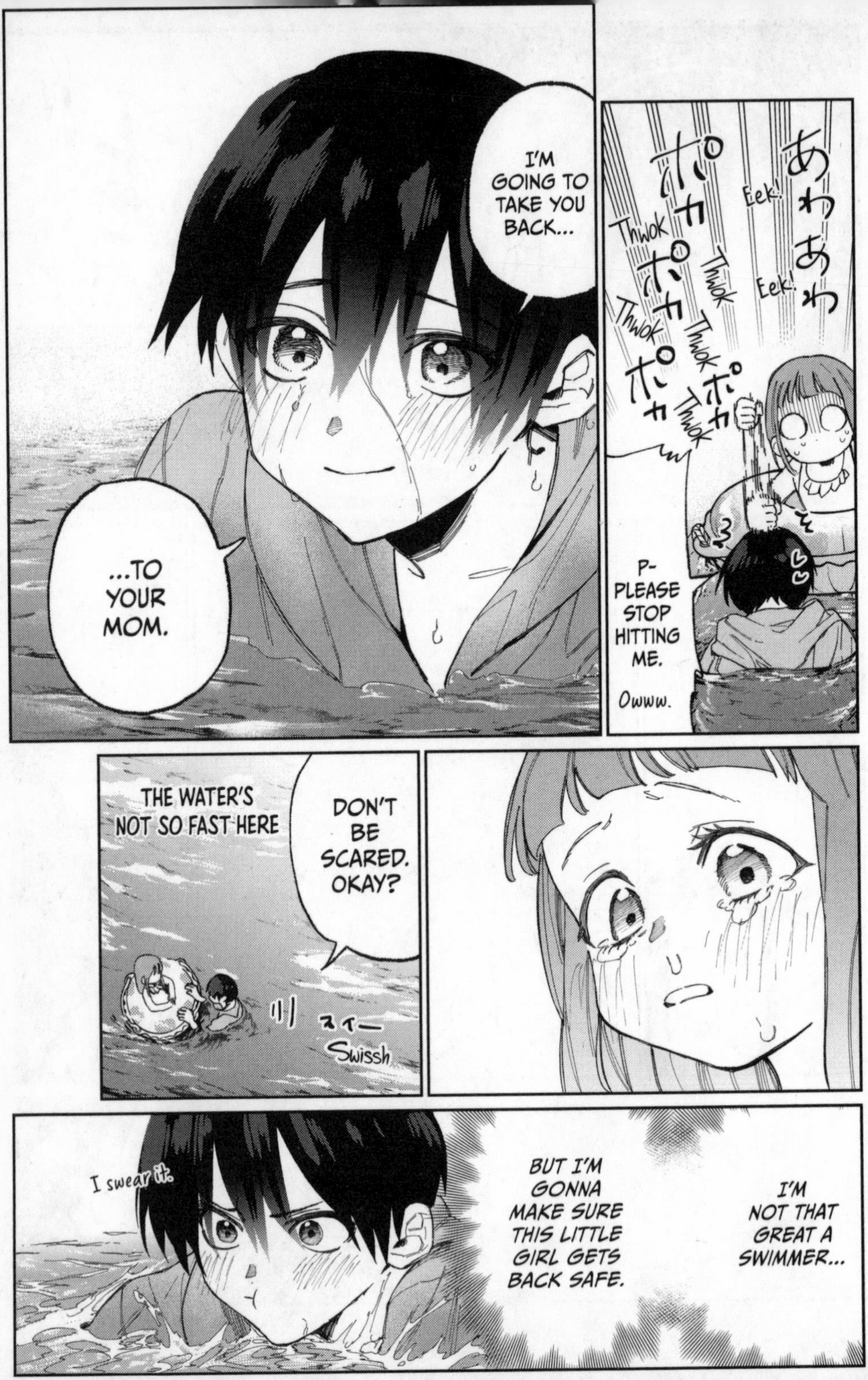

あわあわ
Eek!
Eek!
ポカポカポカポカ
Thwok
Thwok
Thwok
Thwok
Thwok
P-PLEASE STOP HITTING ME.
Owww.
I'M GOING TO TAKE YOU BACK...
...TO YOUR MOM.
DON'T BE SCARED. OKAY?
THE WATER'S NOT SO FAST HERE
スイー
Swissh
I'M NOT THAT GREAT A SWIMMER...
BUT I'M GONNA MAKE SURE THIS LITTLE GIRL GETS BACK SAFE.
I swear it.

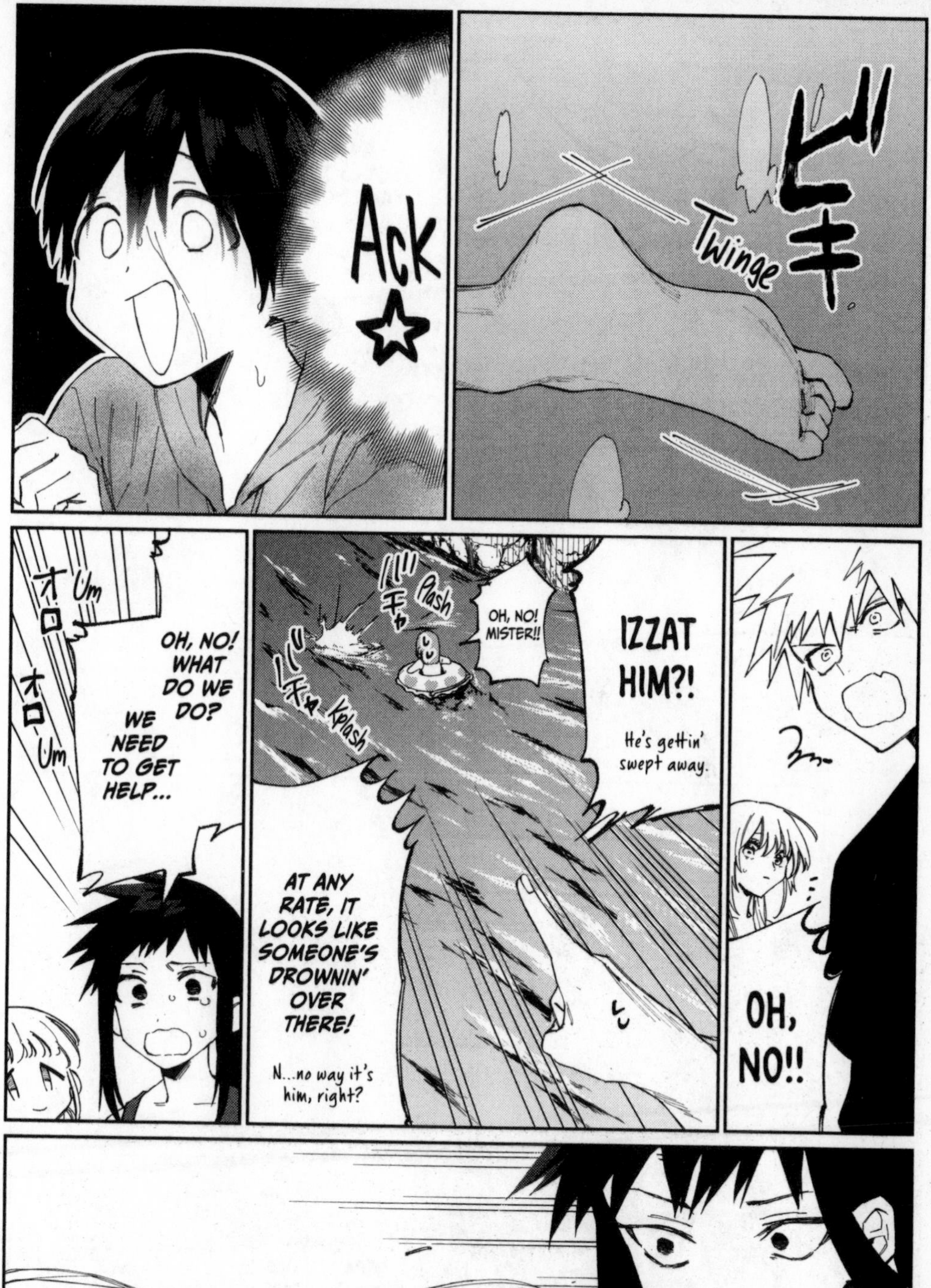
ビキ
Twinge
Ack
IZZAT HIM?!
He's gettin' swept away.
OH, NO!!
Plash
Kplash
OH, NO! MISTER!!
AT ANY RATE, IT LOOKS LIKE SOMEONE'S DROWNIN' OVER THERE!
N...no way it's him, right?
オロ Um
オロ Um
OH, NO! WHAT DO WE DO?
WE NEED TO GET HELP...

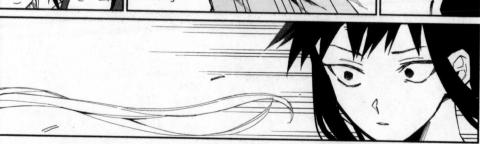

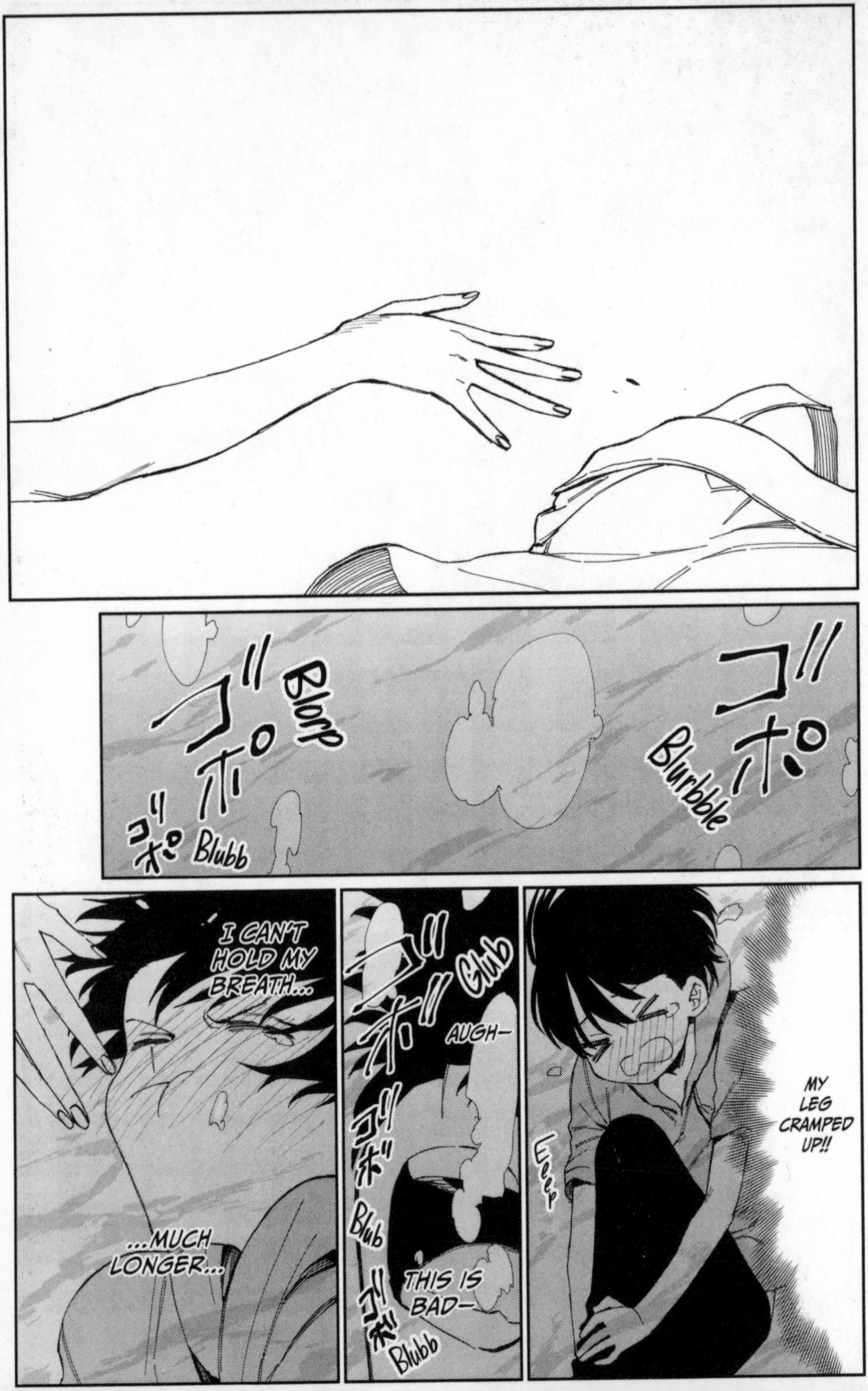
Blurbble
Blorp
Blubb
MY LEG CRAMPED UP!!
Eeep
Glub
AUGH—
Blub
THIS IS BAD—
Blubb
I CAN'T HOLD MY BREATH...
...MUCH LONGER...

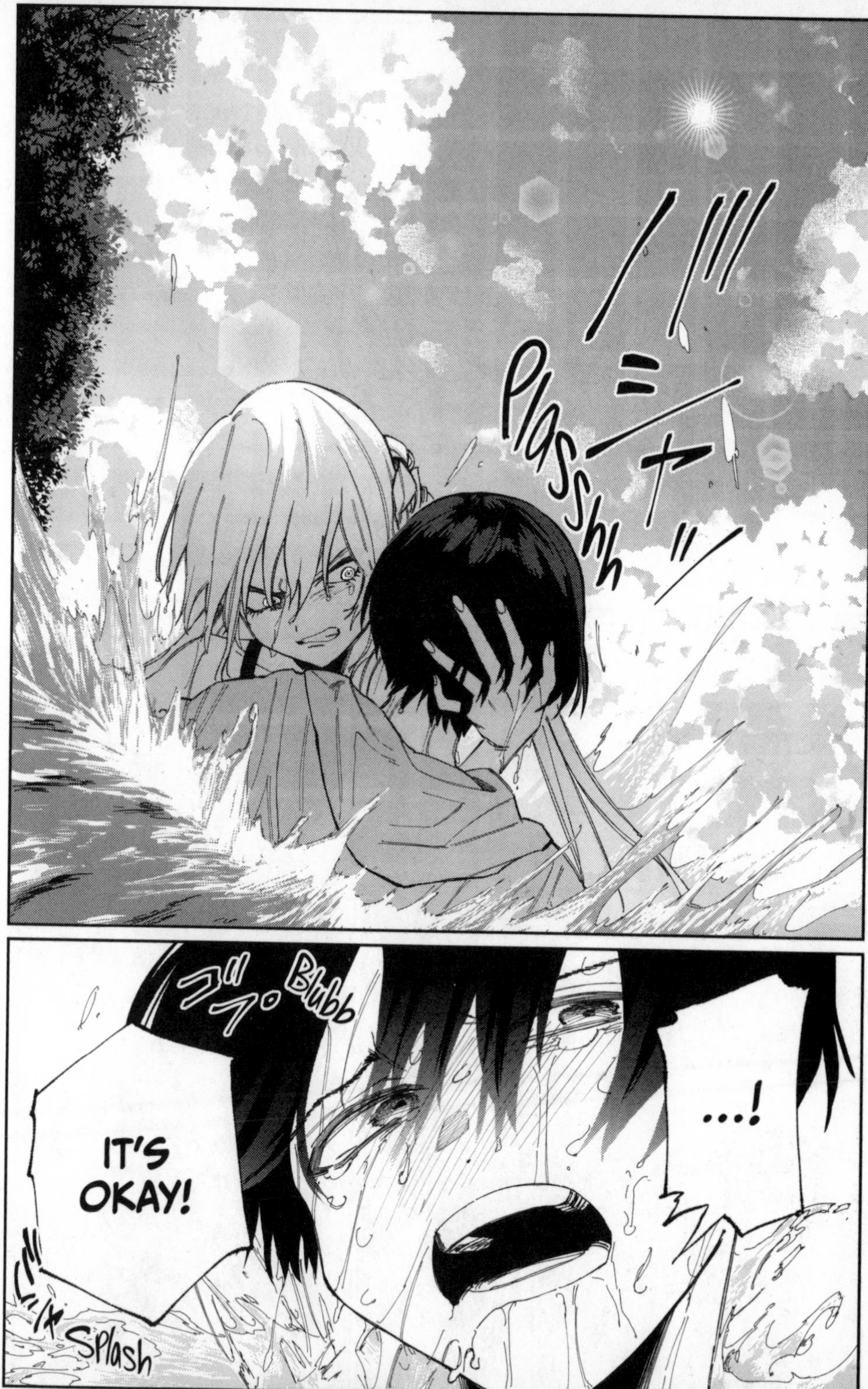
Plasshh
Blubb
...!
IT'S OKAY!
Splash

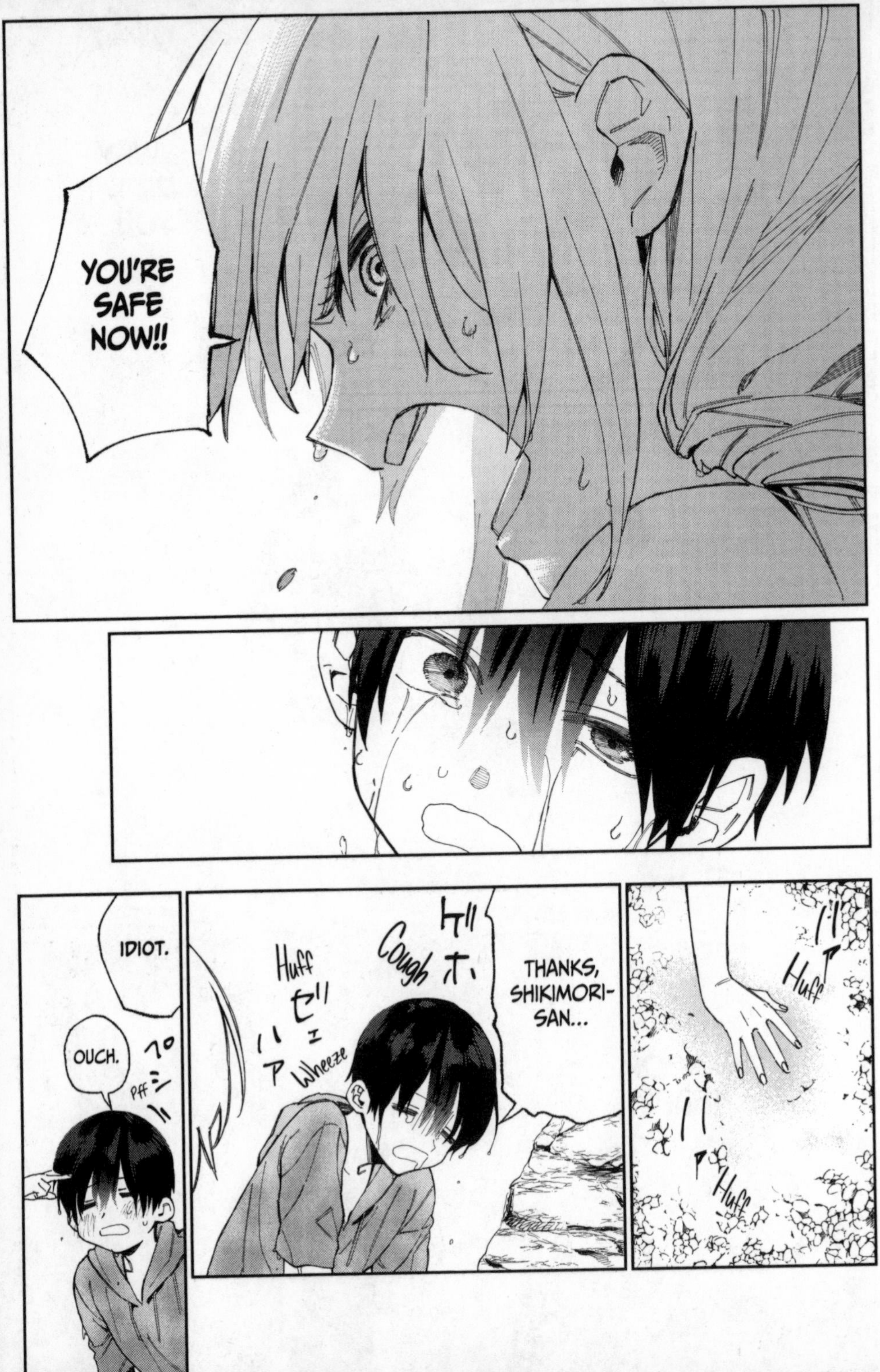
YOU'RE SAFE NOW!!
Huff
Huff
Cough
Huff
Wheeze
THANKS, SHIKIMORI-SAN...
IDIOT.
OUCH.
Pff

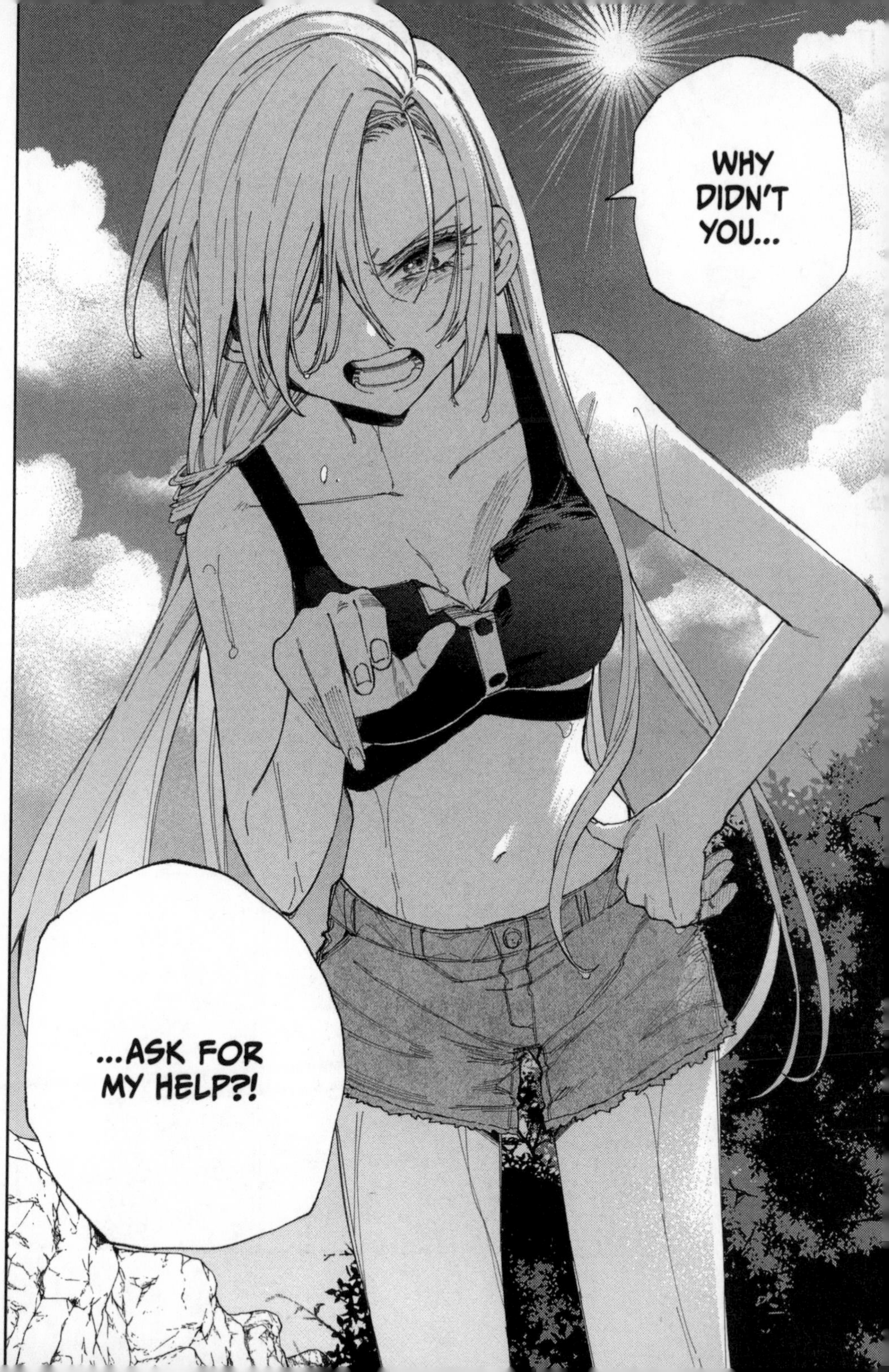
WHY DIDN'T YOU...
...ASK FOR MY HELP?!

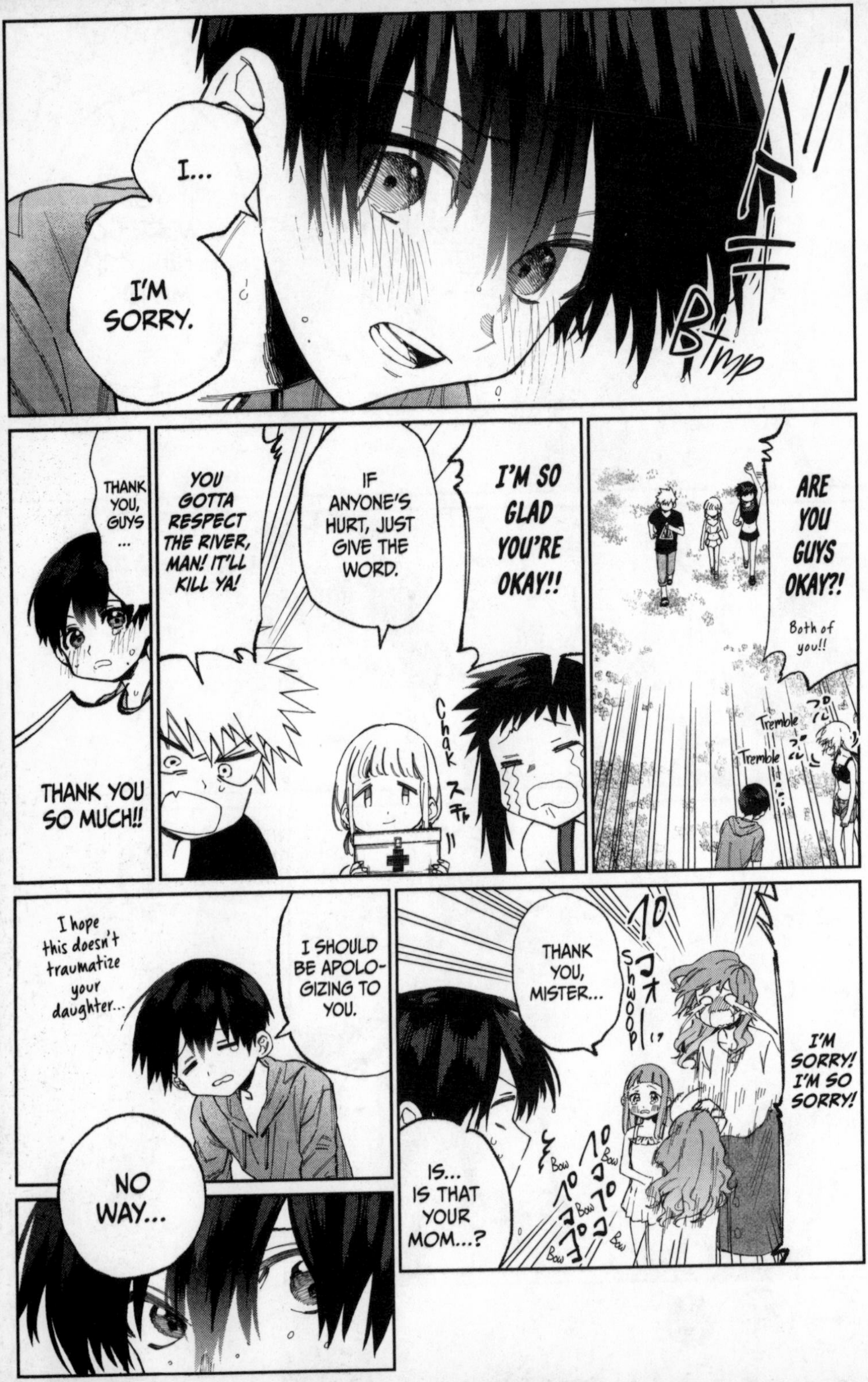
I...
I'M SORRY.
Btmp
ARE YOU GUYS OKAY?!
Both of you!!
Tremble
Tremble
I'M SO GLAD YOU'RE OKAY!!
IF ANYONE'S HURT, JUST GIVE THE WORD.
Chak
YOU GOTTA RESPECT THE RIVER, MAN! IT'LL KILL YA!
THANK YOU, GUYS ...
THANK YOU SO MUCH!!
I'M SORRY! I'M SO SORRY!
THANK YOU, MISTER...
Shwoop
Bow
Bow
Bow
Bow
IS... IS THAT YOUR MOM...?
I SHOULD BE APOLOGIZING TO YOU.
I hope this doesn't traumatize your daughter...
NO WAY...

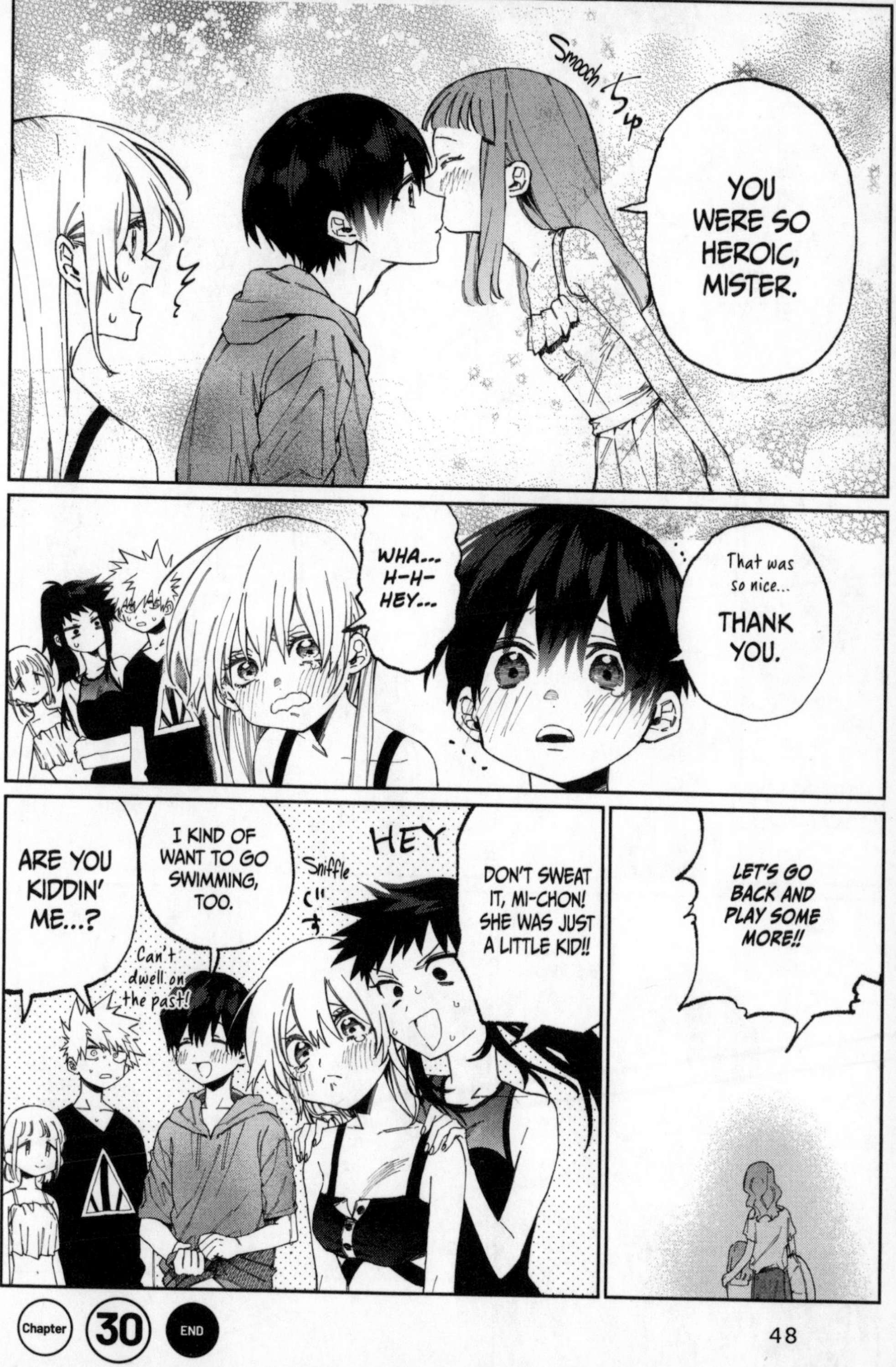
Smooch Sip
YOU WERE SO HEROIC, MISTER.
That was so nice...
THANK YOU.
WHA... H-H-HEY...
LET'S GO BACK AND PLAY SOME MORE!!
DON'T SWEAT IT, MI-CHON! SHE WAS JUST A LITTLE KID!!
HEY
Sniffle
I KIND OF WANT TO GO SWIMMING, TOO.
ARE YOU KIDDIN' ME...?
Can't dwell on the past!

Chapter 30 END

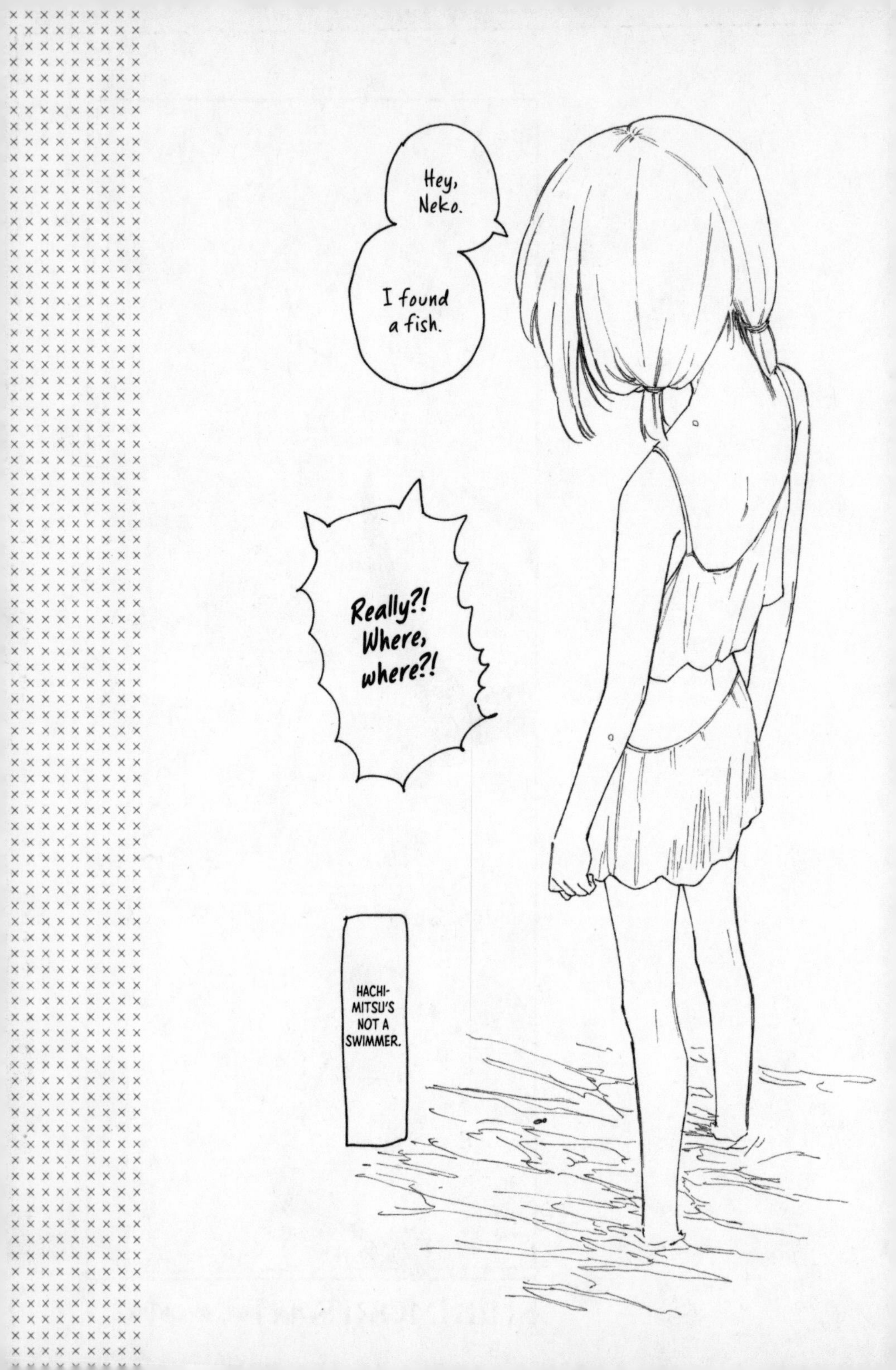

Hey, Neko.
I found a fish.
Really?! Where, where?!
HACHI-MITSU'S NOT A SWIMMER.

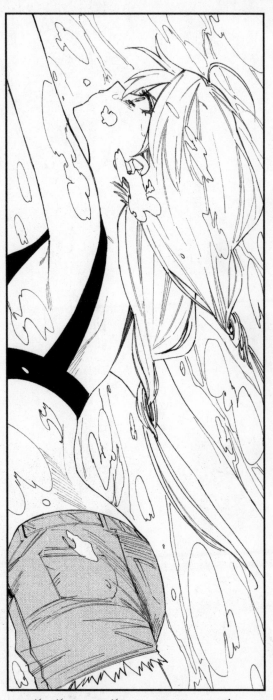

SHIKIMORI'S not just a cutie

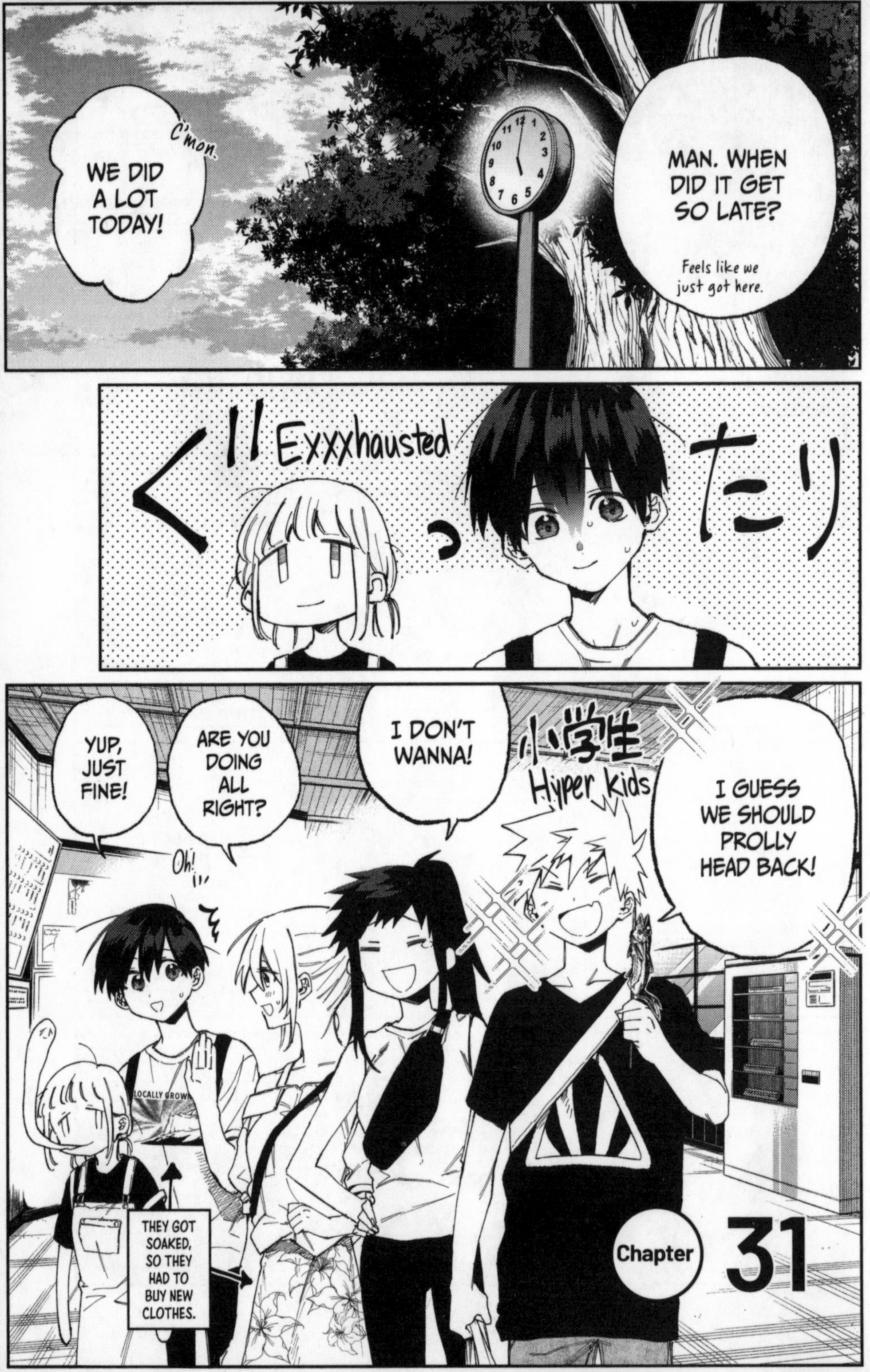
MAN. WHEN DID IT GET SO LATE?
Feels like we just got here.
C'mon.
WE DID A LOT TODAY!
ぐったり
Exxxhausted
I GUESS WE SHOULD PROLLY HEAD BACK!
小学生
Hyper kids
I DON'T WANNA!
ARE YOU DOING ALL RIGHT?
Oh!
YUP, JUST FINE!
LOCALLY GROWN
THEY GOT SOAKED, SO THEY HAD TO BUY NEW CLOTHES.
Chapter 31

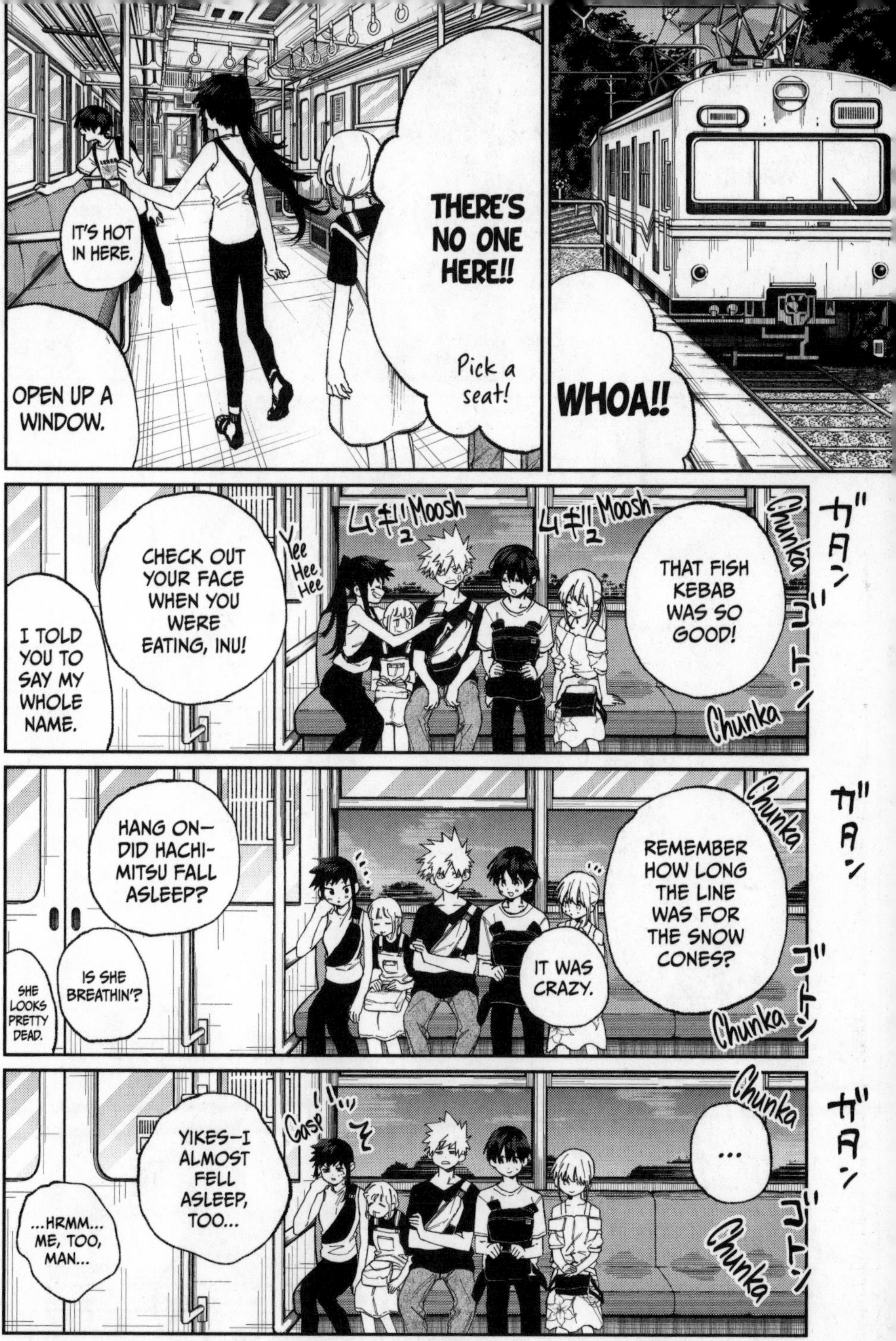
WHOA!!
THERE'S NO ONE HERE!!
Pick a seat!
IT'S HOT IN HERE.
OPEN UP A WINDOW.
ガタン ゴトン
Chunka Chunka
THAT FISH KEBAB WAS SO GOOD!
ムギュ Moosh
ムギュ Moosh
Yee Hee Hee
CHECK OUT YOUR FACE WHEN YOU WERE EATING, INU!
I TOLD YOU TO SAY MY WHOLE NAME.
ガタン ゴトン
Chunka Chunka
REMEMBER HOW LONG THE LINE WAS FOR THE SNOW CONES?
IT WAS CRAZY.
HANG ON—DID HACHI-MITSU FALL ASLEEP?
IS SHE BREATHIN'?
SHE LOOKS PRETTY DEAD.
ガタン ゴトン
Chunka Chunka
...
Gasp
YIKES—I ALMOST FELL ASLEEP, TOO...
...HRMM... ME, TOO, MAN...

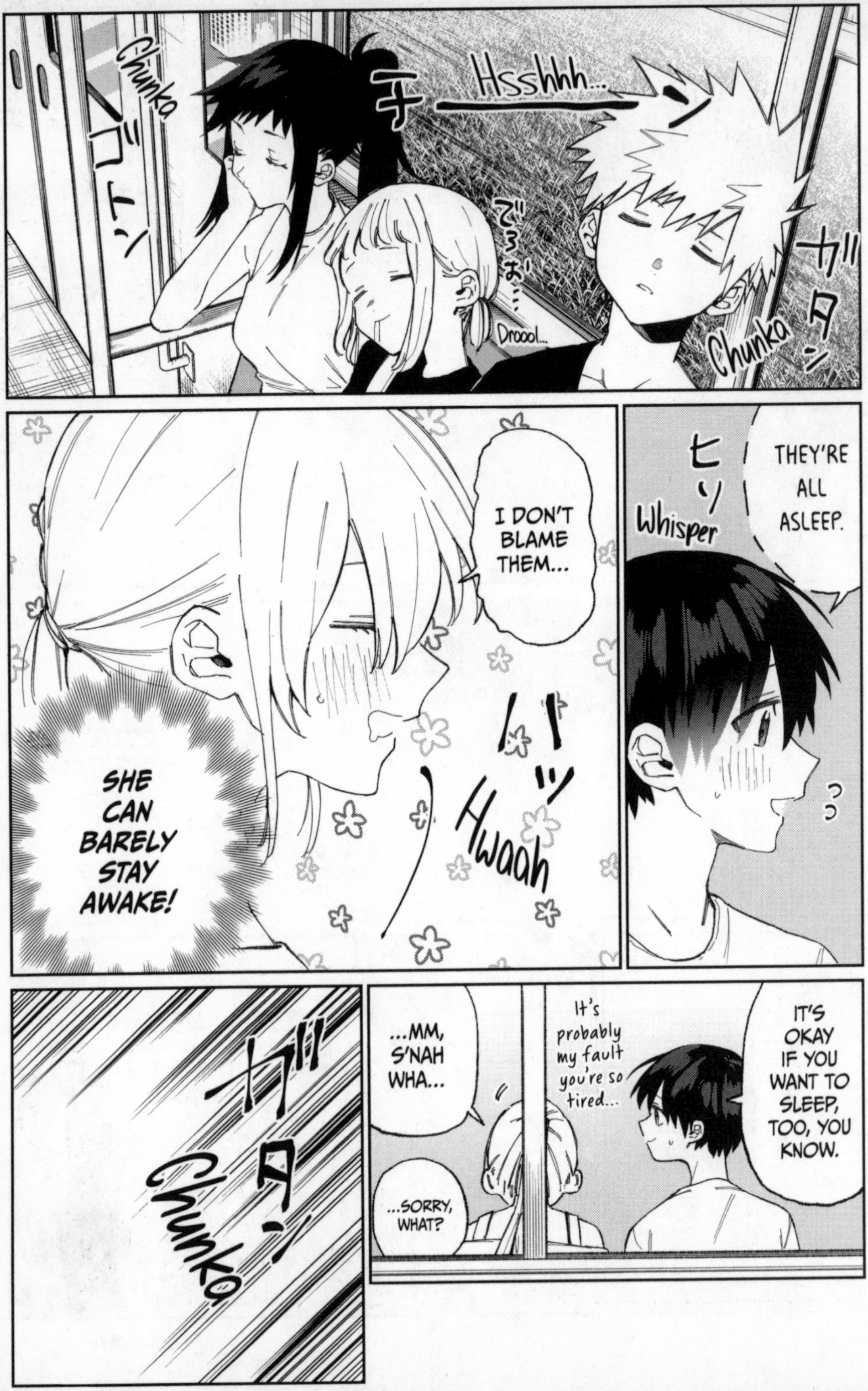
ガタン
Chunka
Hsshhh...
Drooool...
ゴトン
Chunka
ヒソ
Whisper
THEY'RE ALL ASLEEP.
I DON'T BLAME THEM...
ハッ
Hwaah
SHE CAN BARELY STAY AWAKE!
IT'S OKAY IF YOU WANT TO SLEEP, TOO, YOU KNOW.
It's probably my fault you're so tired...
...MM, S'NAH WHA...
...SORRY, WHAT?
ガタン
Chunka

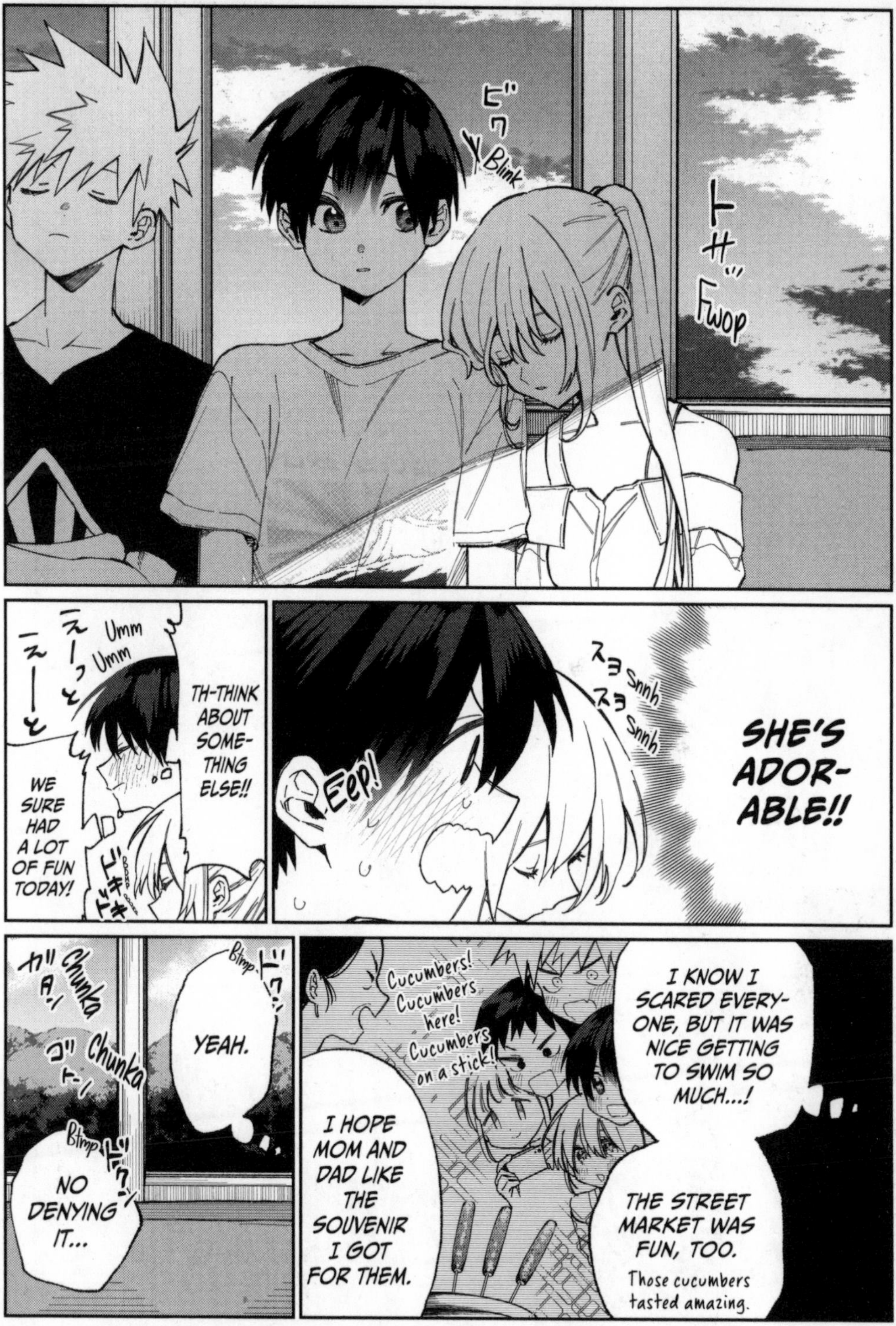
ビクッ
Blink
トサッ
Fwop
スヨ Snnh
スヨ Snnh
Eep!
SHE'S ADORABLE!!
えーっと
えーと
Umm
Umm
TH-THINK ABOUT SOMETHING ELSE!!
WE SURE HAD A LOT OF FUN TODAY!
ドキドキ
I KNOW I SCARED EVERYONE, BUT IT WAS NICE GETTING TO SWIM SO MUCH...!
Cucumbers! Cucumbers here! Cucumbers on a stick!
THE STREET MARKET WAS FUN, TOO.
Those cucumbers tasted amazing.
I HOPE MOM AND DAD LIKE THE SOUVENIR I GOT FOR THEM.
ガタッ Chunka
ゴトッ Chunka
ドクッ Btmp
YEAH.
ドクッ Btmp
NO DENYING IT...

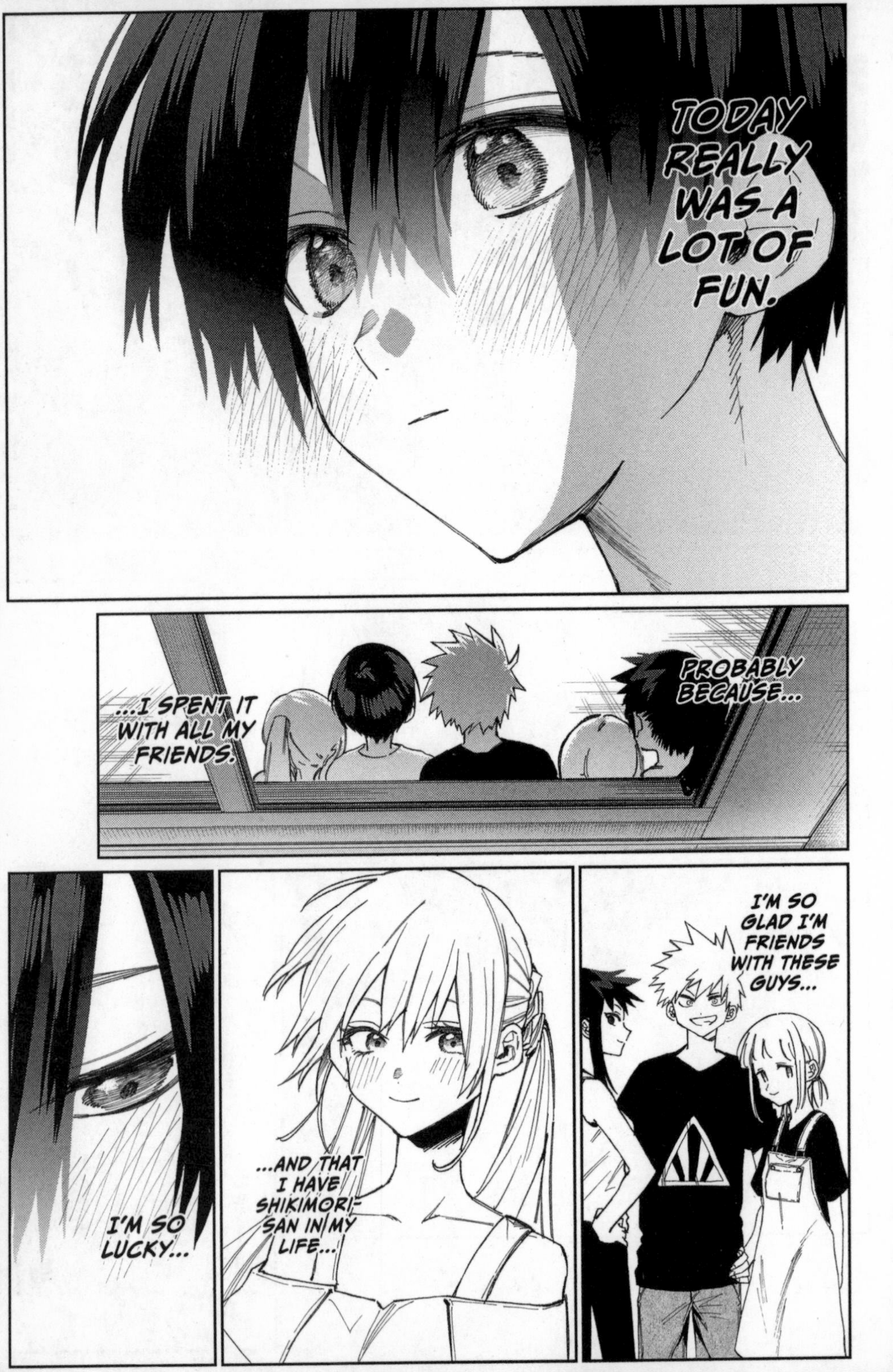
TODAY REALLY WAS A LOT OF FUN.
PROBABLY BECAUSE...
...I SPENT IT WITH ALL MY FRIENDS.
I'M SO GLAD I'M FRIENDS WITH THESE GUYS...
...AND THAT I HAVE SHIKIMORI-SAN IN MY LIFE...
I'M SO LUCKY...

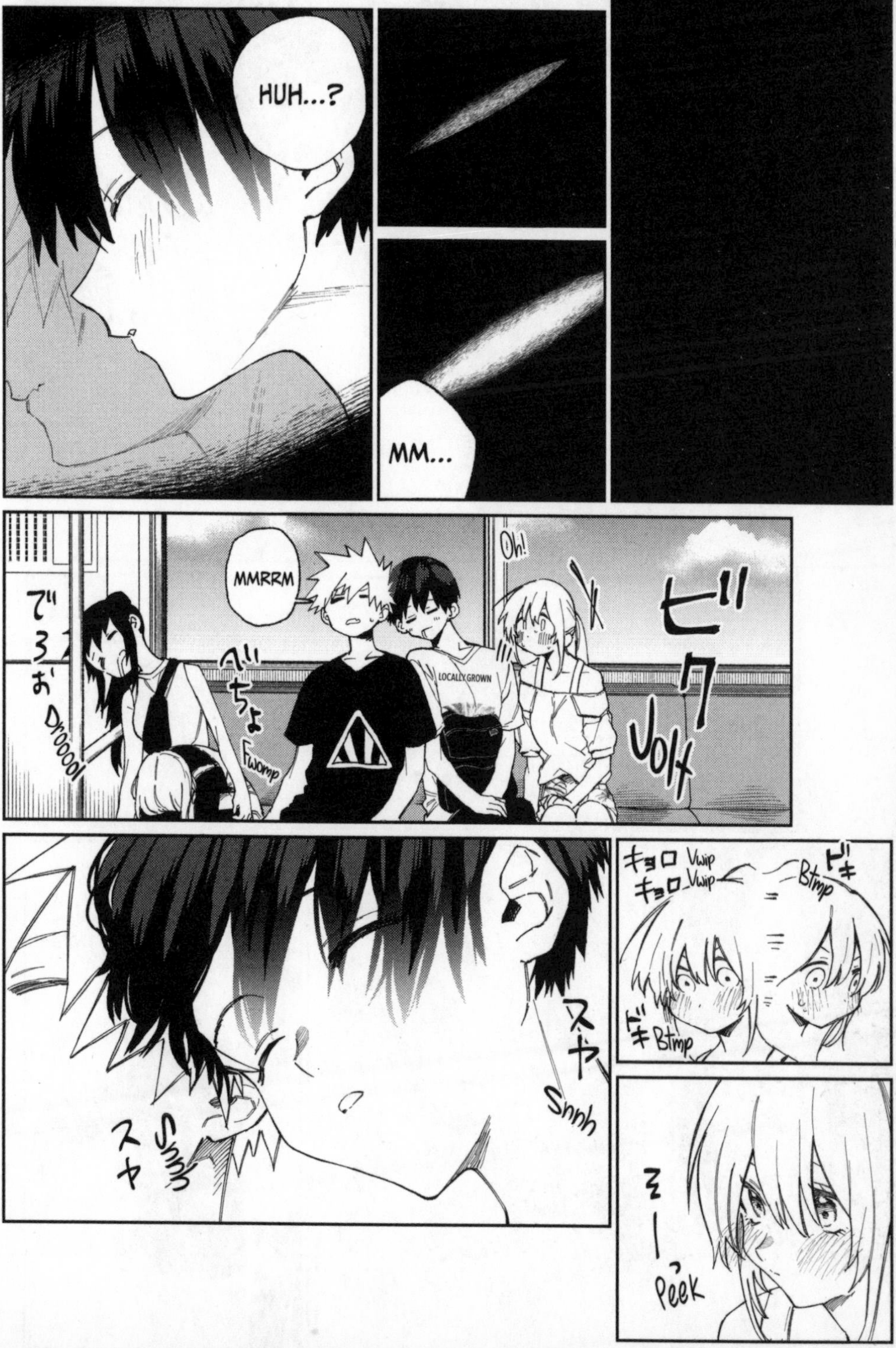
MM...
HUH...?
ビク Jolt
Oh!
MMRRM
べちょ Fwomp
でろぉ Droooo!
キョロ Vwip
キョロ Vwip
ドキ Btmp
ドキ Btmp
ミー Peek
スヤ Snnh
スヤ Snnn

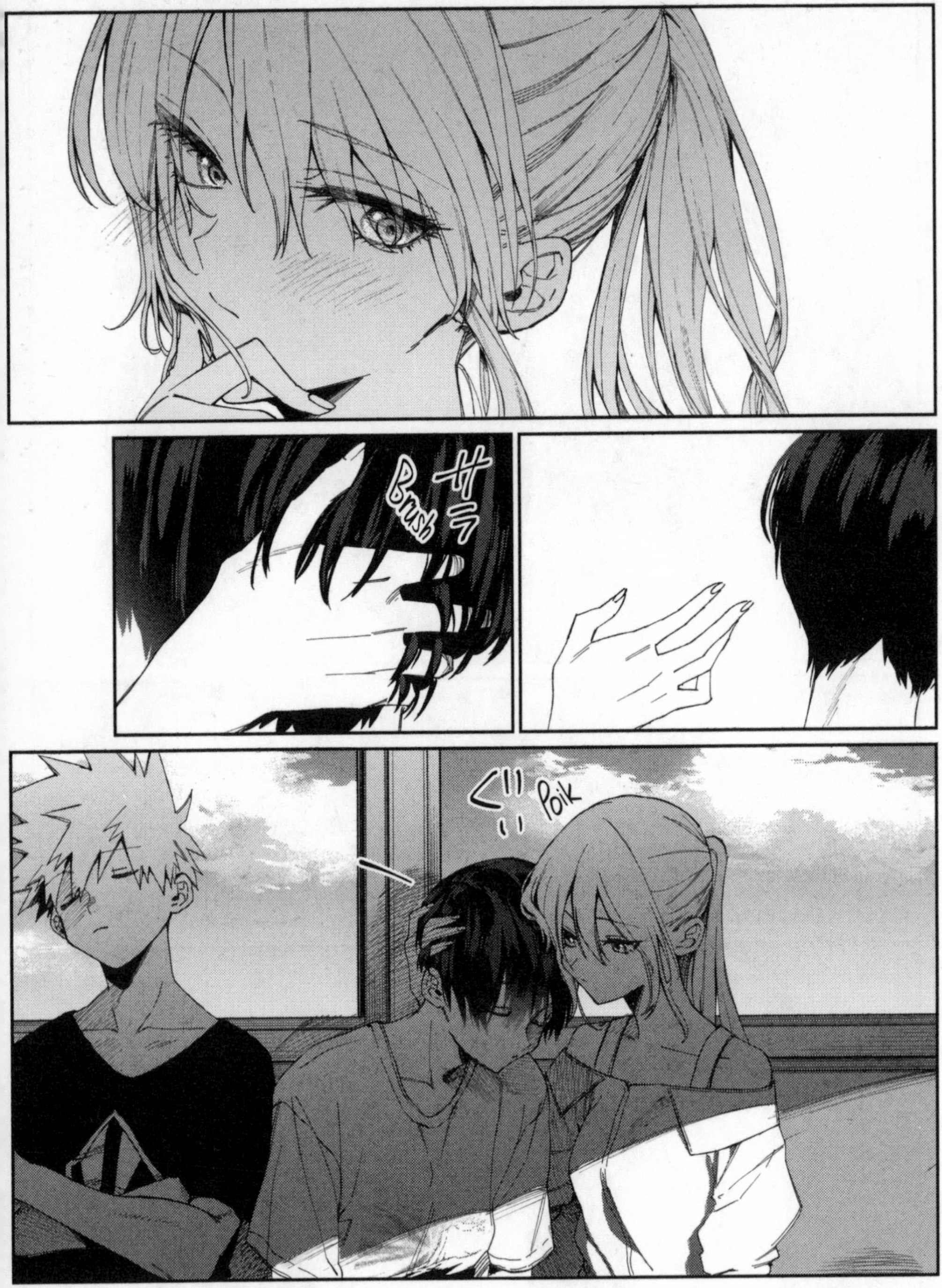
サラ
Brush
ぐい
Poik

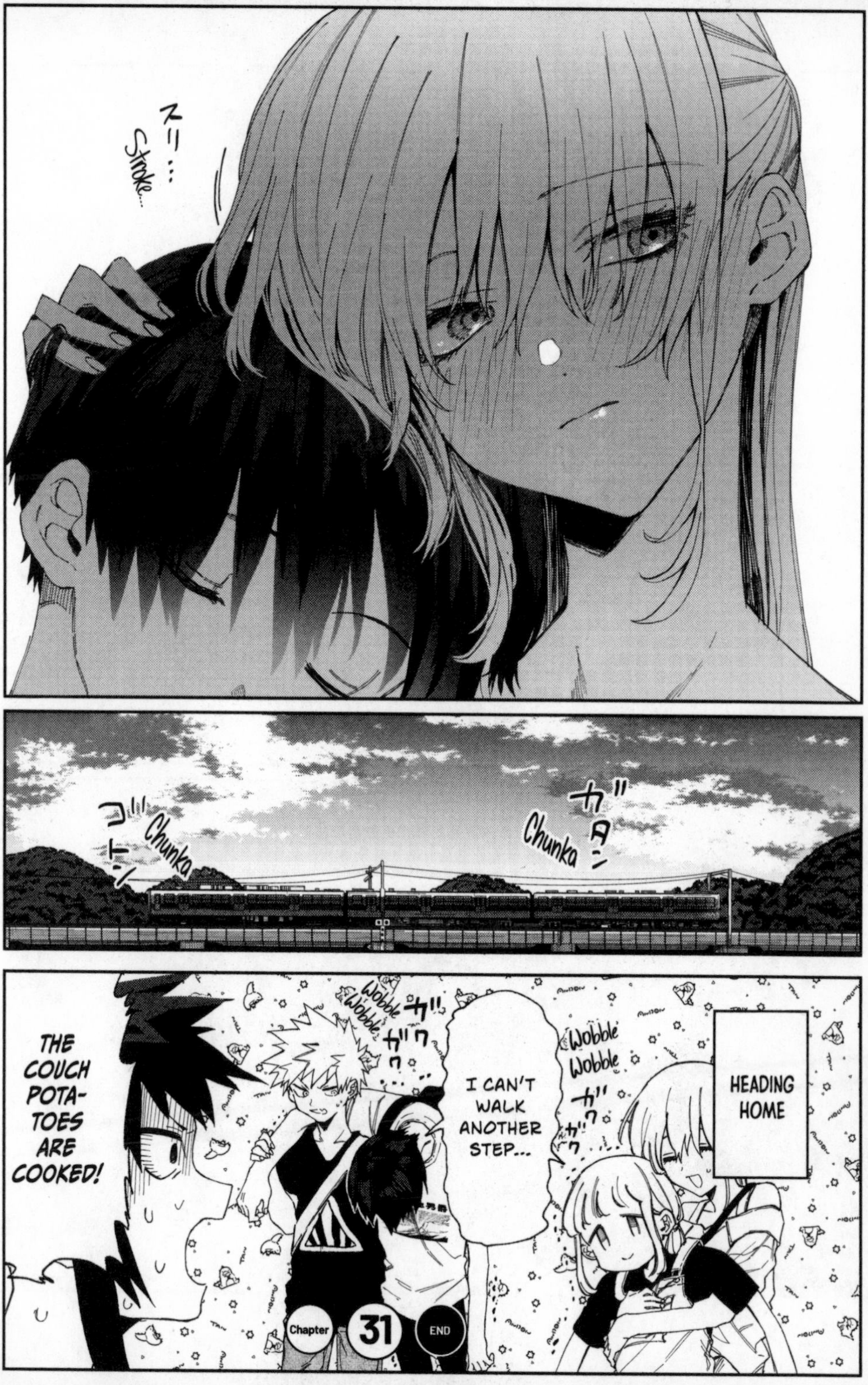
スリ…
Stroke...
ガタン
Chunka
ゴトン
Chunka
HEADING HOME
Wobble Wobble
ガクガク
I CAN'T WALK ANOTHER STEP...
Wobble Wobble
ガクガク
THE COUCH POTA-TOES ARE COOKED!
Chapter 31 END

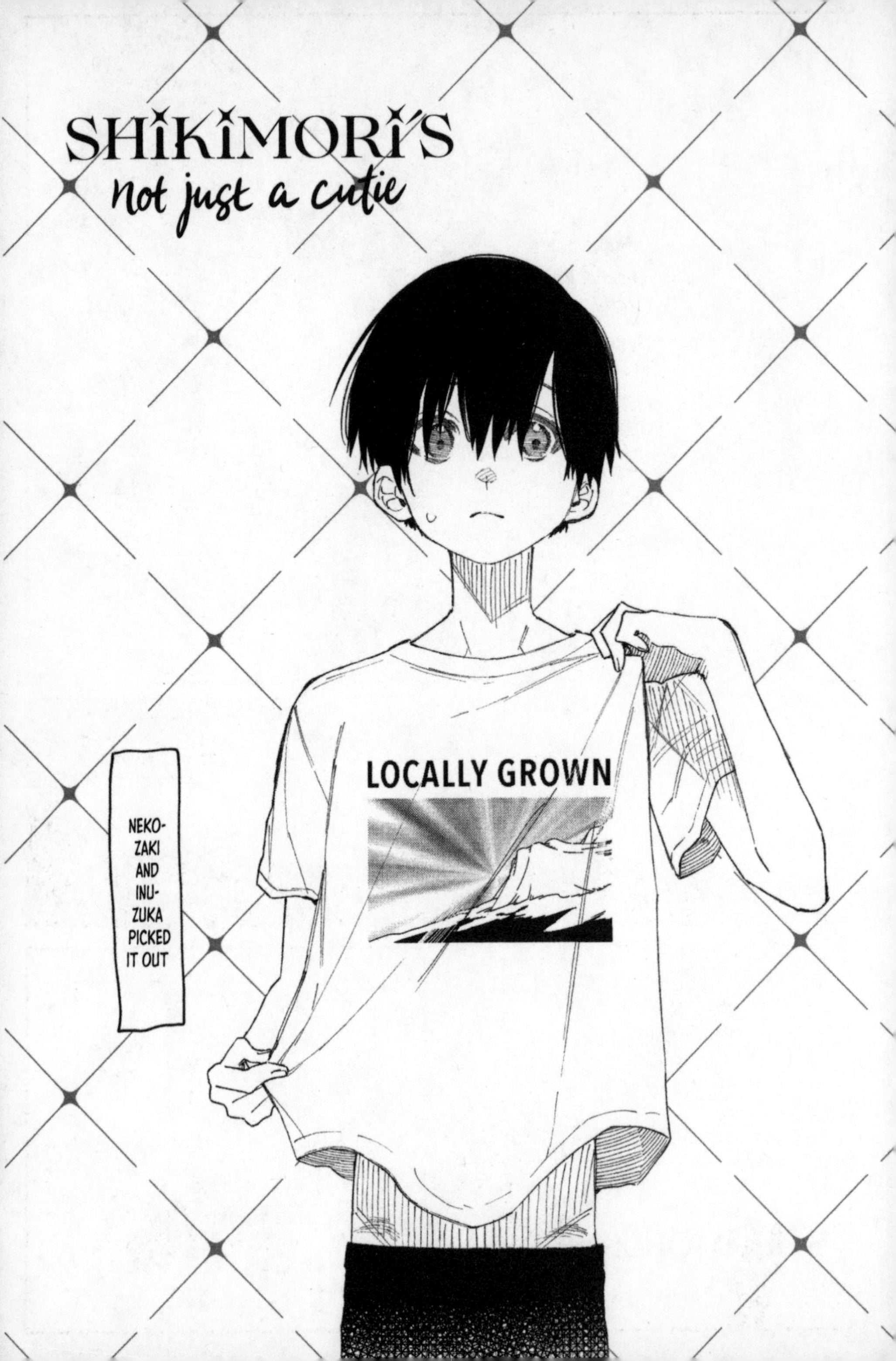
SHIKIMORI'S
not just a cutie
NEKO-ZAKI AND INU-ZUKA PICKED IT OUT
LOCALLY GROWN

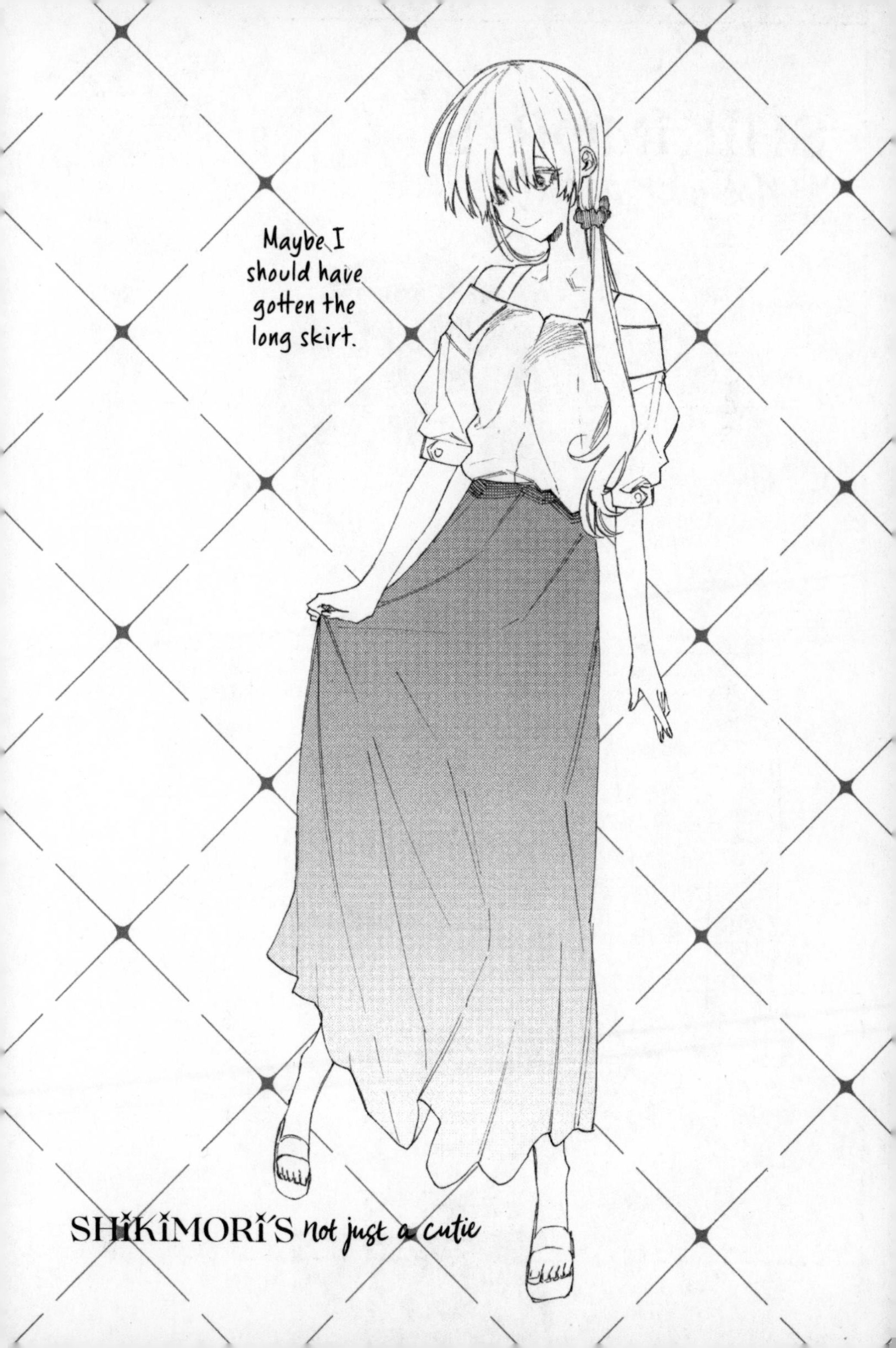
Maybe I should have gotten the long skirt.
SHIKIMORI'S not just a cutie

Chapter 32

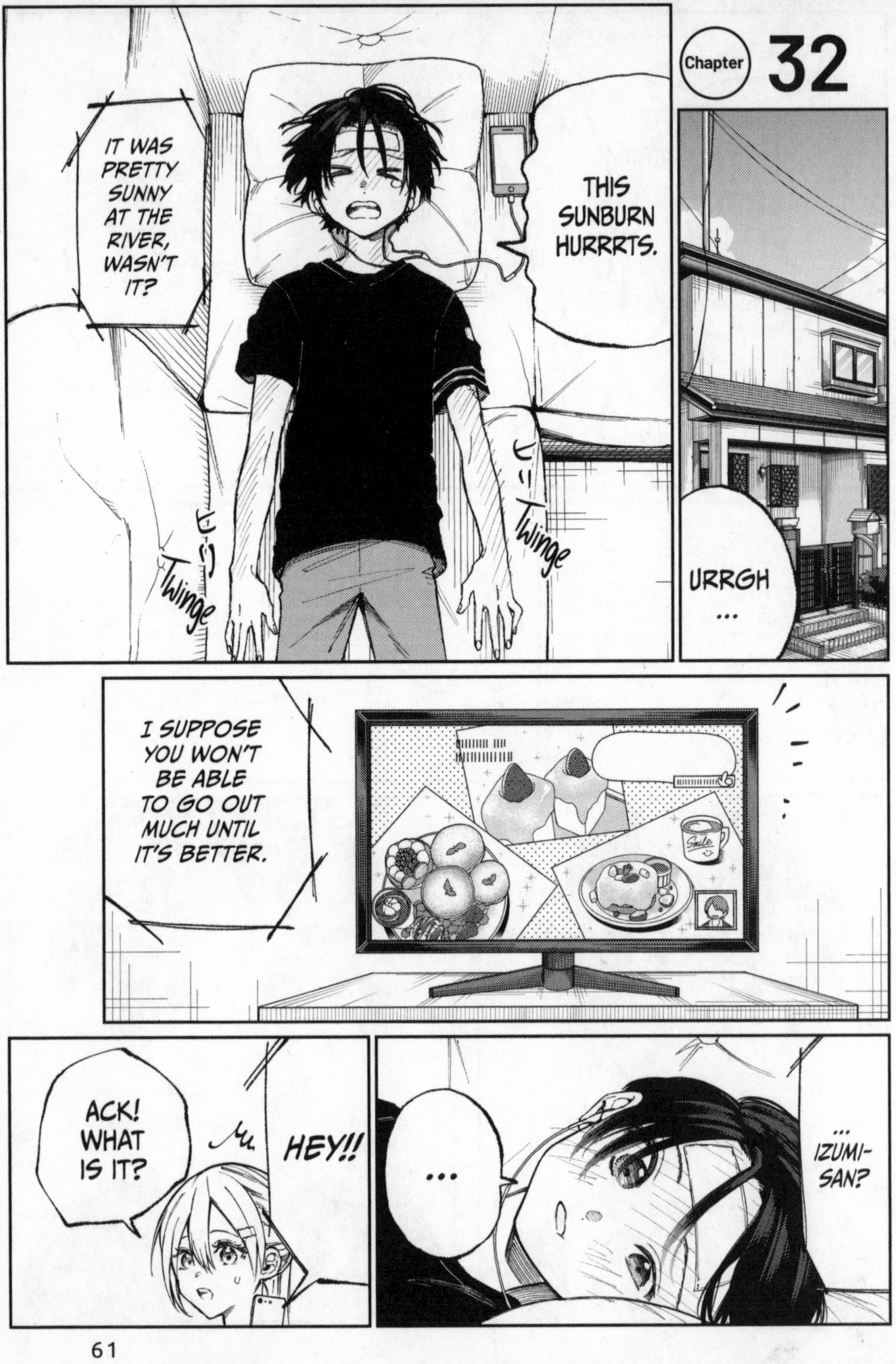

URRGH ...
THIS SUNBURN HURRRTS.
IT WAS PRETTY SUNNY AT THE RIVER, WASN'T IT?
Twinge
Twinge
I SUPPOSE YOU WON'T BE ABLE TO GO OUT MUCH UNTIL IT'S BETTER.
... IZUMI-SAN?
...
HEY!!
ACK! WHAT IS IT?

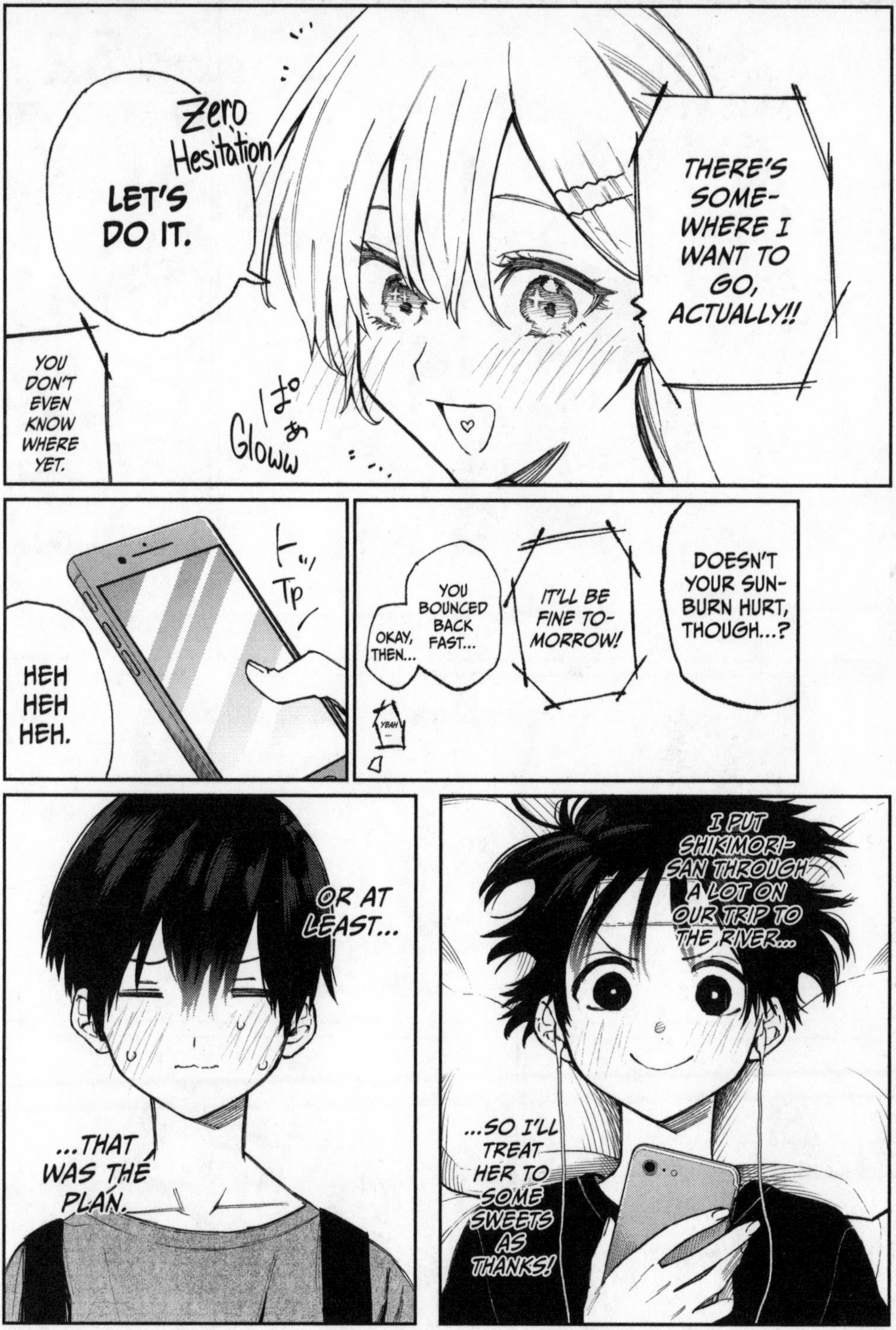
THERE'S SOME-WHERE I WANT TO GO, ACTUALLY!!
Zero Hesitation
LET'S DO IT.
YOU DON'T EVEN KNOW WHERE YET.
ぱぁ
Gloww
DOESN'T YOUR SUN-BURN HURT, THOUGH...?
IT'LL BE FINE TO-MORROW!
YOU BOUNCED BACK FAST...
OKAY, THEN...
トッ
Tp
HEH HEH HEH.
I PUT SHIKIMORI-SAN THROUGH A LOT ON OUR TRIP TO THE RIVER...
...SO I'LL TREAT HER TO SOME SWEETS AS THANKS!
OR AT LEAST...
...THAT WAS THE PLAN.

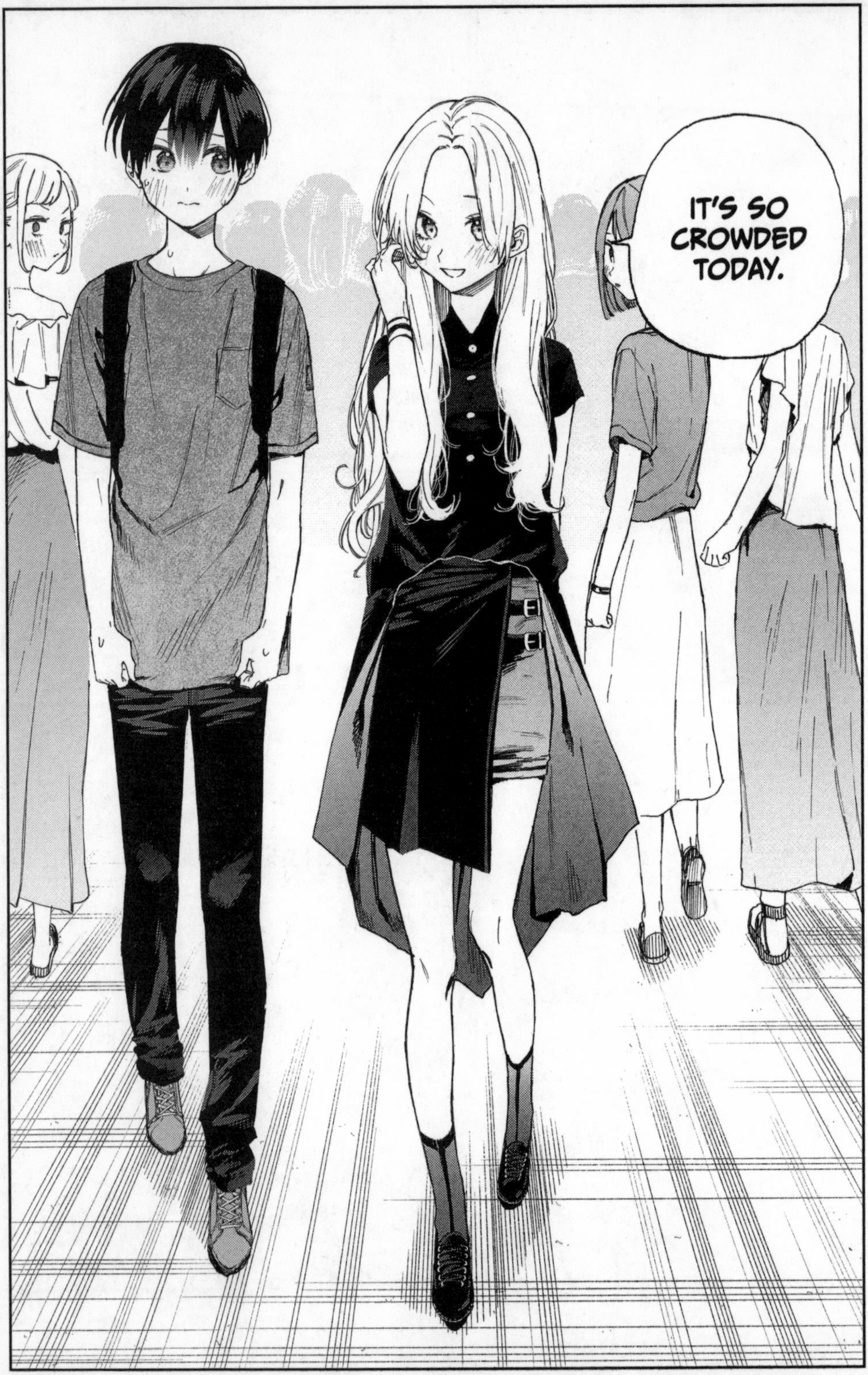
IT'S SO CROWDED TODAY.

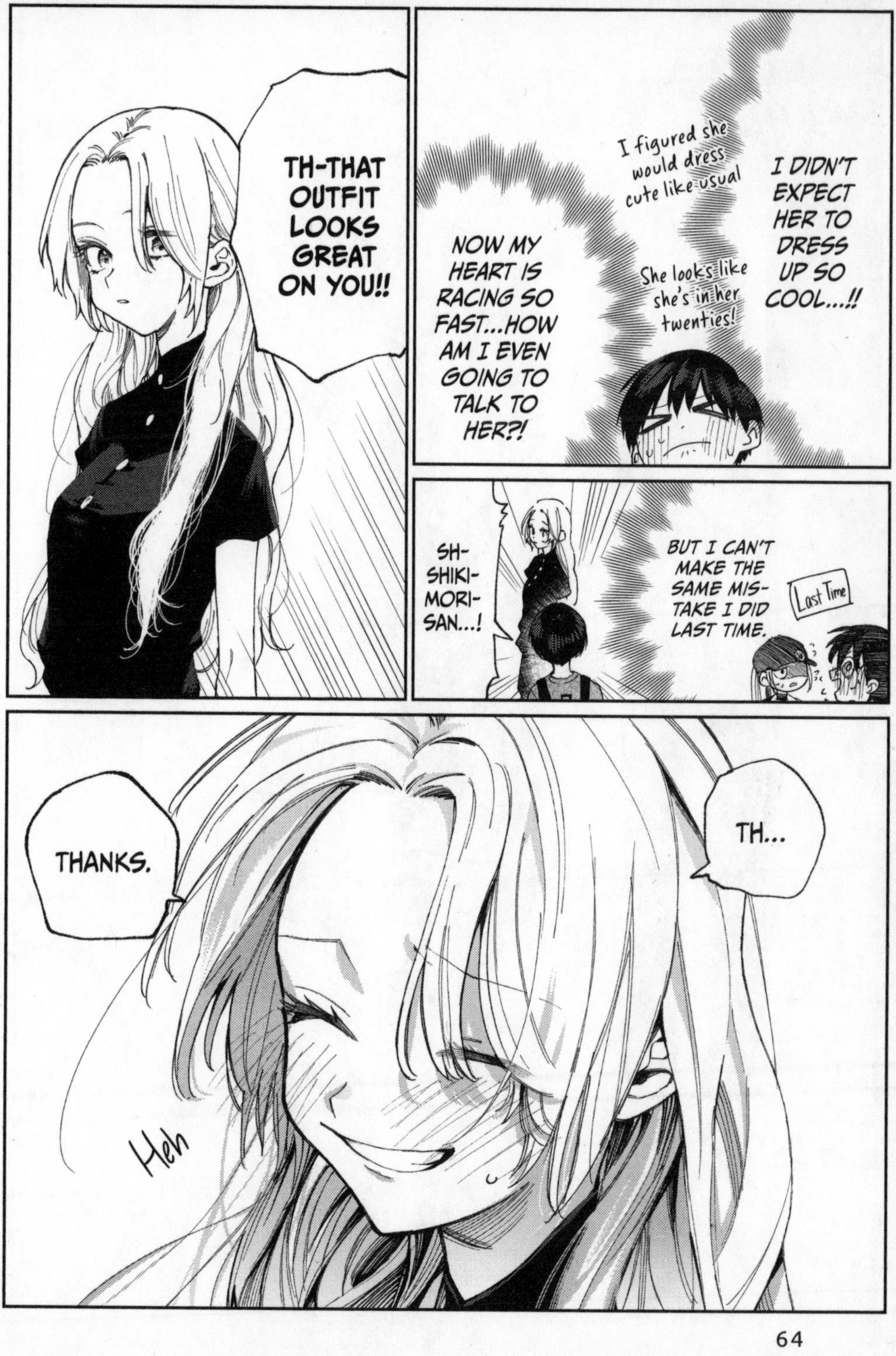
I DIDN'T EXPECT HER TO DRESS UP SO COOL...!!
I figured she would dress cute like usual
She looks like she's in her twenties!
NOW MY HEART IS RACING SO FAST...HOW AM I EVEN GOING TO TALK TO HER?!
BUT I CAN'T MAKE THE SAME MIS-TAKE I DID LAST TIME.
Last Time
SH-SHIKI-MORI-SAN...!
TH-THAT OUTFIT LOOKS GREAT ON YOU!!
TH...
THANKS.
Heh

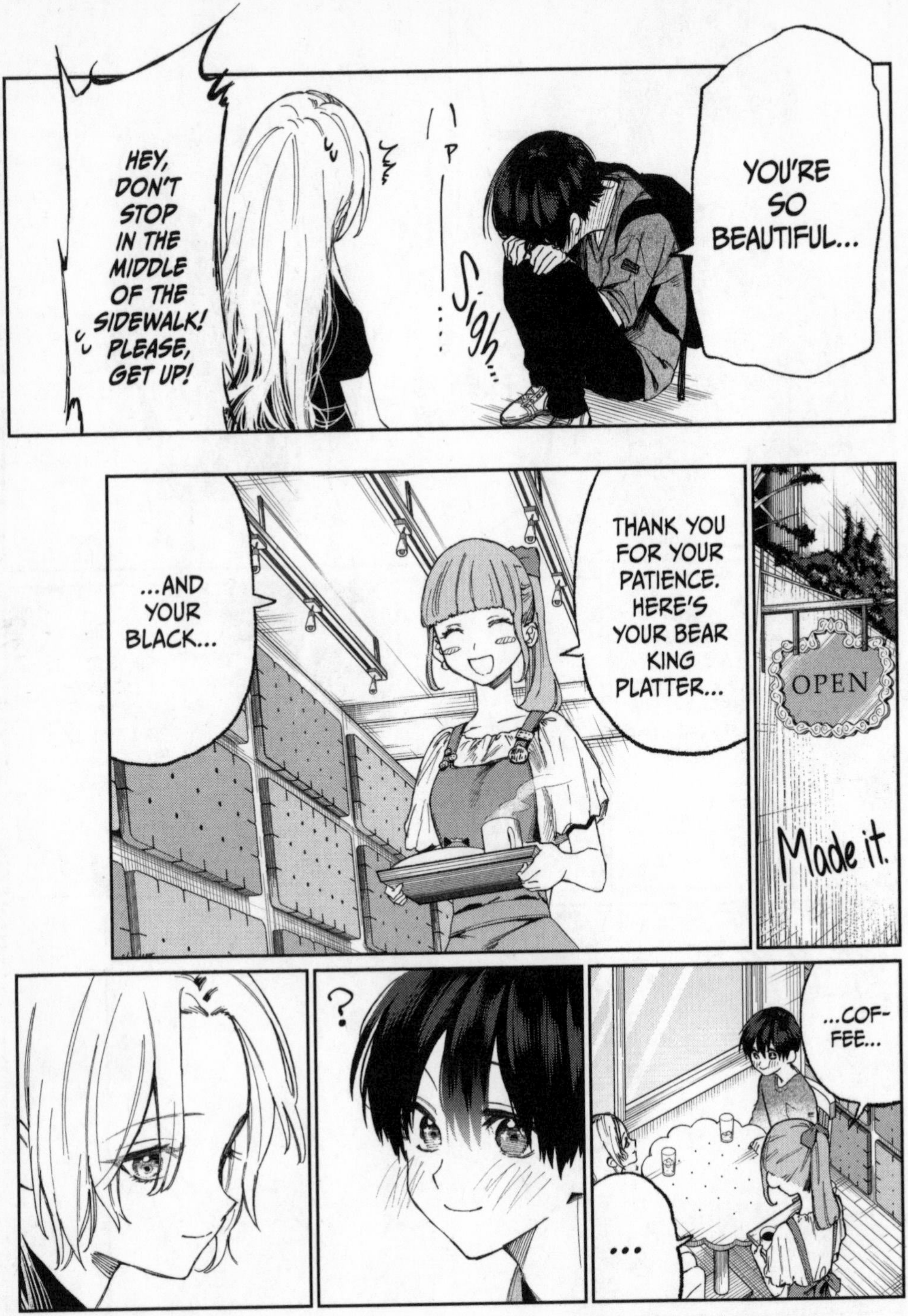
YOU'RE SO BEAUTIFUL...
Sigh...
HEY, DON'T STOP IN THE MIDDLE OF THE SIDEWALK! PLEASE, GET UP!
OPEN
Made it.
THANK YOU FOR YOUR PATIENCE. HERE'S YOUR BEAR KING PLATTER...
...AND YOUR BLACK...
...COF-FEE...
...
?

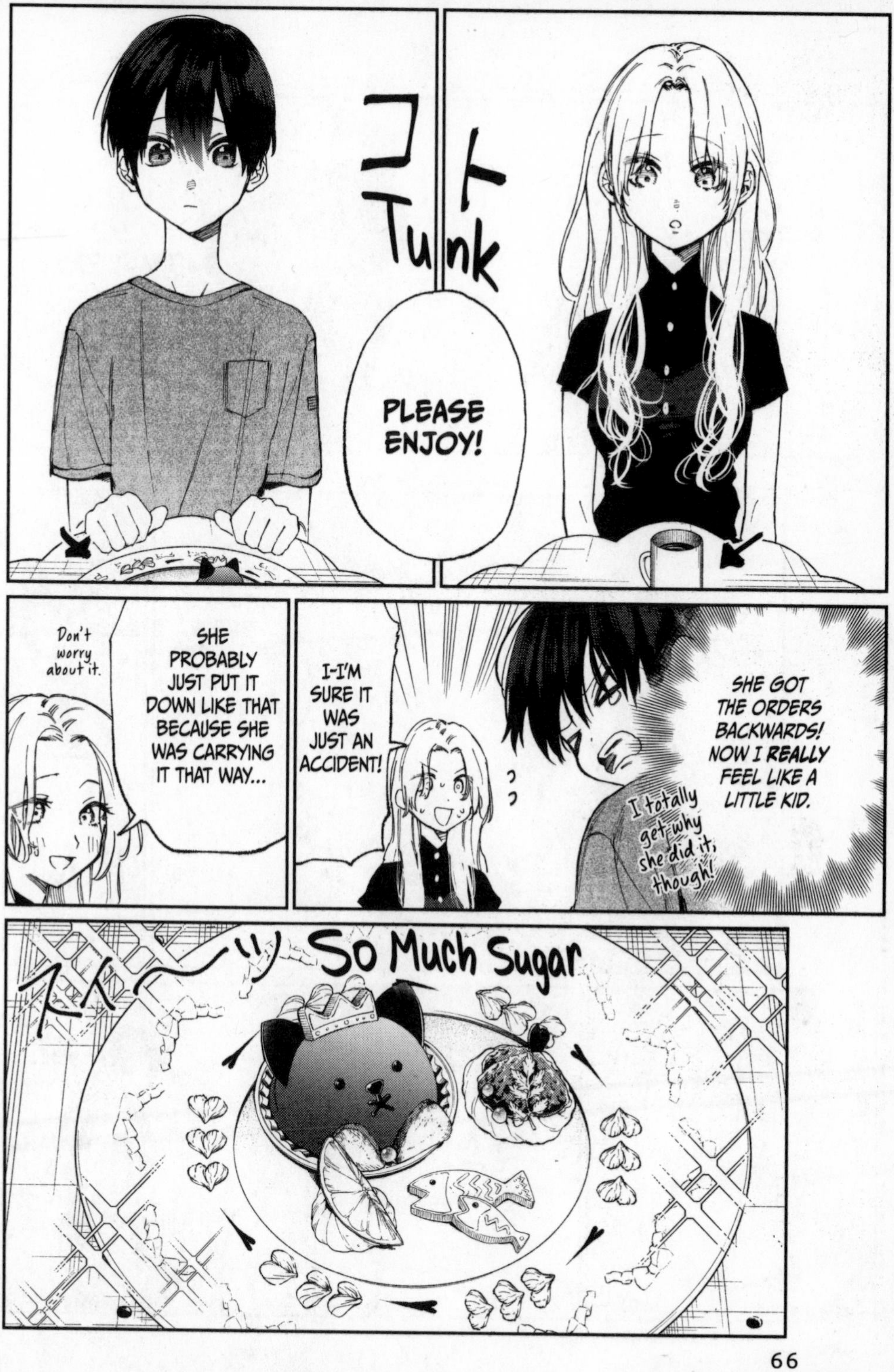
コト
Tunk
PLEASE ENJOY!
SHE GOT THE ORDERS BACKWARDS! NOW I REALLY FEEL LIKE A LITTLE KID.
I totally get why she did it, though!
I-I'M SURE IT WAS JUST AN ACCIDENT!
SHE PROBABLY JUST PUT IT DOWN LIKE THAT BECAUSE SHE WAS CARRYING IT THAT WAY...
Don't worry about it.
So Much Sugar

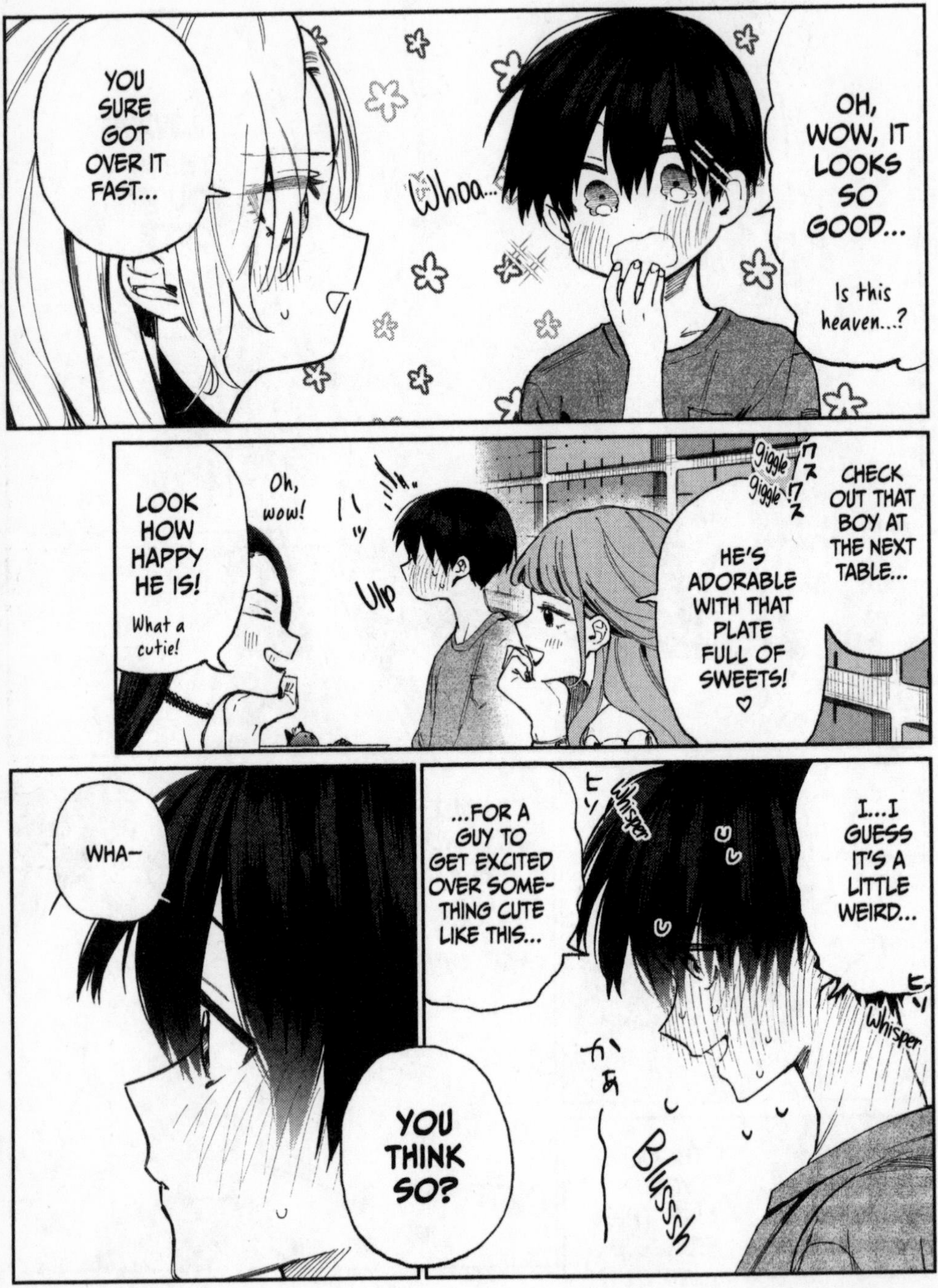
OH, WOW, IT LOOKS SO GOOD...
Is this heaven...?
Whoa...
YOU SURE GOT OVER IT FAST...
CHECK OUT THAT BOY AT THE NEXT TABLE...
giggle giggle
HE'S ADORABLE WITH THAT PLATE FULL OF SWEETS! ♡
Ulp
Oh, wow!
LOOK HOW HAPPY HE IS!
What a cutie!
I...I GUESS IT'S A LITTLE WEIRD...
Whisper
...FOR A GUY TO GET EXCITED OVER SOME-THING CUTE LIKE THIS...
Whisper
Blussh
WHA-
YOU THINK SO?

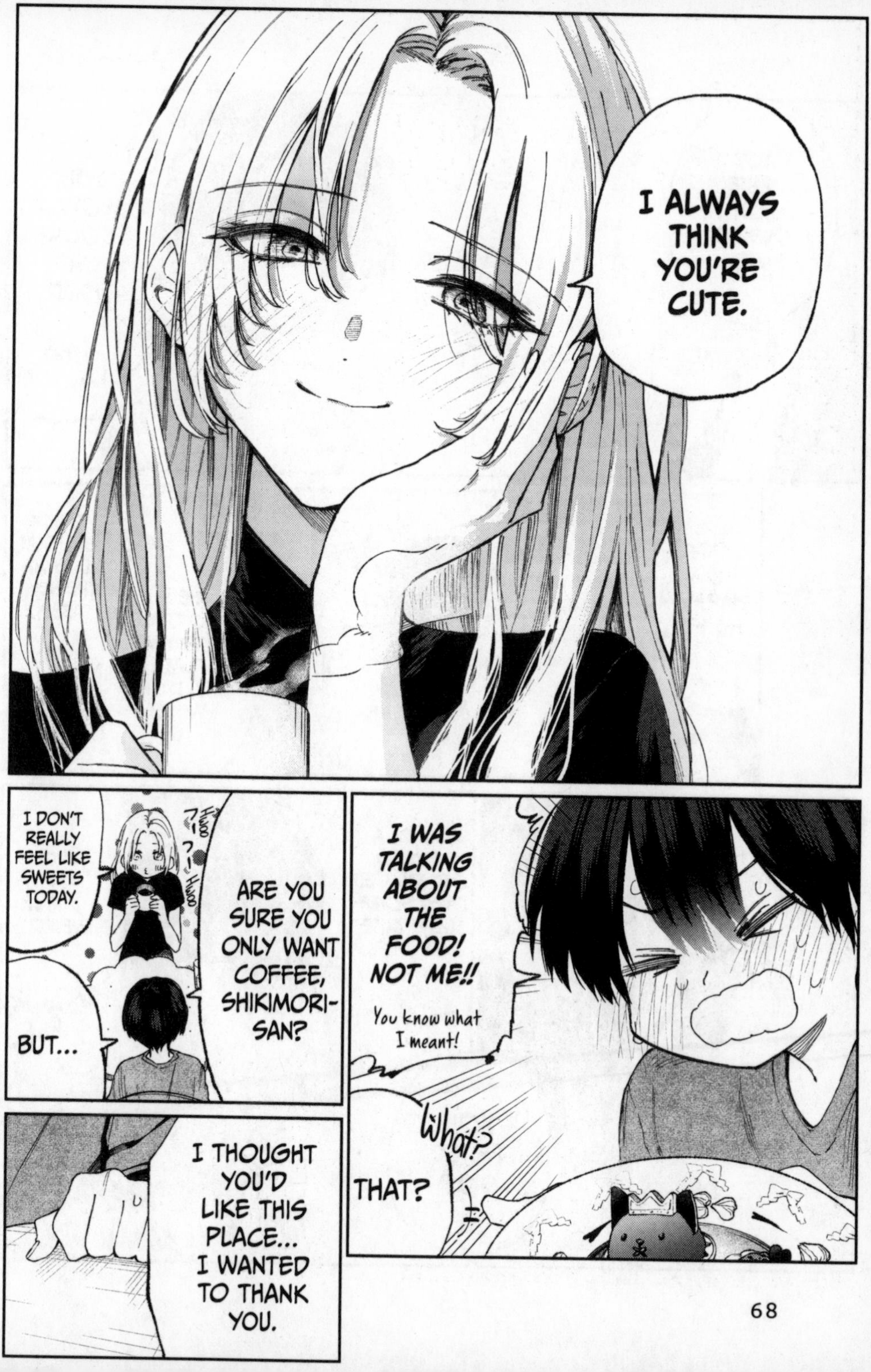
I ALWAYS THINK YOU'RE CUTE.
THAT?
What?
I WAS TALKING ABOUT THE FOOD! NOT ME!!
You know what I meant!
ARE YOU SURE YOU ONLY WANT COFFEE, SHIKIMORI-SAN?
I DON'T REALLY FEEL LIKE SWEETS TODAY.
BUT...
I THOUGHT YOU'D LIKE THIS PLACE... I WANTED TO THANK YOU.

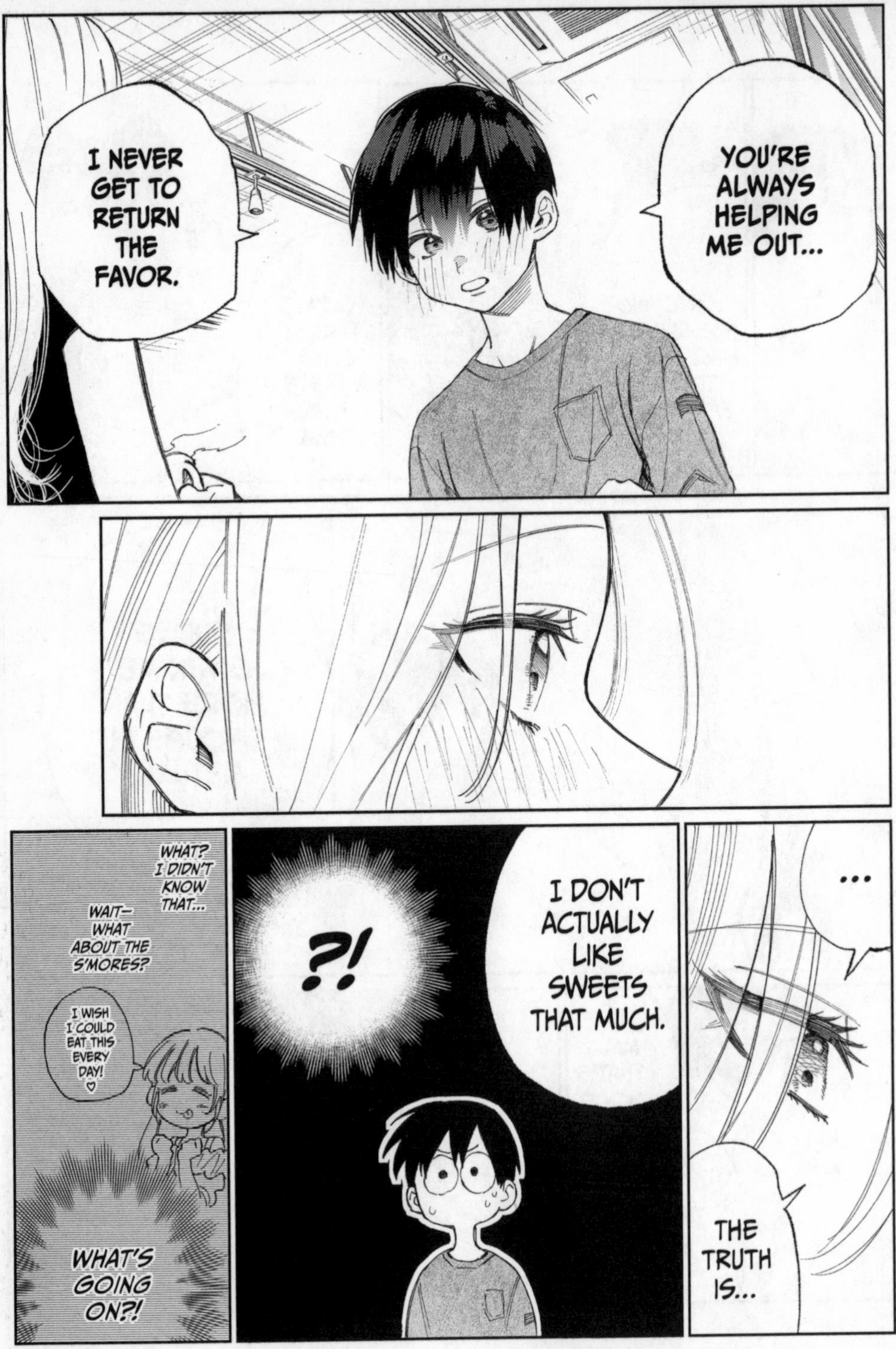

YOU'RE ALWAYS HELPING ME OUT...
I NEVER GET TO RETURN THE FAVOR.
...
THE TRUTH IS...
I DON'T ACTUALLY LIKE SWEETS THAT MUCH.
?!
WHAT? I DIDN'T KNOW THAT...
WAIT— WHAT ABOUT THE S'MORES?
I WISH I COULD EAT THIS EVERY DAY! ♡
WHAT'S GOING ON?!

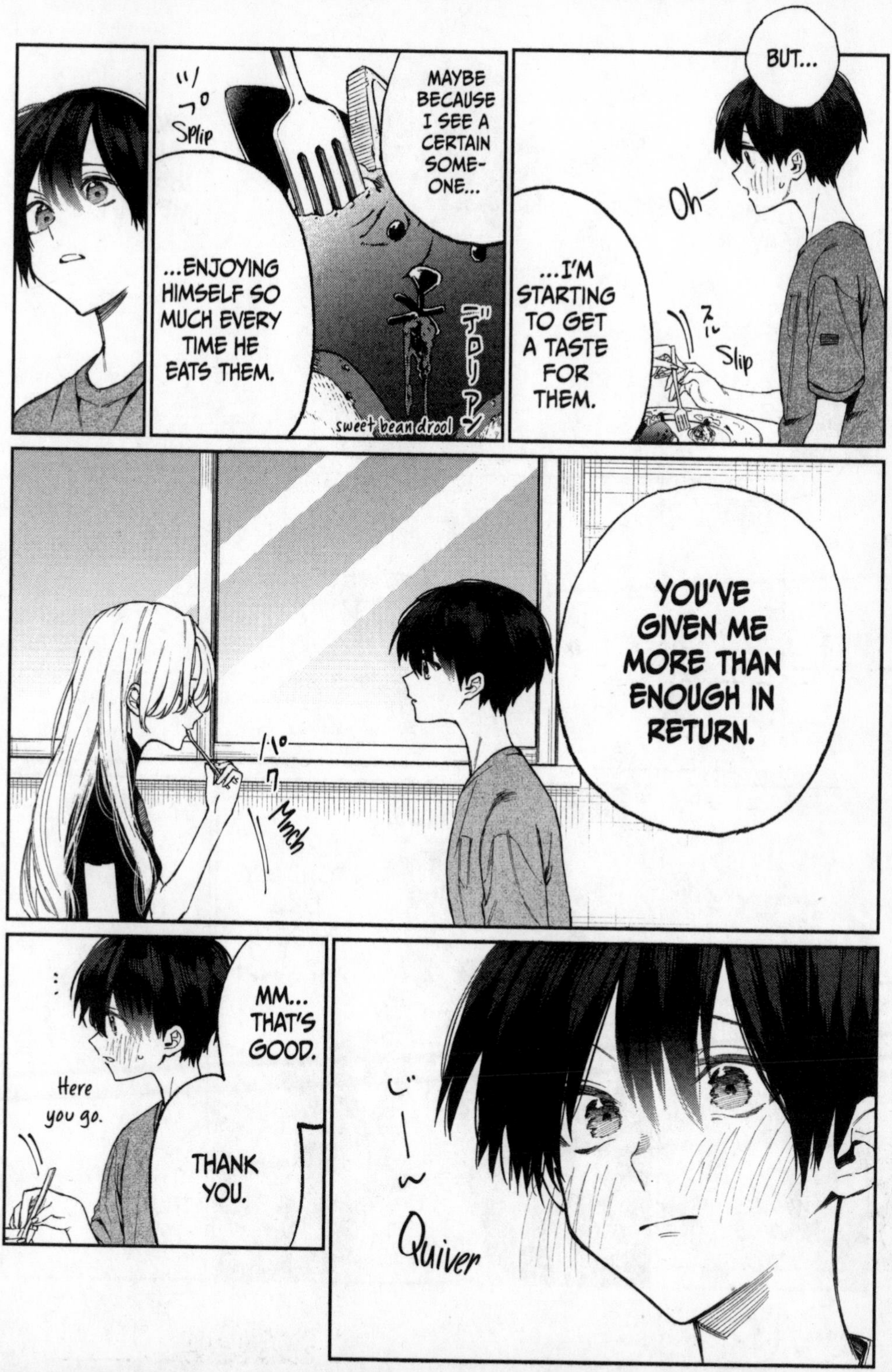
BUT...
Oh—
...I'M STARTING TO GET A TASTE FOR THEM.
Slip
MAYBE BECAUSE I SEE A CERTAIN SOME-ONE...
...ENJOYING HIMSELF SO MUCH EVERY TIME HE EATS THEM.
Splip
sweet bean drool
YOU'VE GIVEN ME MORE THAN ENOUGH IN RETURN.
Mnch
Quiver
MM... THAT'S GOOD.
Here you go.
THANK YOU.

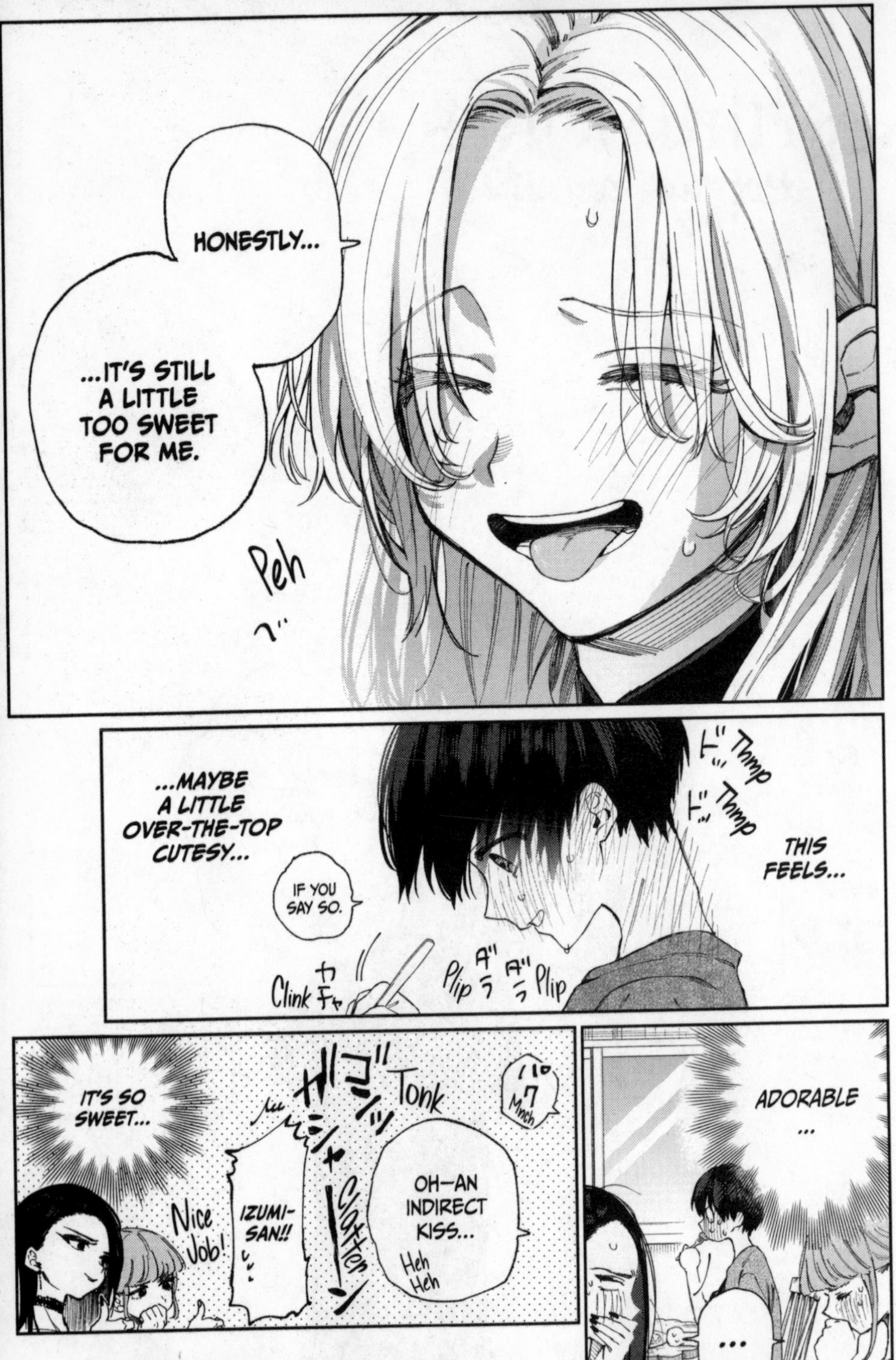

HONESTLY...
...IT'S STILL A LITTLE TOO SWEET FOR ME.
Peh
ドッ Thmp
ドッ Thmp
THIS FEELS...
IF YOU SAY SO.
...MAYBE A LITTLE OVER-THE-TOP CUTESY...
ダラ Plip
ダラ Plip
カチャ Clink
ADORABLE ...
...
ハク Mnch
ゴンッ Tonk
OH—AN INDIRECT KISS...
Heh Heh
ガシャーン Clatter
IZUMI-SAN!!
Nice Job!
IT'S SO SWEET...

Chapter 32 END

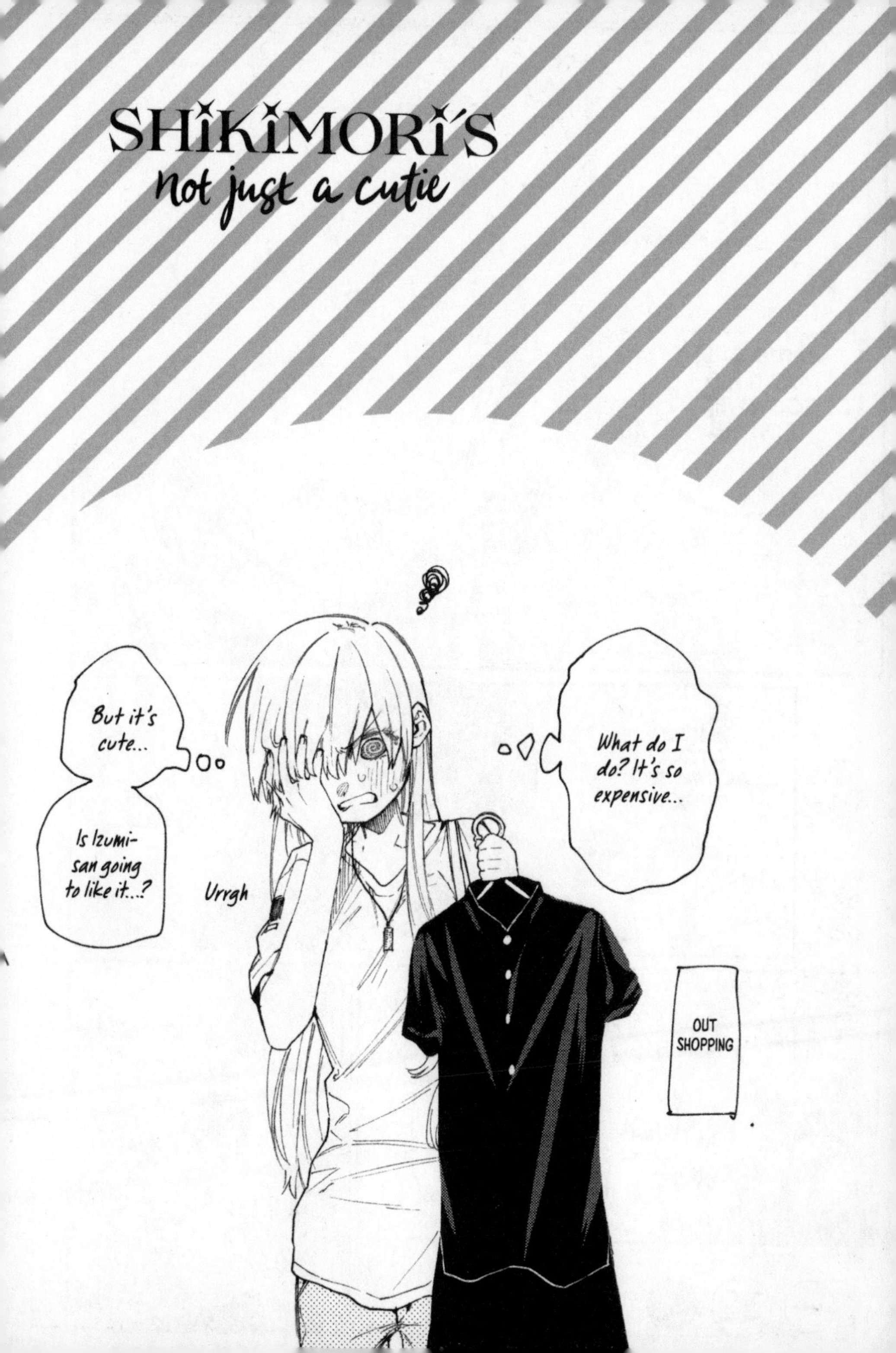
SHIKIMORI'S
Not just a cutie
What do I do? It's so expensive...
But it's cute...
Is Izumi-san going to like it...?
Urrgh
OUT SHOPPING

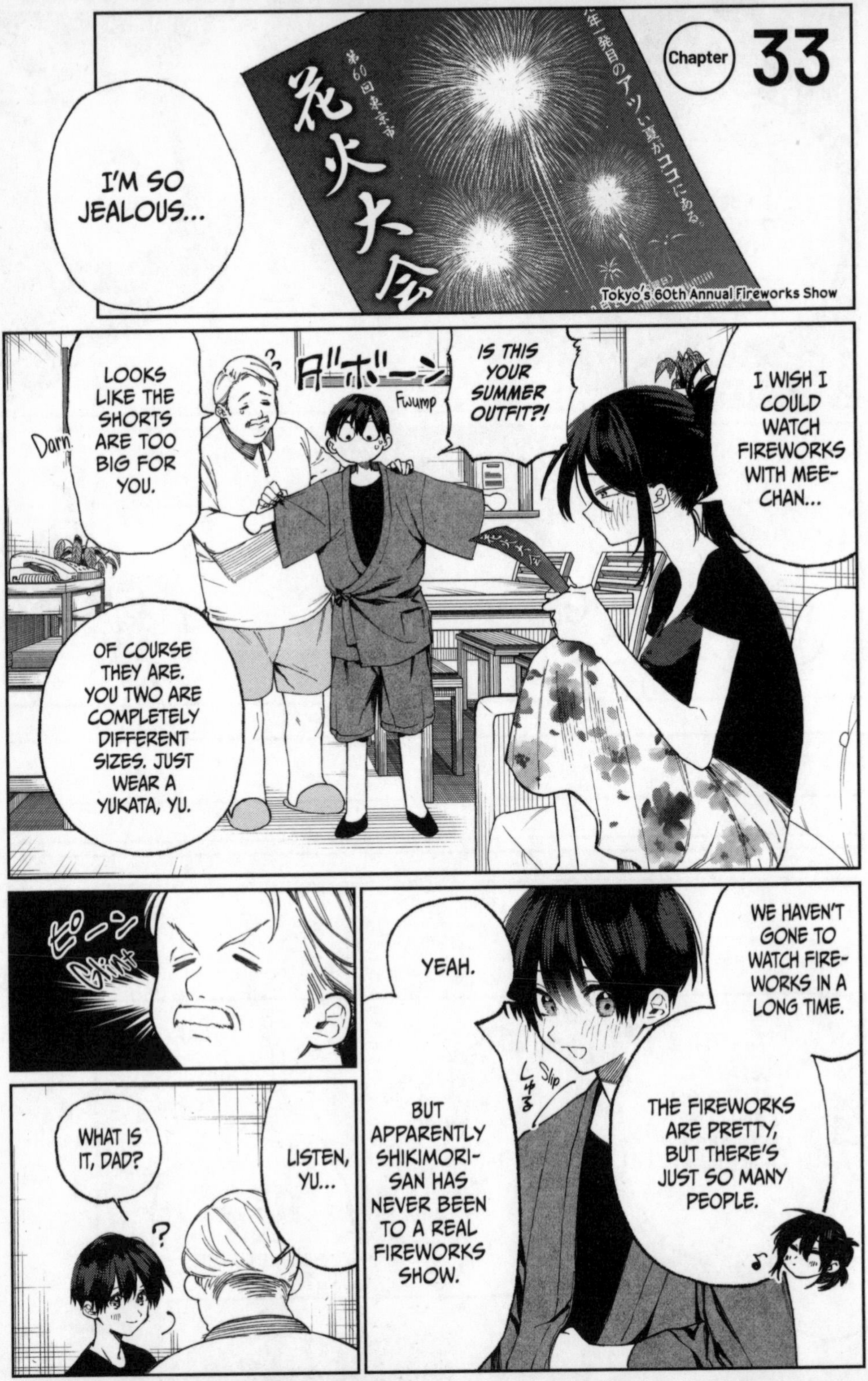
Chapter 33
第60回東京市
花火大会
年一発目のアツい夏がココにある。
Tokyo's 60th Annual Fireworks Show
I'M SO JEALOUS...
I WISH I COULD WATCH FIREWORKS WITH MEE-CHAN...
IS THIS YOUR SUMMER OUTFIT?!
ボーン
Fwump
LOOKS LIKE THE SHORTS ARE TOO BIG FOR YOU.
Darn.
OF COURSE THEY ARE. YOU TWO ARE COMPLETELY DIFFERENT SIZES. JUST WEAR A YUKATA, YU.
WE HAVEN'T GONE TO WATCH FIRE-WORKS IN A LONG TIME.
YEAH.
THE FIREWORKS ARE PRETTY, BUT THERE'S JUST SO MANY PEOPLE.
しゅる
Slip
BUT APPARENTLY SHIKIMORI-SAN HAS NEVER BEEN TO A REAL FIREWORKS SHOW.
ピーン
Glint
LISTEN, YU...
WHAT IS IT, DAD?

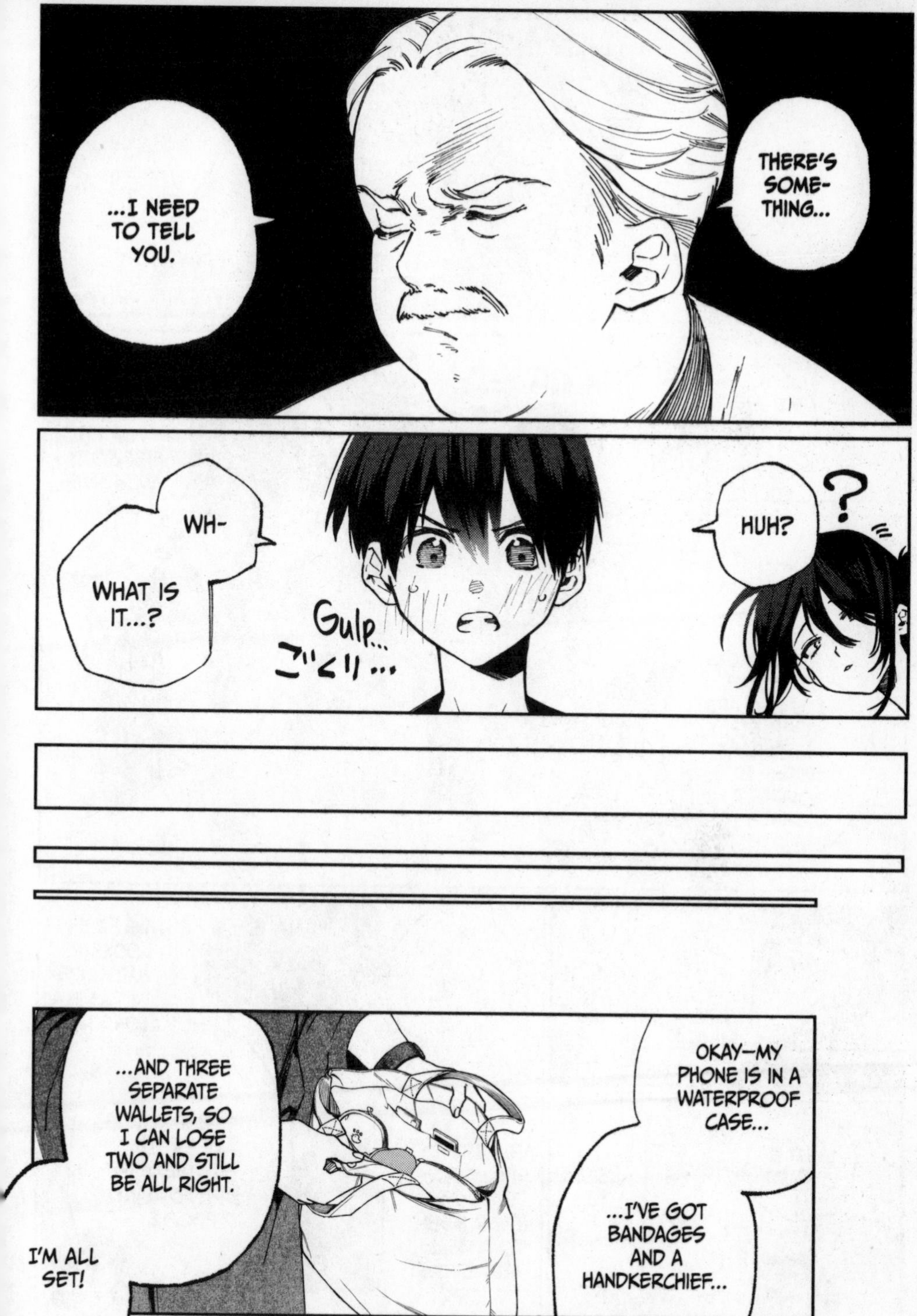
THERE'S SOME-THING...
...I NEED TO TELL YOU.
HUH?
?
Gulp...
ごくり...
WH-
WHAT IS IT...?
OKAY—MY PHONE IS IN A WATERPROOF CASE...
...I'VE GOT BANDAGES AND A HANDKERCHIEF...
...AND THREE SEPARATE WALLETS, SO I CAN LOSE TWO AND STILL BE ALL RIGHT.
I'M ALL SET!

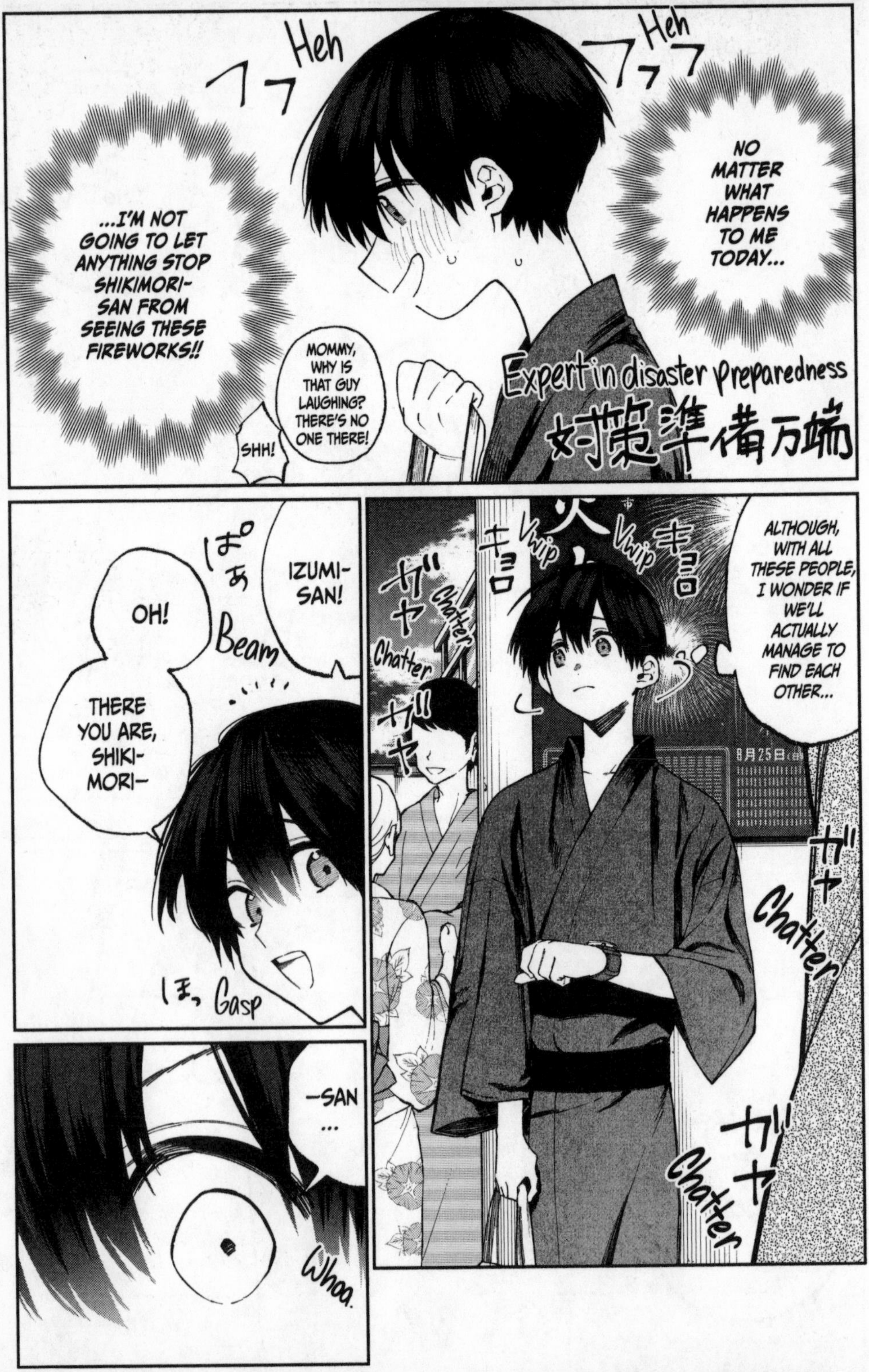

Heh
Heh
NO MATTER WHAT HAPPENS TO ME TODAY...
...I'M NOT GOING TO LET ANYTHING STOP SHIKIMORI-SAN FROM SEEING THESE FIREWORKS!!
MOMMY, WHY IS THAT GUY LAUGHING? THERE'S NO ONE THERE!
SHH!
Expert in disaster preparedness
対策準備万端
ALTHOUGH, WITH ALL THESE PEOPLE, I WONDER IF WE'LL ACTUALLY MANAGE TO FIND EACH OTHER...
Vwip
Vwip
Chatter
Chatter
Chatter
Chatter
IZUMI-SAN!
OH!
Beam
THERE YOU ARE, SHIKI-MORI–
Gasp
–SAN ...
Whoa.

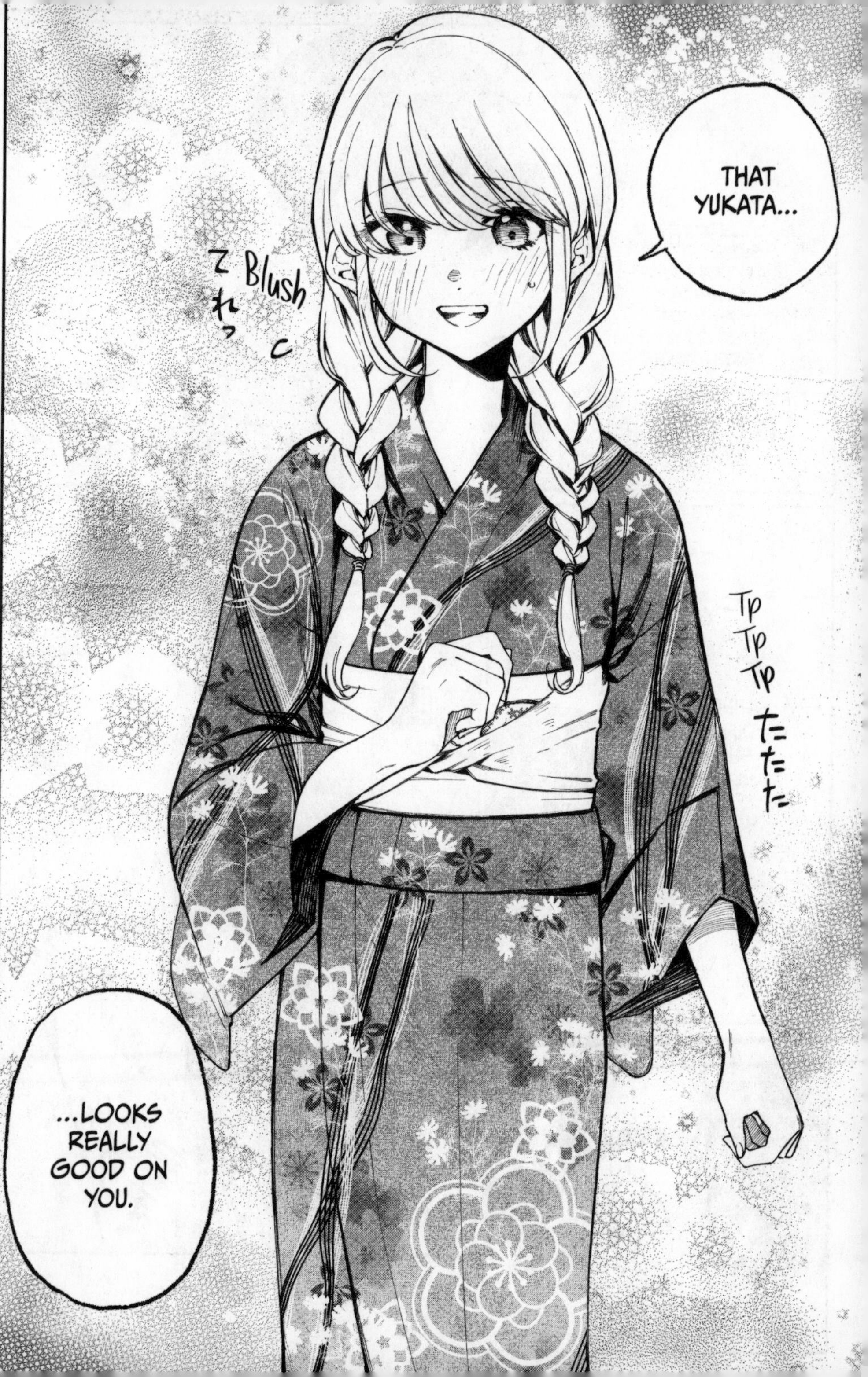
THAT YUKATA...
Blush てれっ
Tp Tp Tp たたた
...LOOKS REALLY GOOD ON YOU.

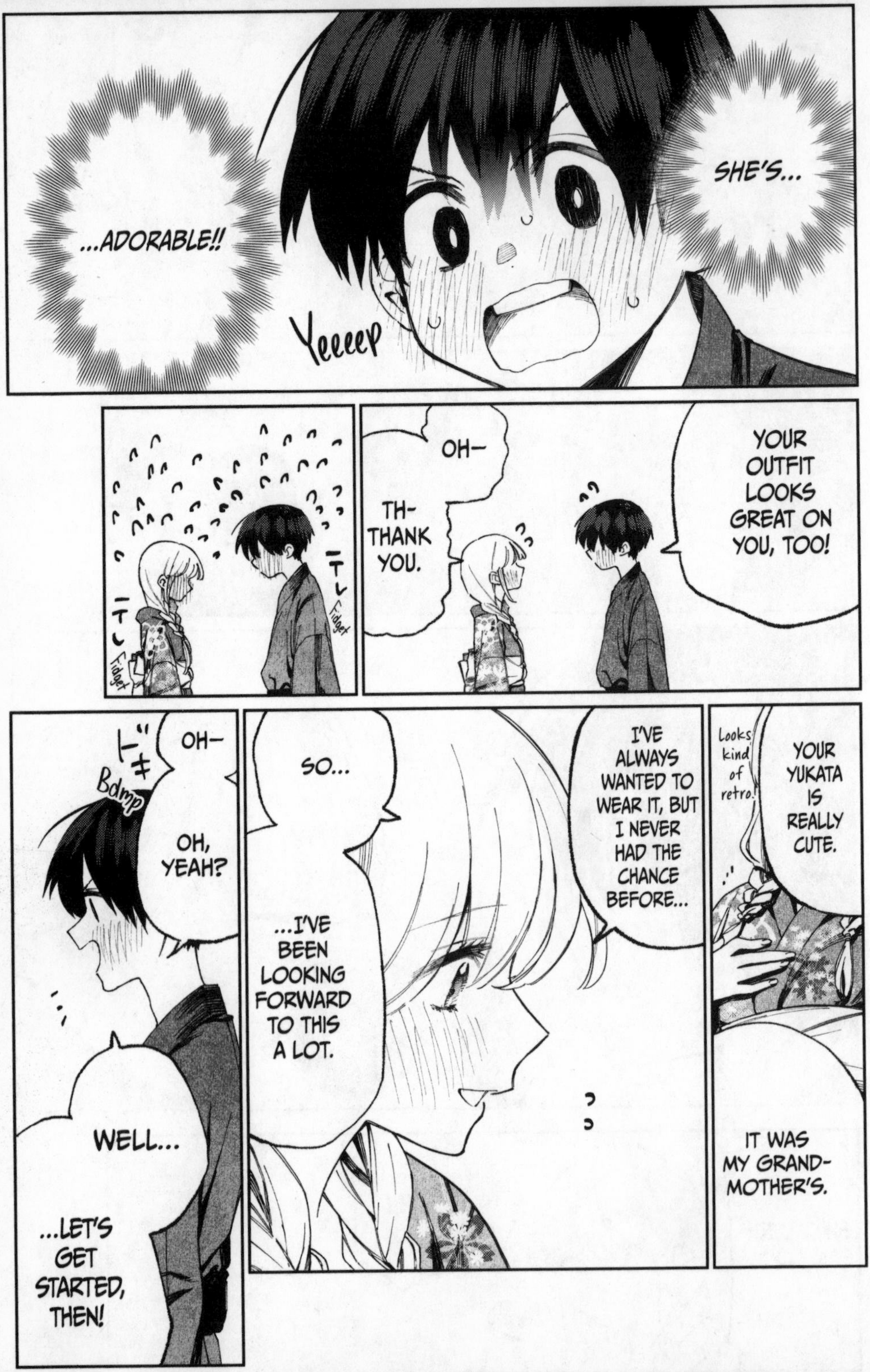
SHE'S...
...ADORABLE!!
Yeeeep
YOUR OUTFIT LOOKS GREAT ON YOU, TOO!
OH—
TH- THANK YOU.
Fidget
Fidget
YOUR YUKATA IS REALLY CUTE.
Looks kind of retro.
IT WAS MY GRAND-MOTHER'S.
I'VE ALWAYS WANTED TO WEAR IT, BUT I NEVER HAD THE CHANCE BEFORE...
SO...
...I'VE BEEN LOOKING FORWARD TO THIS A LOT.
OH—
Bdmp
OH, YEAH?
WELL...
...LET'S GET STARTED, THEN!

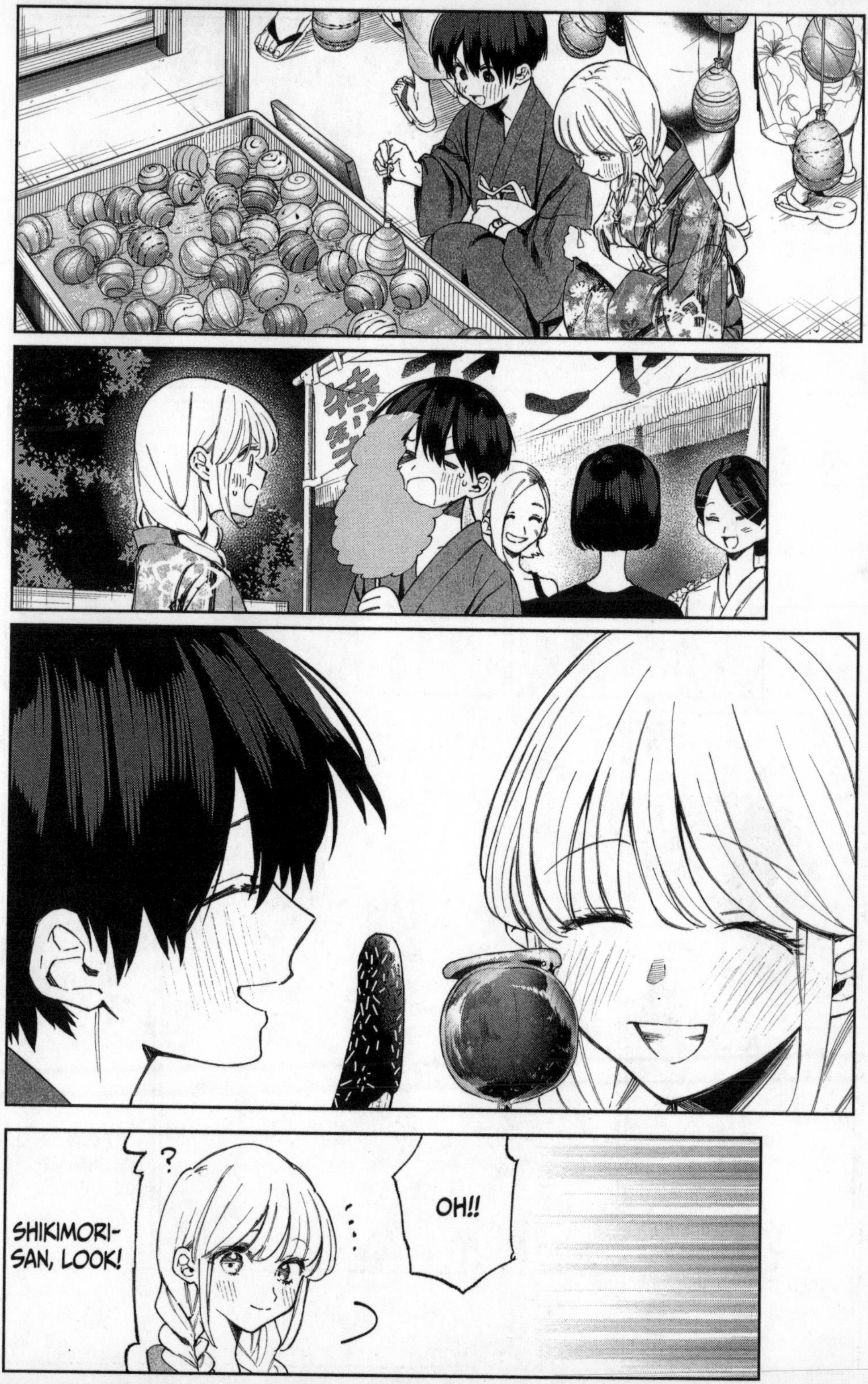
OH!!
?
...
SHIKIMORI-SAN, LOOK!

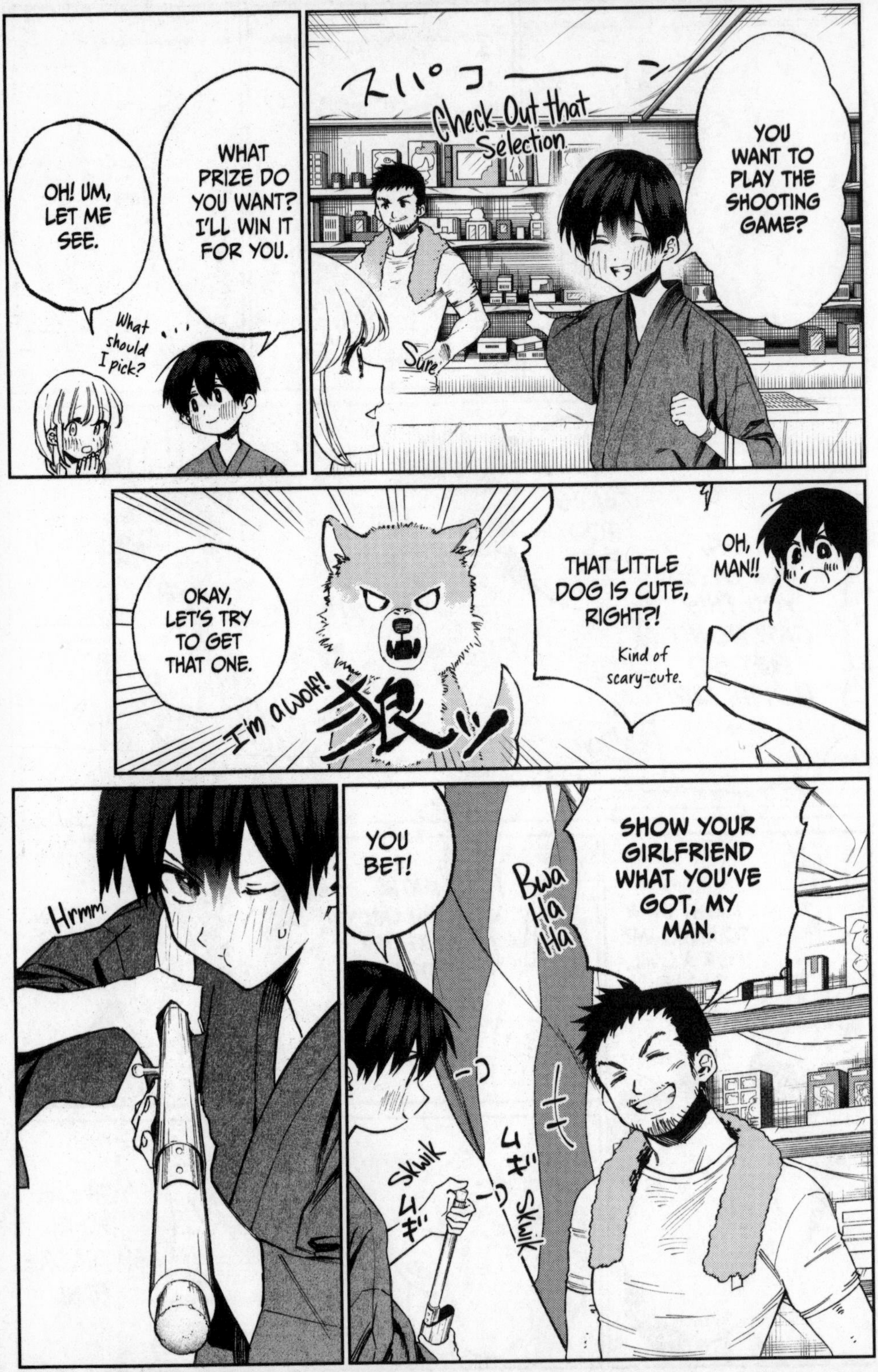
スパコーーーン
Check Out that Selection
YOU WANT TO PLAY THE SHOOTING GAME?
Sure
WHAT PRIZE DO YOU WANT? I'LL WIN IT FOR YOU.
...
OH! UM, LET ME SEE.
What should I pick?
OH, MAN!!
THAT LITTLE DOG IS CUTE, RIGHT?!
Kind of scary-cute.
狼ッ
I'm a wolf!
OKAY, LET'S TRY TO GET THAT ONE.
SHOW YOUR GIRLFRIEND WHAT YOU'VE GOT, MY MAN.
Bwa Ha Ha
YOU BET!
キーッ
ムギ Skwik
ムギ Skwik
Hrmm.

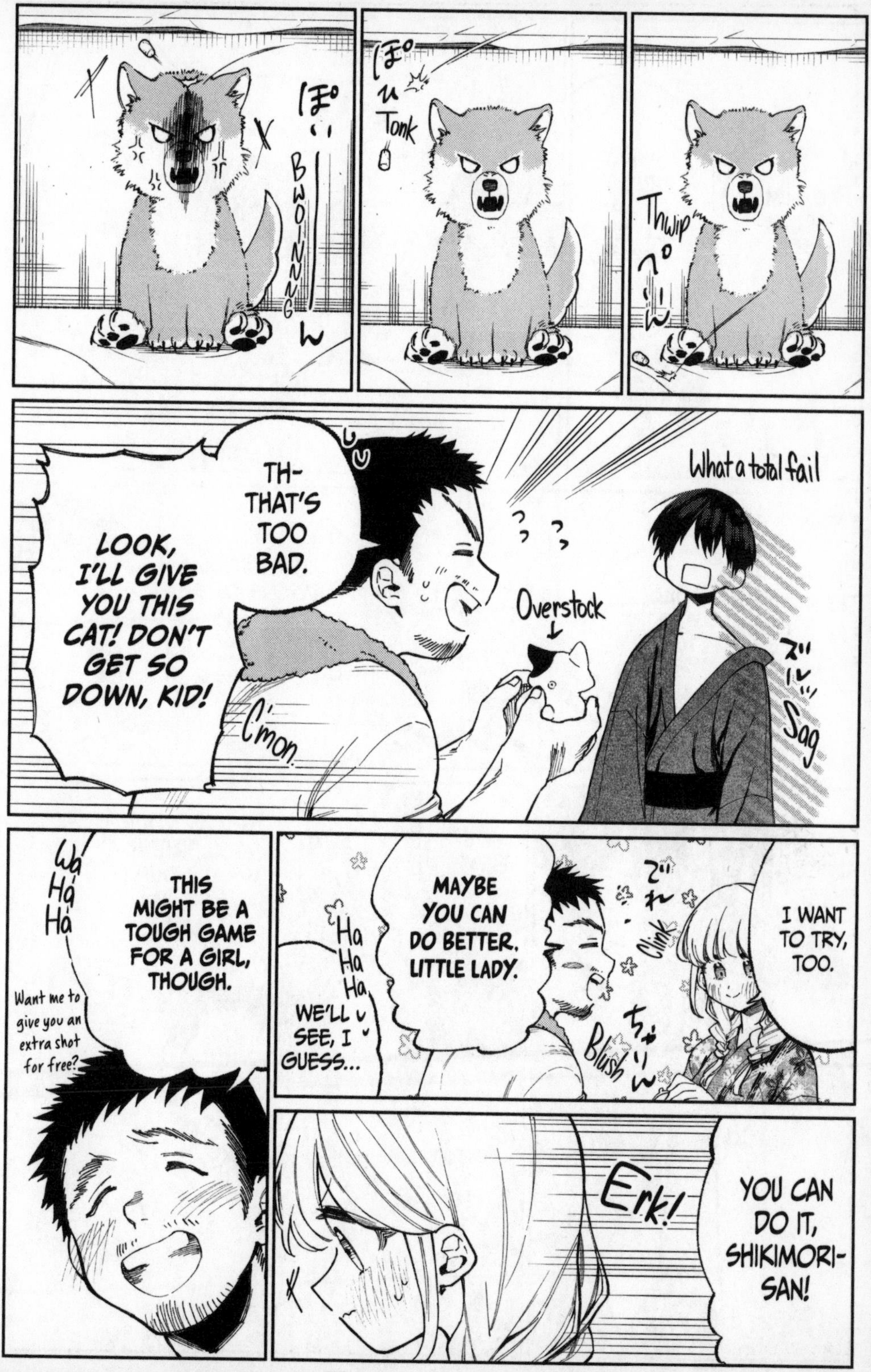
Thwip
Tonk
BWOINNNG
What a total fail
Sag
TH- THAT'S TOO BAD.
Overstock
LOOK, I'LL GIVE YOU THIS CAT! DON'T GET SO DOWN, KID!
C'mon.
I WANT TO TRY, TOO.
Clink
Blush
MAYBE YOU CAN DO BETTER, LITTLE LADY.
Ha Ha Ha
WE'LL SEE, I GUESS...
YOU CAN DO IT, SHIKIMORI-SAN!
Erk!
Wa Ha Ha
THIS MIGHT BE A TOUGH GAME FOR A GIRL, THOUGH.
Want me to give you an extra shot for free?

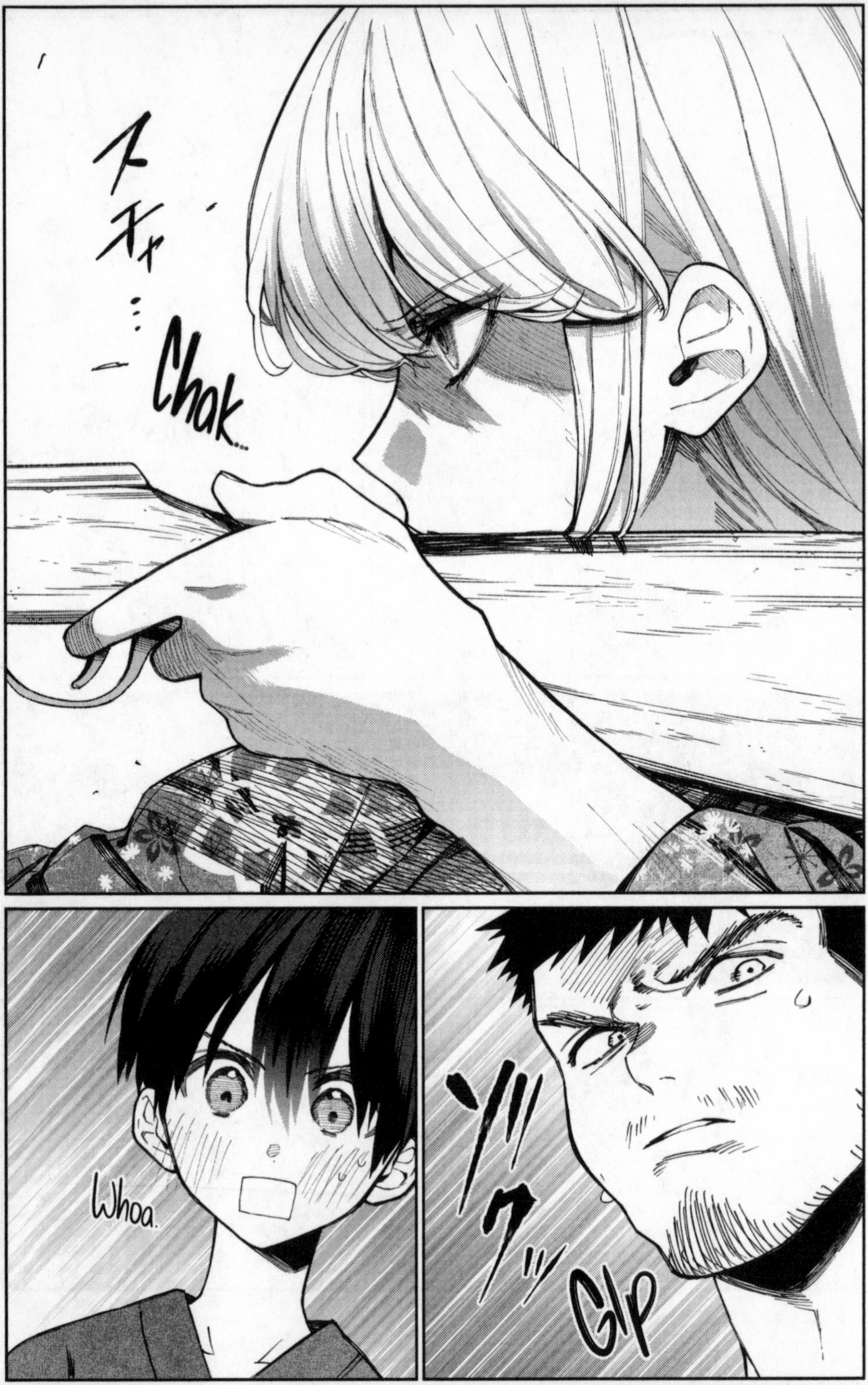
スチャ…
Chak...
ゾクッ
Glp
Whoa.

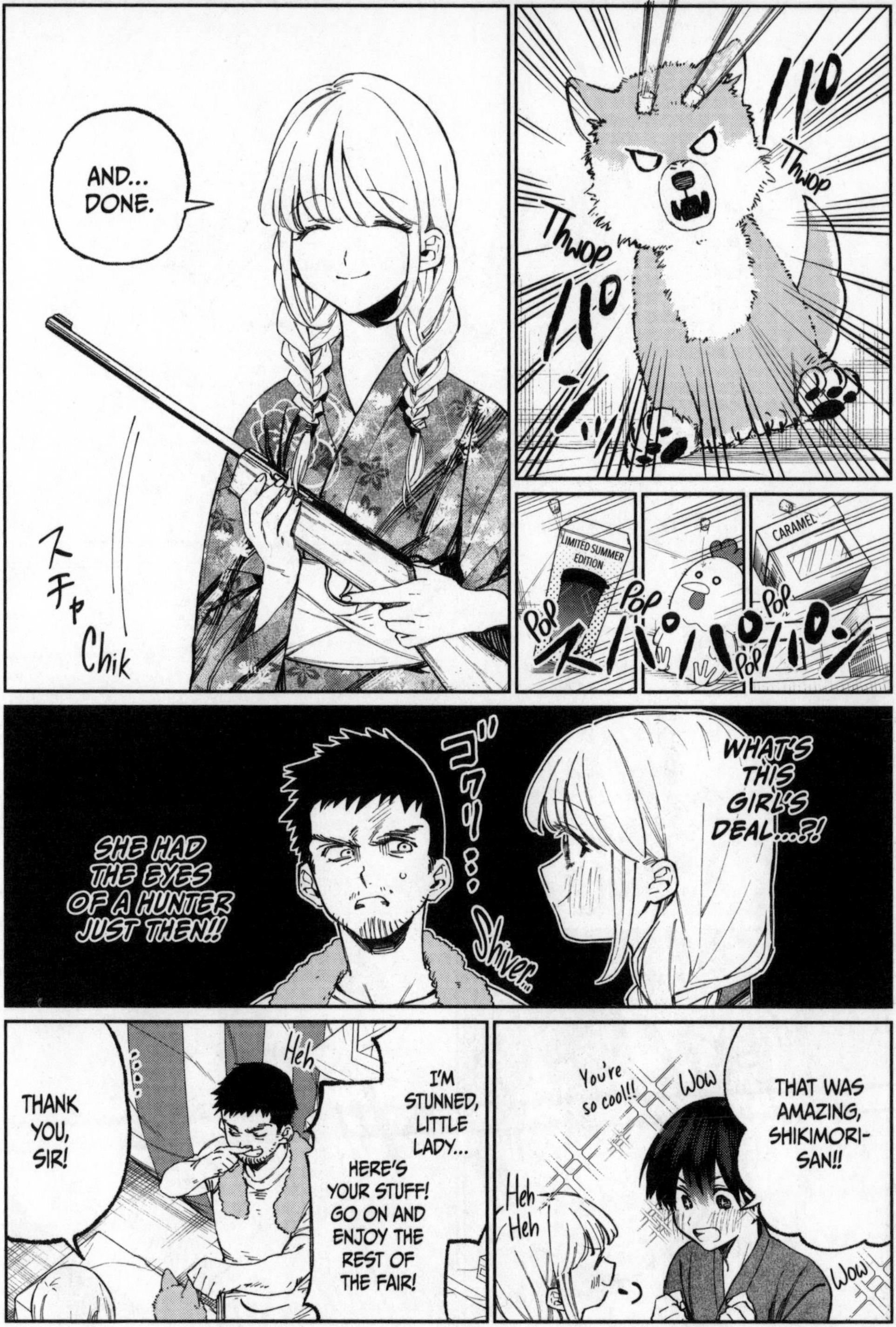
Thwop
Thwop
CARAMEL
Pop
Pop
Pop
LIMITED SUMMER EDITION
Pop
Pop
AND... DONE.
スチャ
Chik
WHAT'S THIS GIRL'S DEAL...?!
Shiver...
SHE HAD THE EYES OF A HUNTER JUST THEN!!
THAT WAS AMAZING, SHIKIMORI-SAN!!
Wow
You're so cool!!
Wow
Heh Heh
I'M STUNNED, LITTLE LADY...
HERE'S YOUR STUFF! GO ON AND ENJOY THE REST OF THE FAIR!
Heh
THANK YOU, SIR!

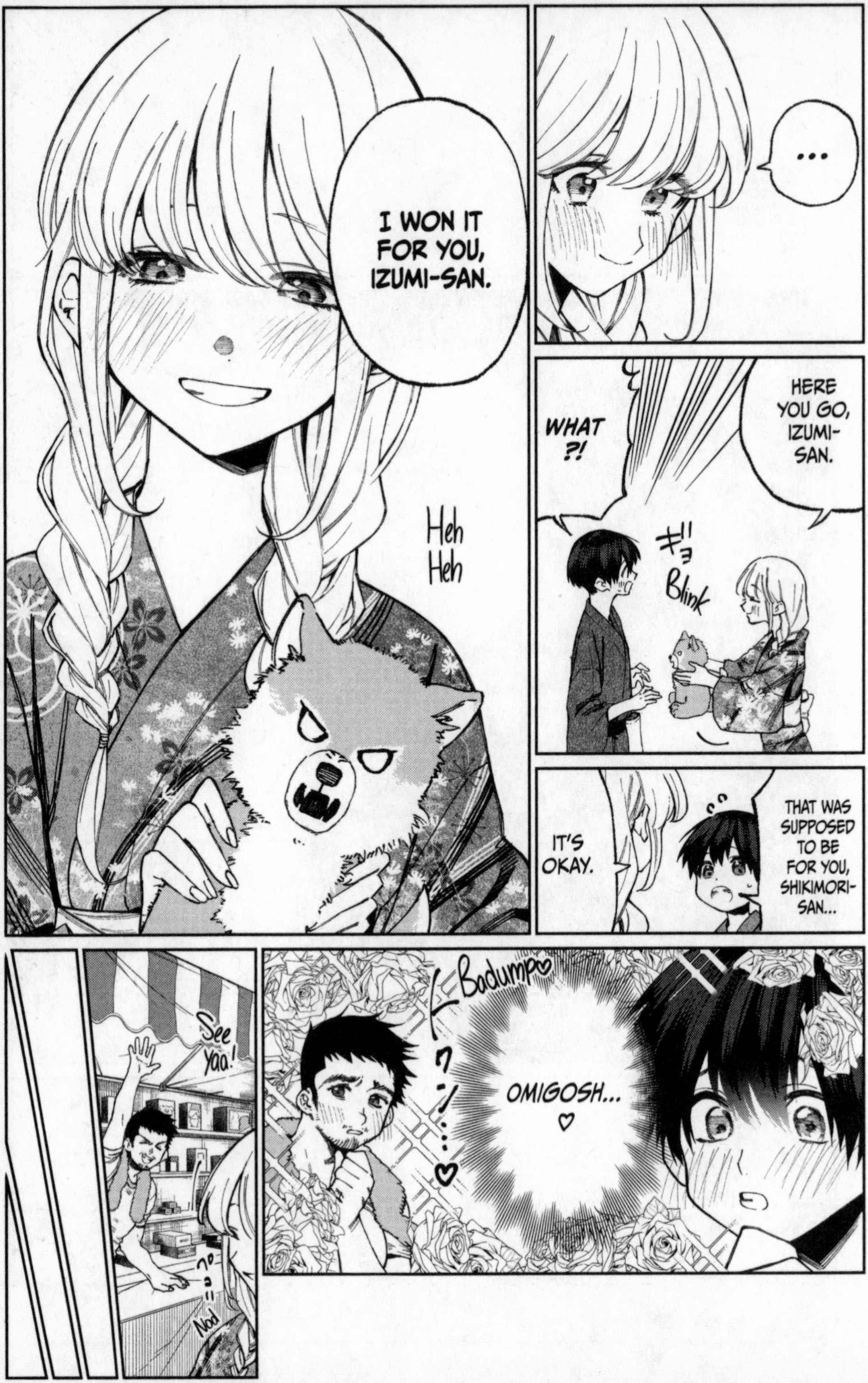
...
HERE YOU GO, IZUMI-SAN.
WHAT ?!
Blink
THAT WAS SUPPOSED TO BE FOR YOU, SHIKIMORI-SAN...
IT'S OKAY.
I WON IT FOR YOU, IZUMI-SAN.
Heh Heh
Badump♥
OMIGOSH... ♡
See yaa!
Nod

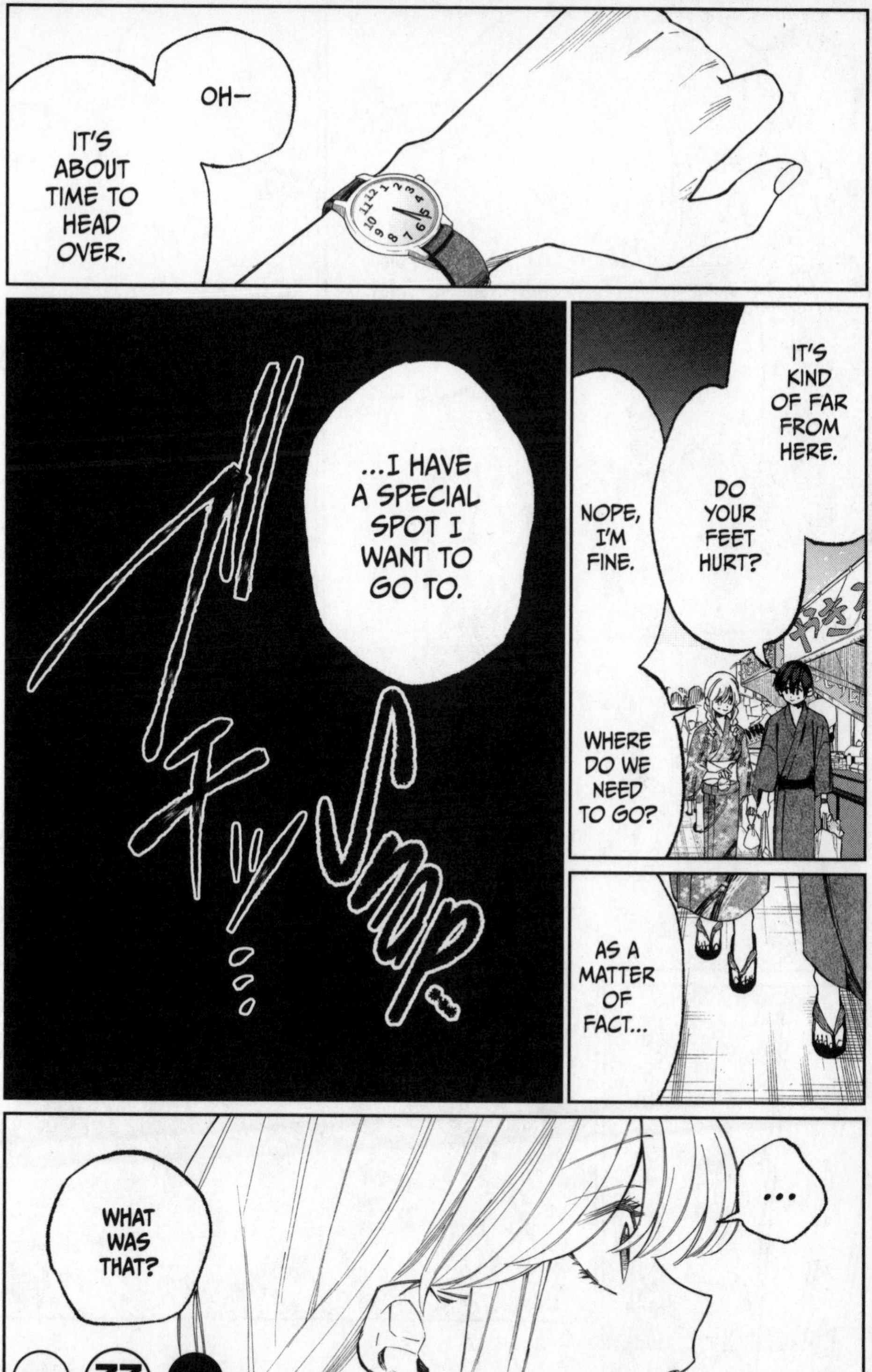
OH—
IT'S ABOUT TIME TO HEAD OVER.
IT'S KIND OF FAR FROM HERE.
DO YOUR FEET HURT?
NOPE, I'M FINE.
WHERE DO WE NEED TO GO?
AS A MATTER OF FACT...
...I HAVE A SPECIAL SPOT I WANT TO GO TO.
Snap...
...
WHAT WAS THAT?
Chapter 33 END

MISS Shikimori IS NOT JUST CUTE

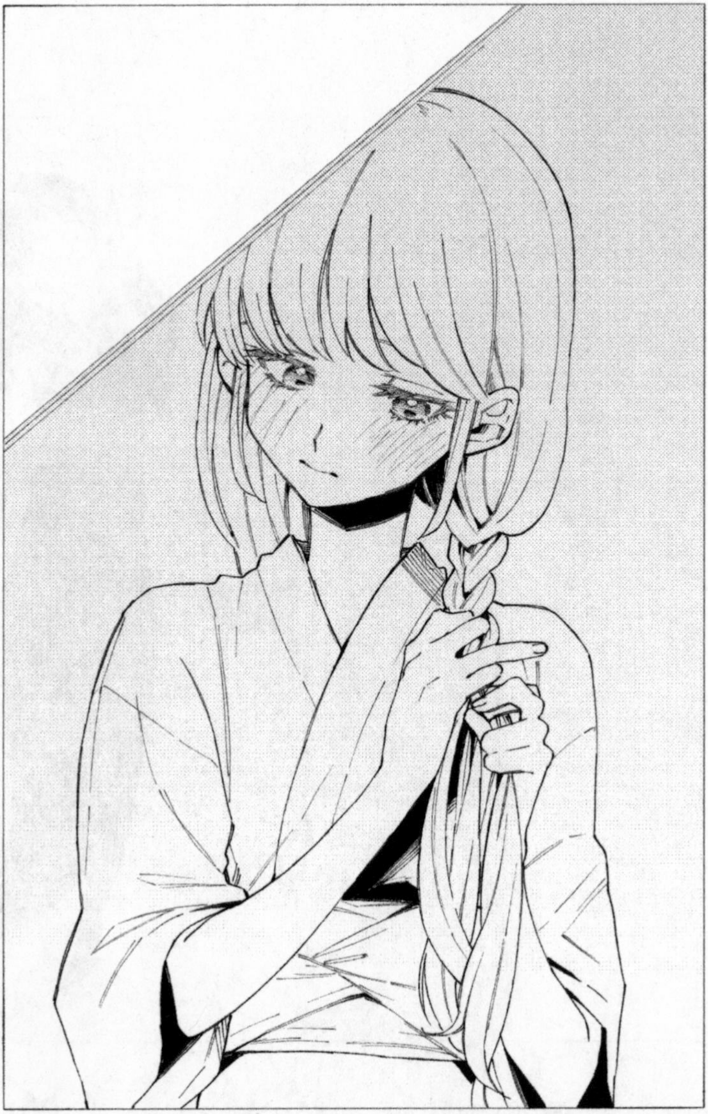

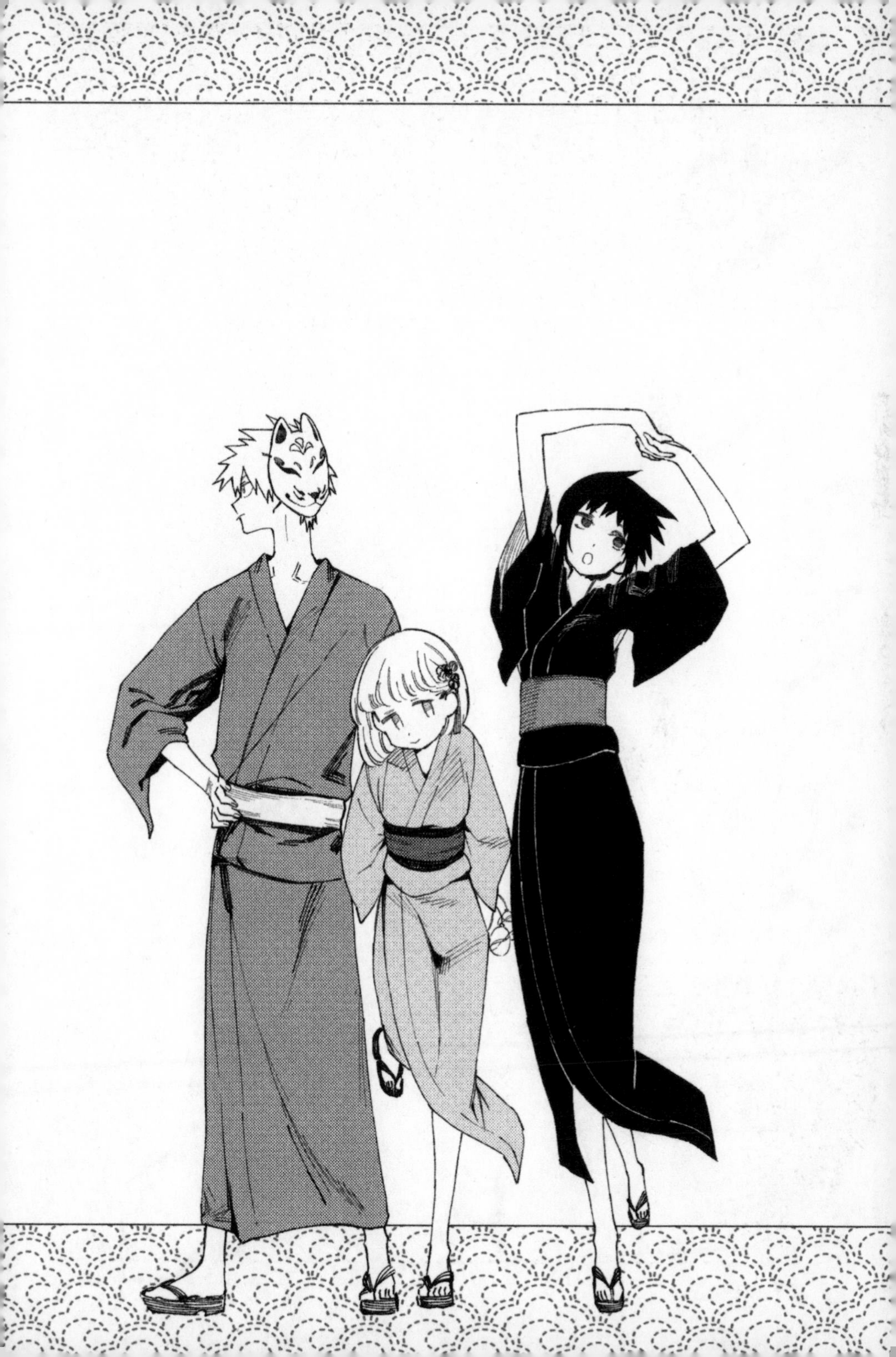

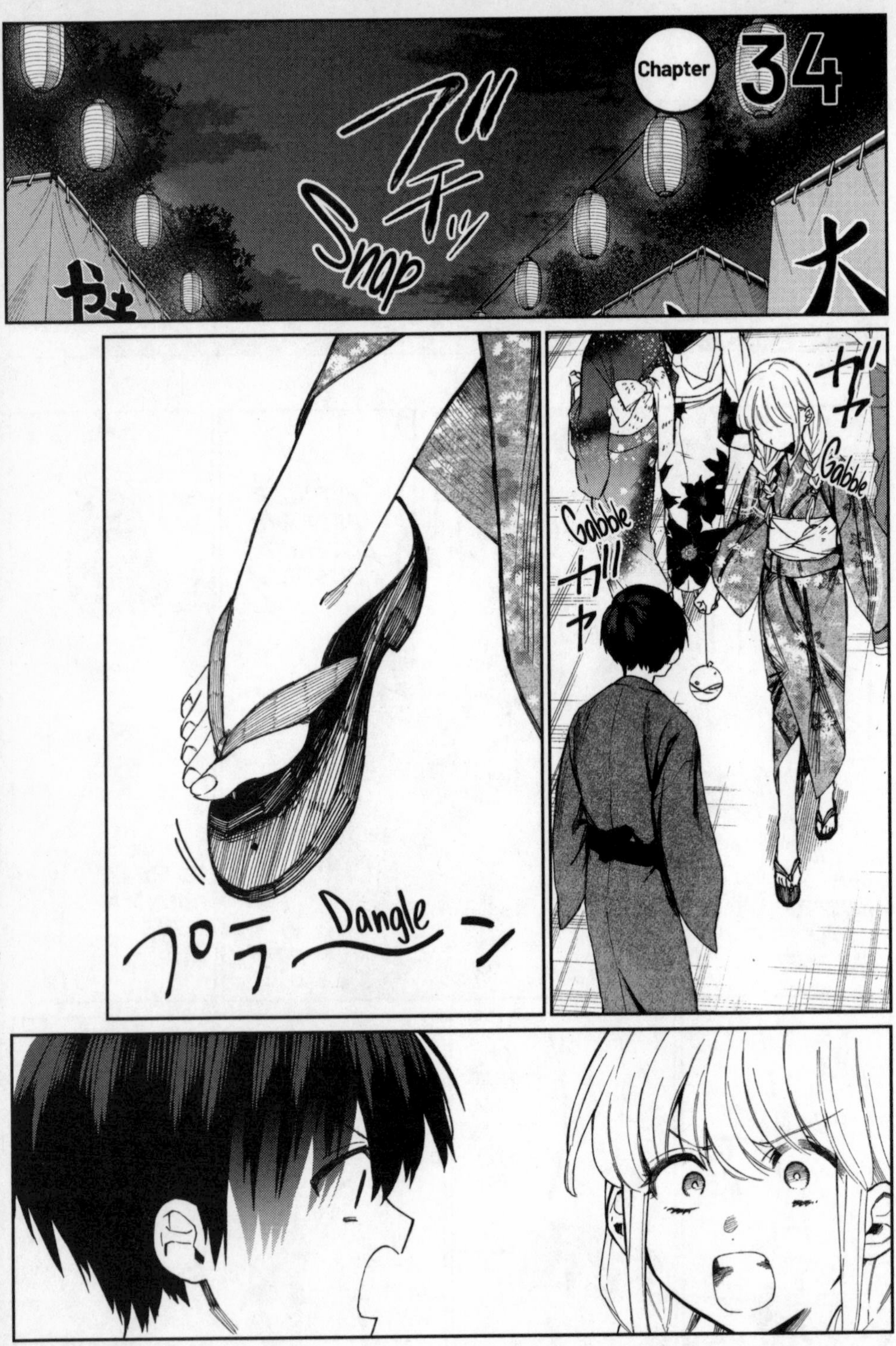
Chapter 34
ブチッ
Snap
ガヤ
Gabble
Gabble
ガヤ
プラーン
Dangle

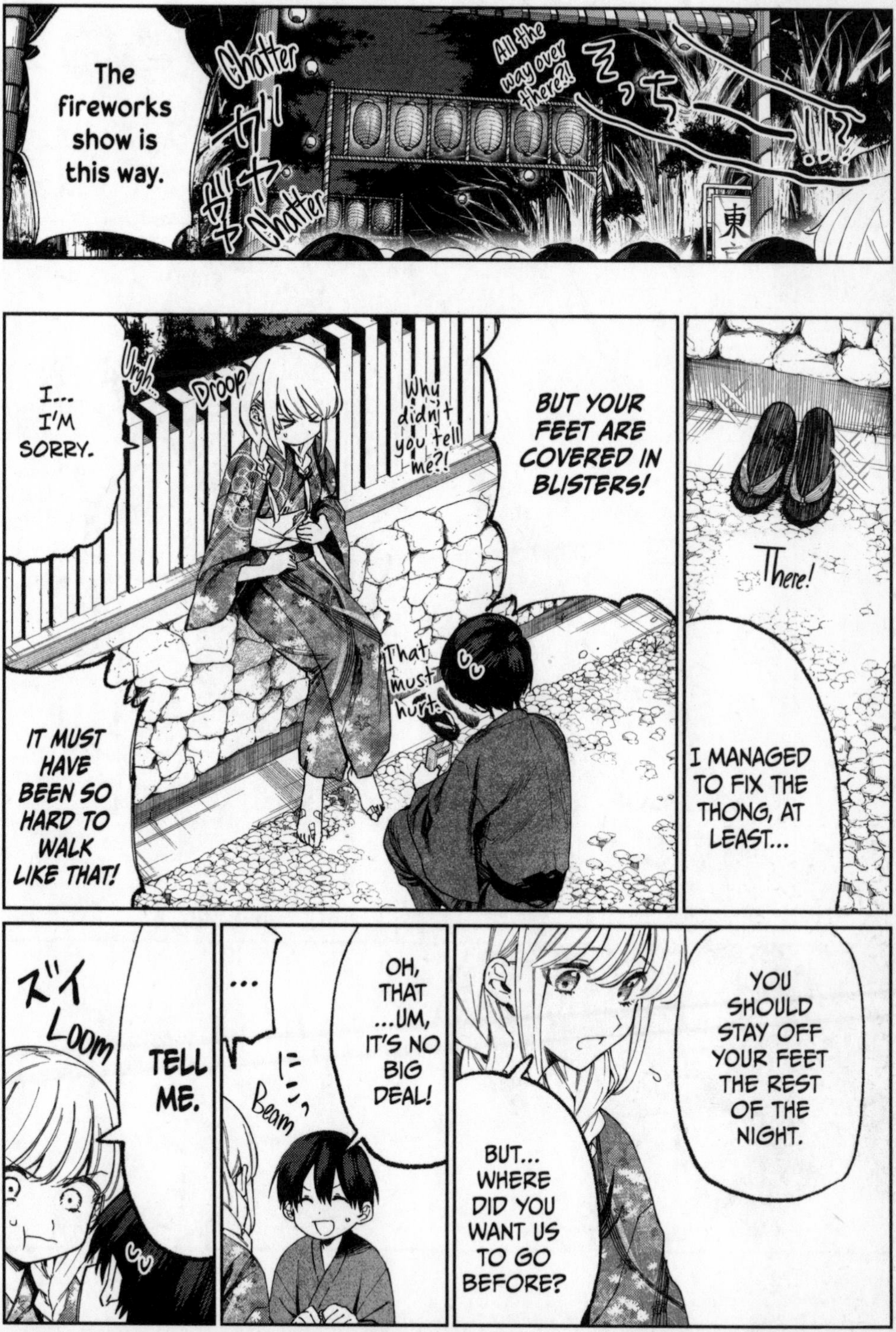
All the way over there?!
Chatter
Chatter
The fireworks show is this way.
There!
I MANAGED TO FIX THE THONG, AT LEAST...
BUT YOUR FEET ARE COVERED IN BLISTERS!
Why didn't you tell me?!
Droop
Urgh...
I... I'M SORRY.
That must hurt.
IT MUST HAVE BEEN SO HARD TO WALK LIKE THAT!
YOU SHOULD STAY OFF YOUR FEET THE REST OF THE NIGHT.
BUT... WHERE DID YOU WANT US TO GO BEFORE?
OH, THAT ...UM, IT'S NO BIG DEAL!
...
Beam
TELL ME.
Loom

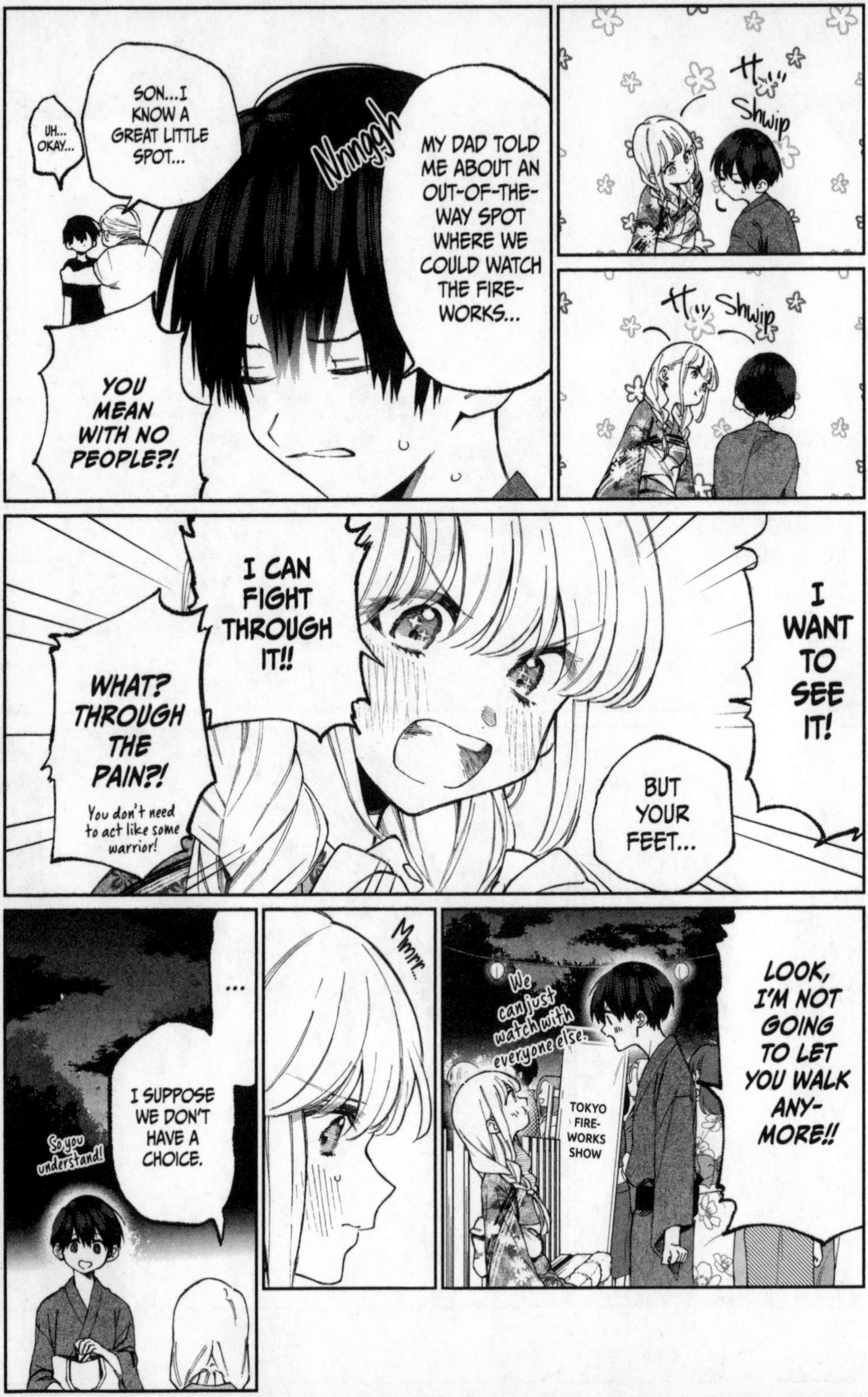

Shwip
Shwip
MY DAD TOLD ME ABOUT AN OUT-OF-THE-WAY SPOT WHERE WE COULD WATCH THE FIRE-WORKS...
Nnnggh
SON...I KNOW A GREAT LITTLE SPOT...
UH... OKAY...
YOU MEAN WITH NO PEOPLE?!
I WANT TO SEE IT!
BUT YOUR FEET...
I CAN FIGHT THROUGH IT!!
WHAT? THROUGH THE PAIN?!
You don't need to act like some warrior!
LOOK, I'M NOT GOING TO LET YOU WALK ANY-MORE!!
We can just watch with everyone else.
TOKYO FIRE-WORKS SHOW
Mmmr...
...
I SUPPOSE WE DON'T HAVE A CHOICE.
So you understand!

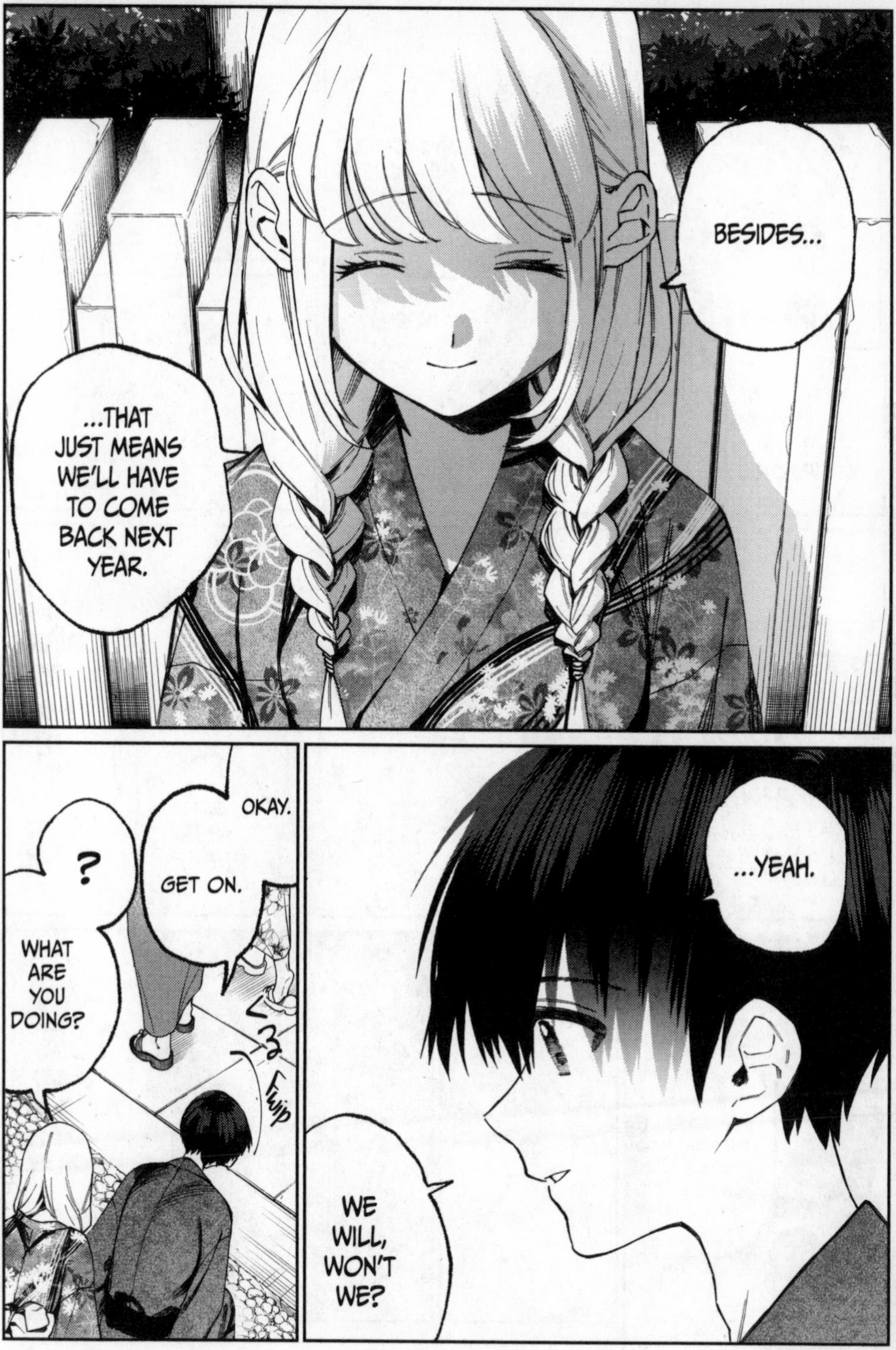
BESIDES...
...THAT JUST MEANS WE'LL HAVE TO COME BACK NEXT YEAR.
...YEAH.
WE WILL, WON'T WE?
OKAY. GET ON.
? WHAT ARE YOU DOING?
Fwip

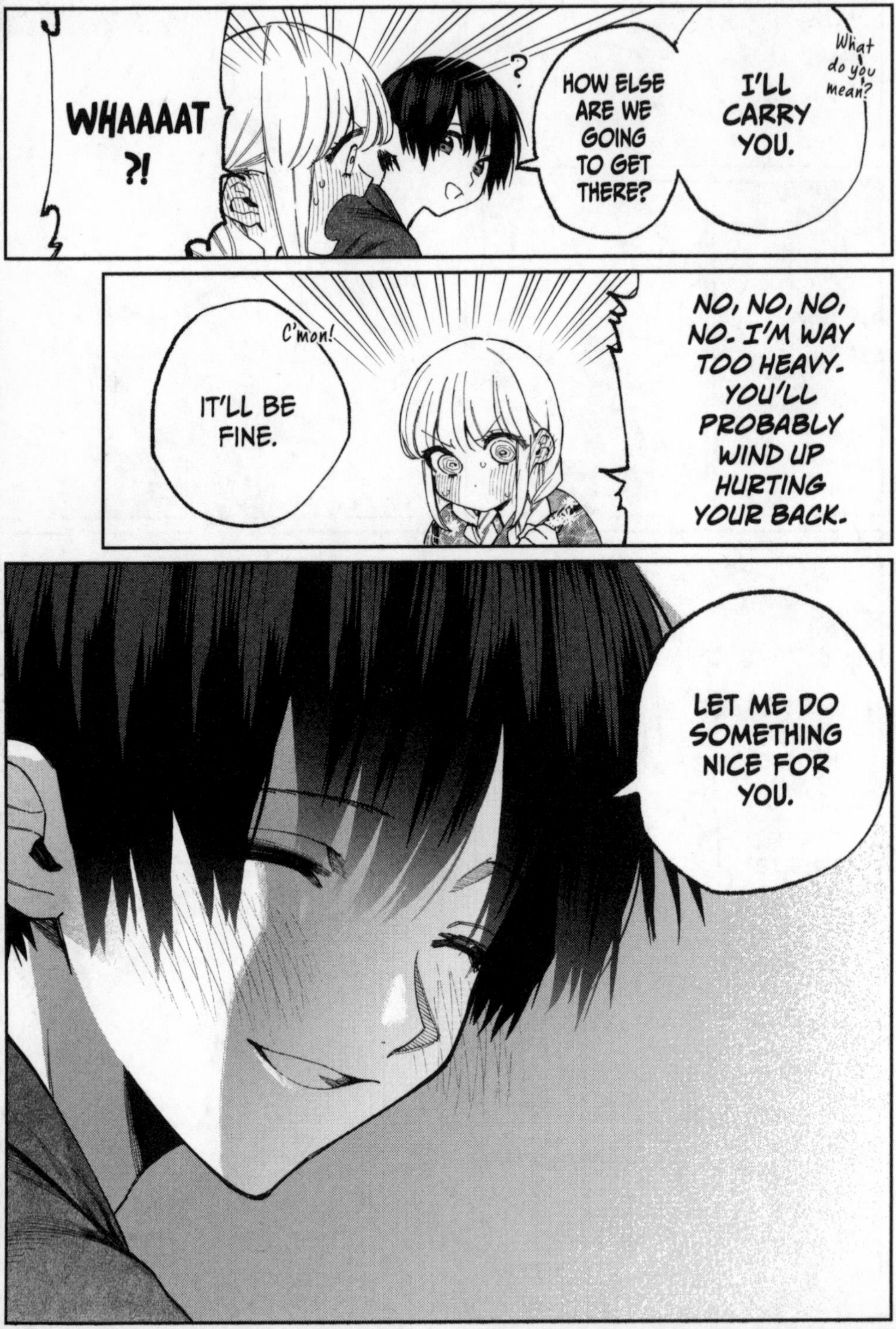
What do you mean?
I'LL CARRY YOU.
HOW ELSE ARE WE GOING TO GET THERE?
WHAAAAT ?!
NO, NO, NO, NO. I'M WAY TOO HEAVY. YOU'LL PROBABLY WIND UP HURTING YOUR BACK.
C'mon!
IT'LL BE FINE.
LET ME DO SOMETHING NICE FOR YOU.

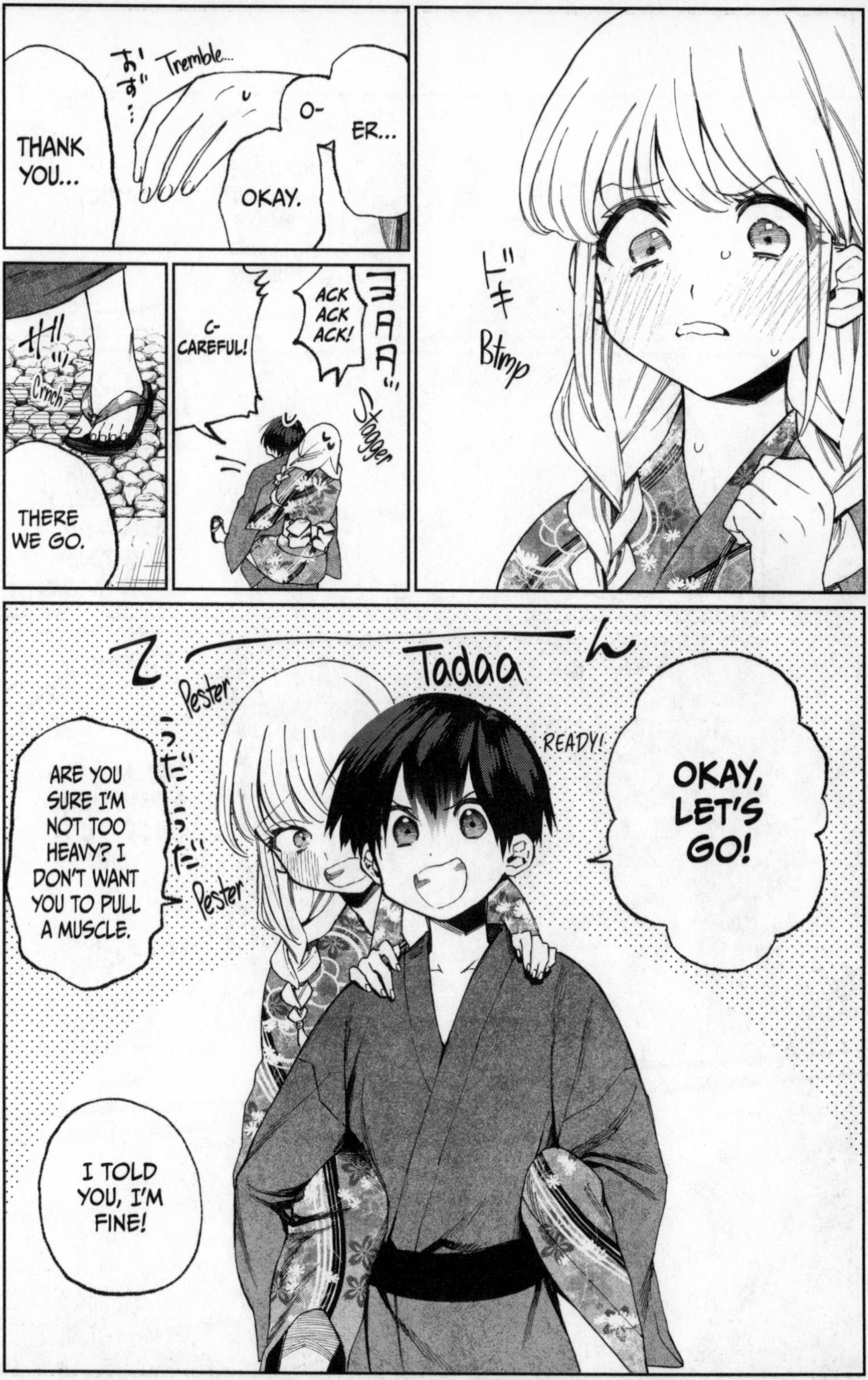
ドキ
Btmp
O-
ER...
OKAY.
おず...
Tremble...
THANK YOU...
ヨタタ
Stagger
ACK ACK ACK!
C-CAREFUL!
ザリ
Crnch
THERE WE GO.
Tadaa
OKAY, LET'S GO!
READY!
うだうだ
Pester
Pester
ARE YOU SURE I'M NOT TOO HEAVY? I DON'T WANT YOU TO PULL A MUSCLE.
I TOLD YOU, I'M FINE!

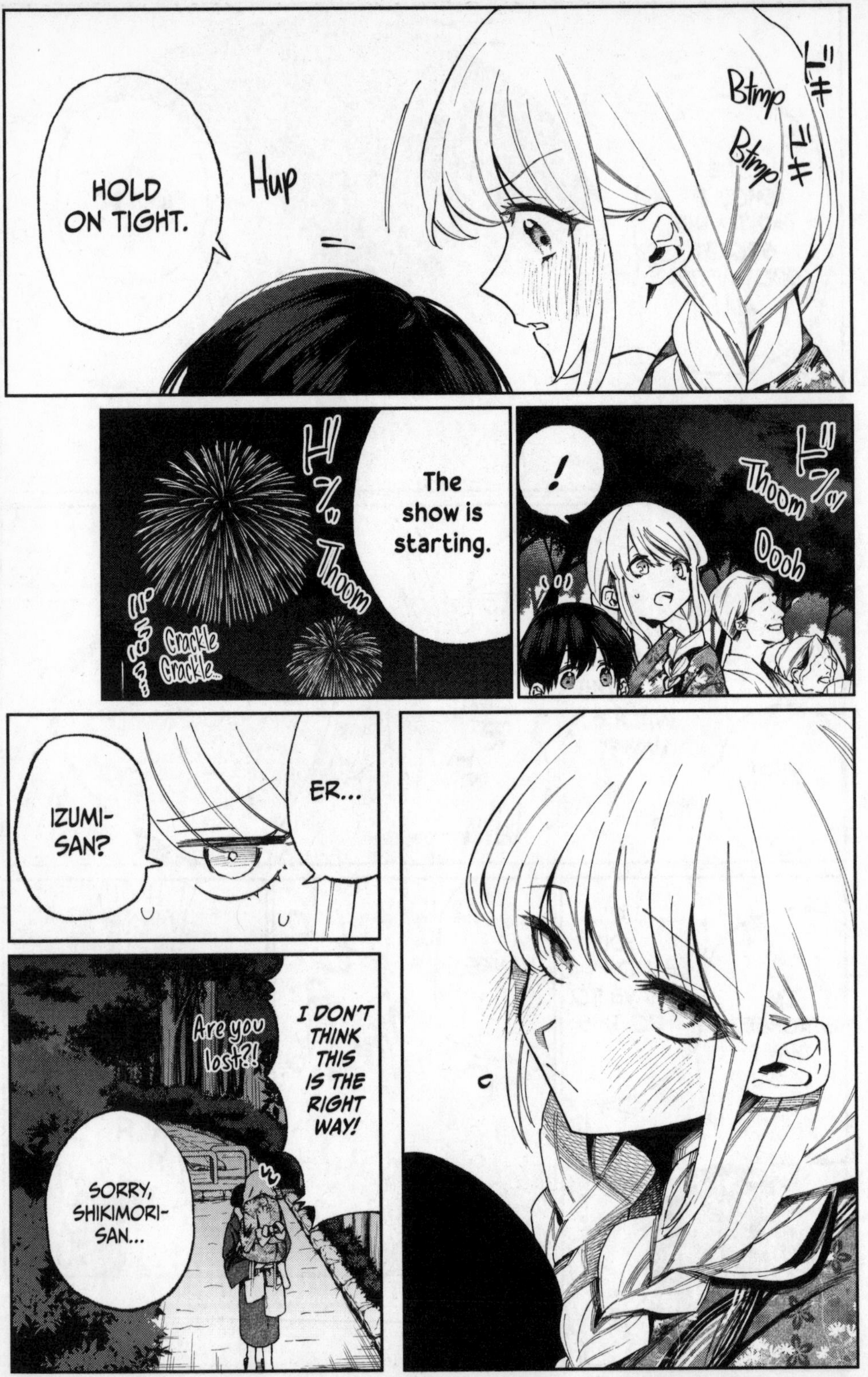
ドキ
Btmp
ドキ
Btmp
Hup
HOLD ON TIGHT.
Thoom
!
Oooh
The show is starting.
Thoom
Crackle Crackle...
ER...
IZUMI-SAN?
I DON'T THINK THIS IS THE RIGHT WAY!
Are you lost?!
SORRY, SHIKIMORI-SAN...

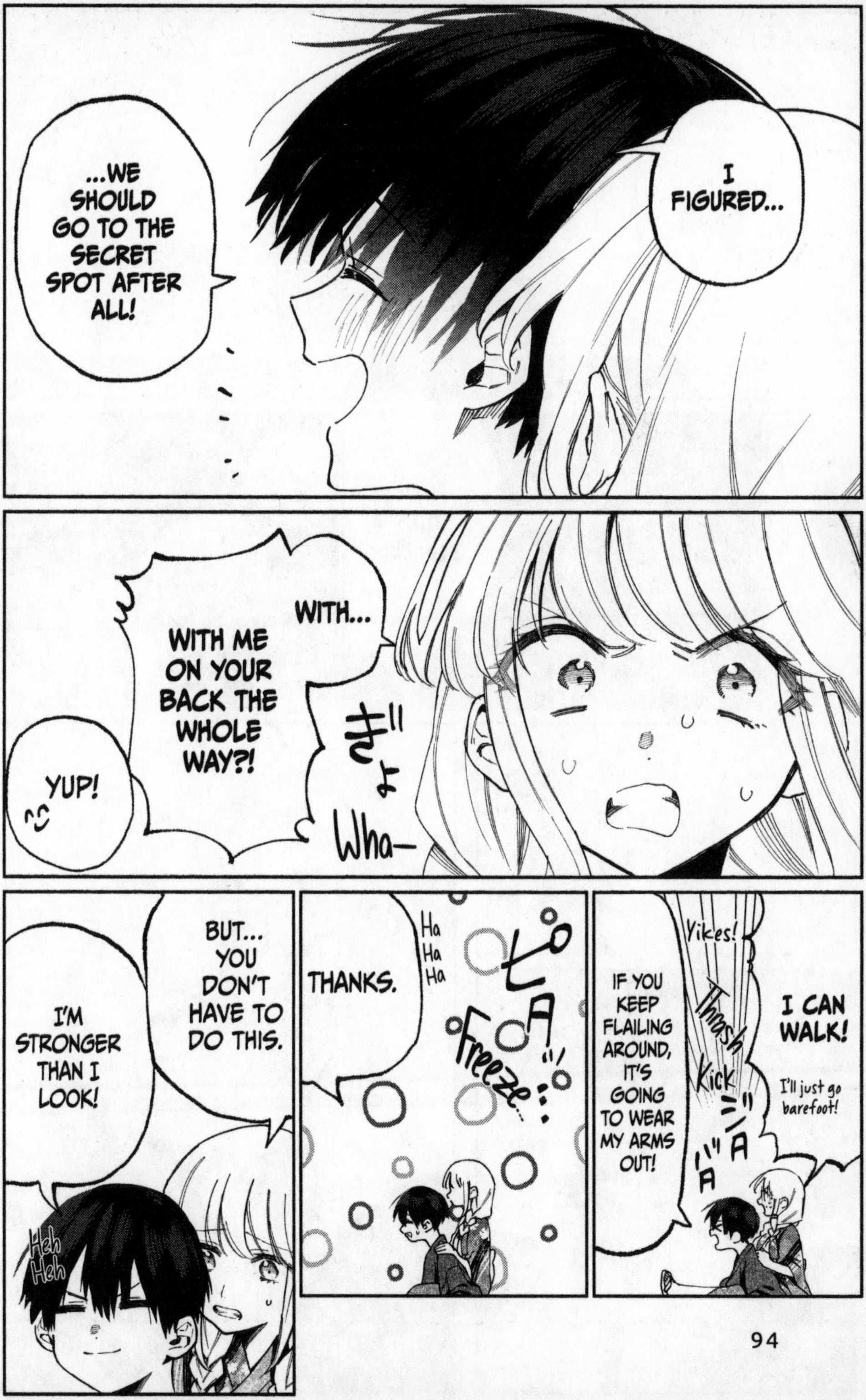
I FIGURED...
...WE SHOULD GO TO THE SECRET SPOT AFTER ALL!
Wha–
ぎょ
WITH...
WITH ME ON YOUR BACK THE WHOLE WAY?!
YUP!
I CAN WALK!
I'll just go barefoot!
Yikes!
Thrash
Kick
IF YOU KEEP FLAILING AROUND, IT'S GOING TO WEAR MY ARMS OUT!
ピ
Freeze...
Ha Ha Ha
THANKS.
BUT... YOU DON'T HAVE TO DO THIS.
I'M STRONGER THAN I LOOK!
Heh Heh

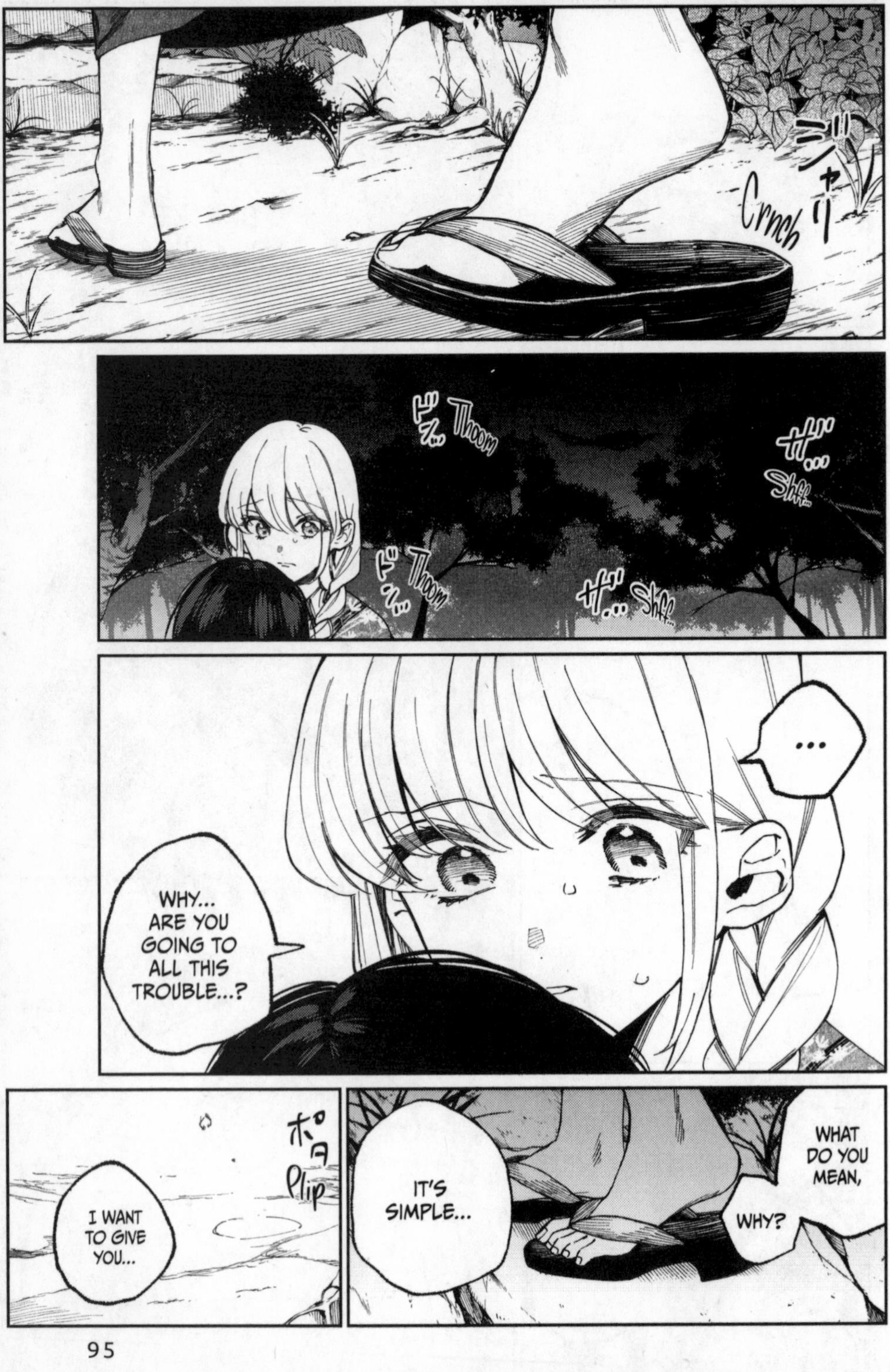
ジャリ
Crnch
ザ…
Shff...
ドス…
Thoom
ド…
Thoom
ザ…
Shff...
...
WHY... ARE YOU GOING TO ALL THIS TROUBLE...?
WHAT DO YOU MEAN,
WHY?
IT'S SIMPLE...
ポタ
Plip
I WANT TO GIVE YOU...

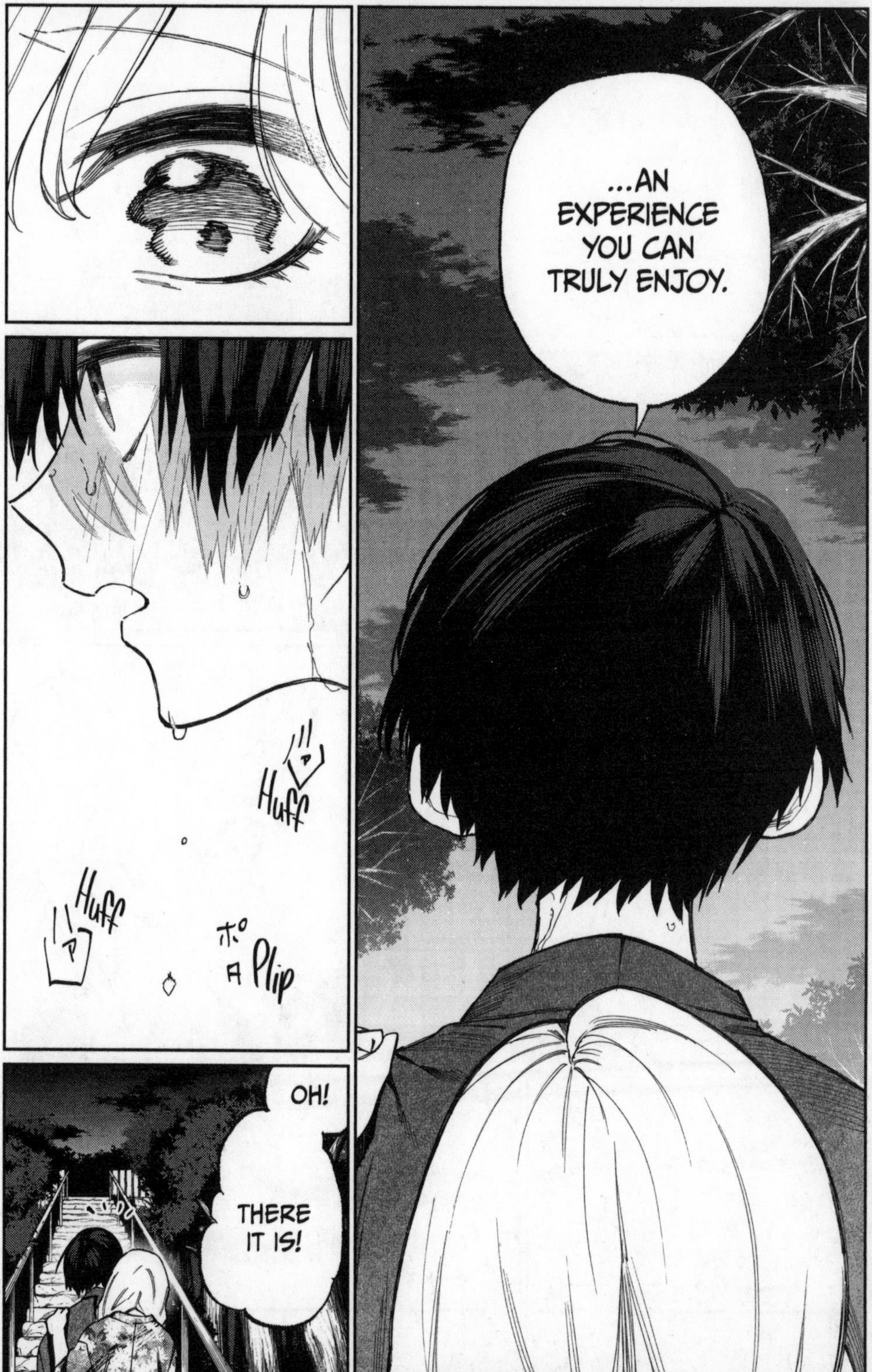
...AN EXPERIENCE YOU CAN TRULY ENJOY.
Huff
Huff
Plip
OH!
THERE IT IS!

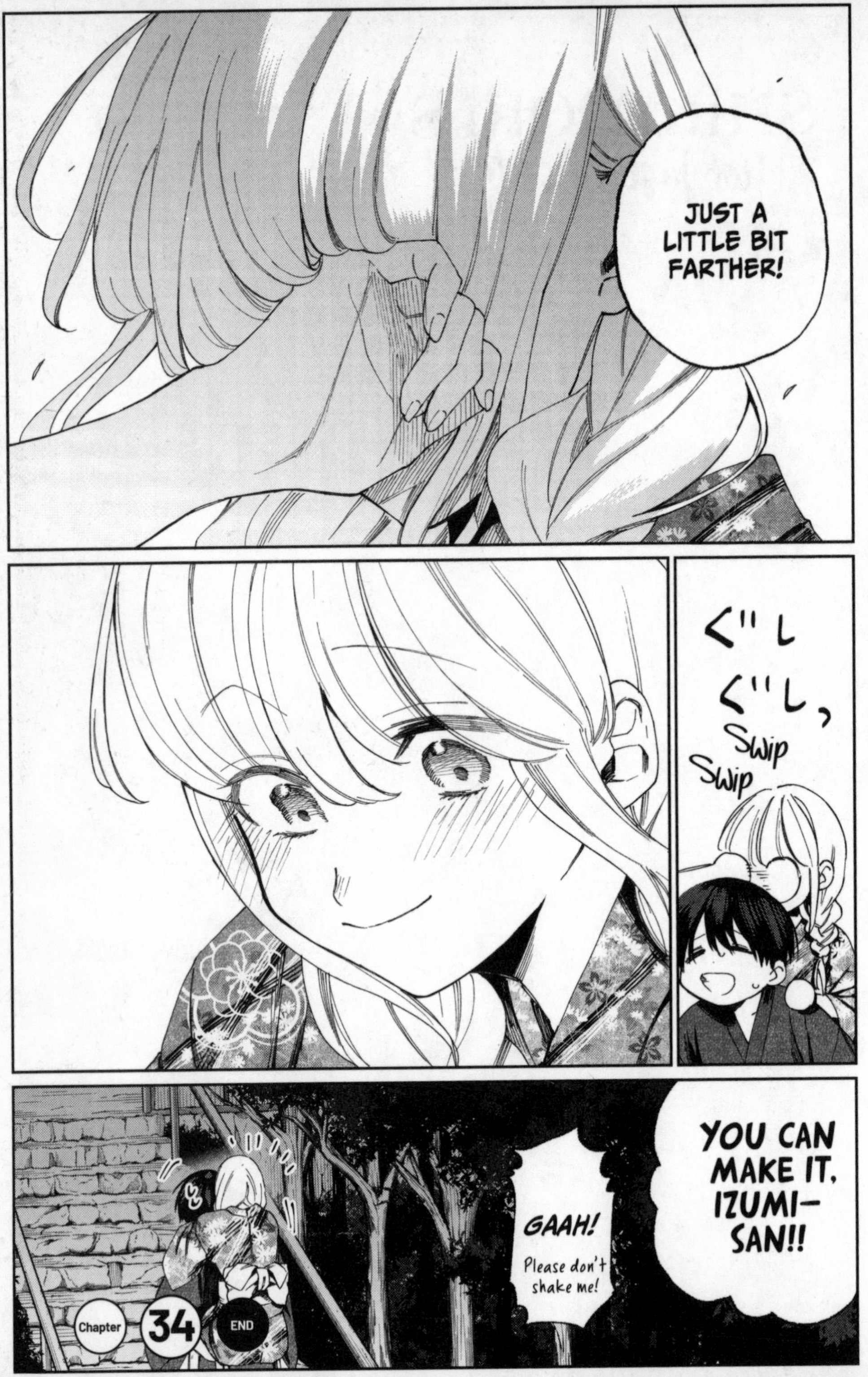
JUST A LITTLE BIT FARTHER!
ぐしぐし
Swip Swip
YOU CAN MAKE IT, IZUMI-SAN!!
GAAH!
Please don't shake me!
Chapter 34 END

SHIKIMORI'S
not just a cutie

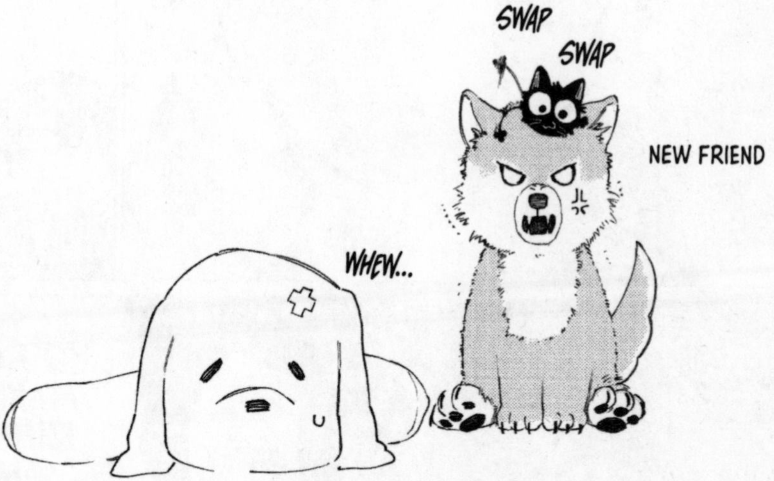
SWAP
SWAP
NEW FRIEND
WHEW...

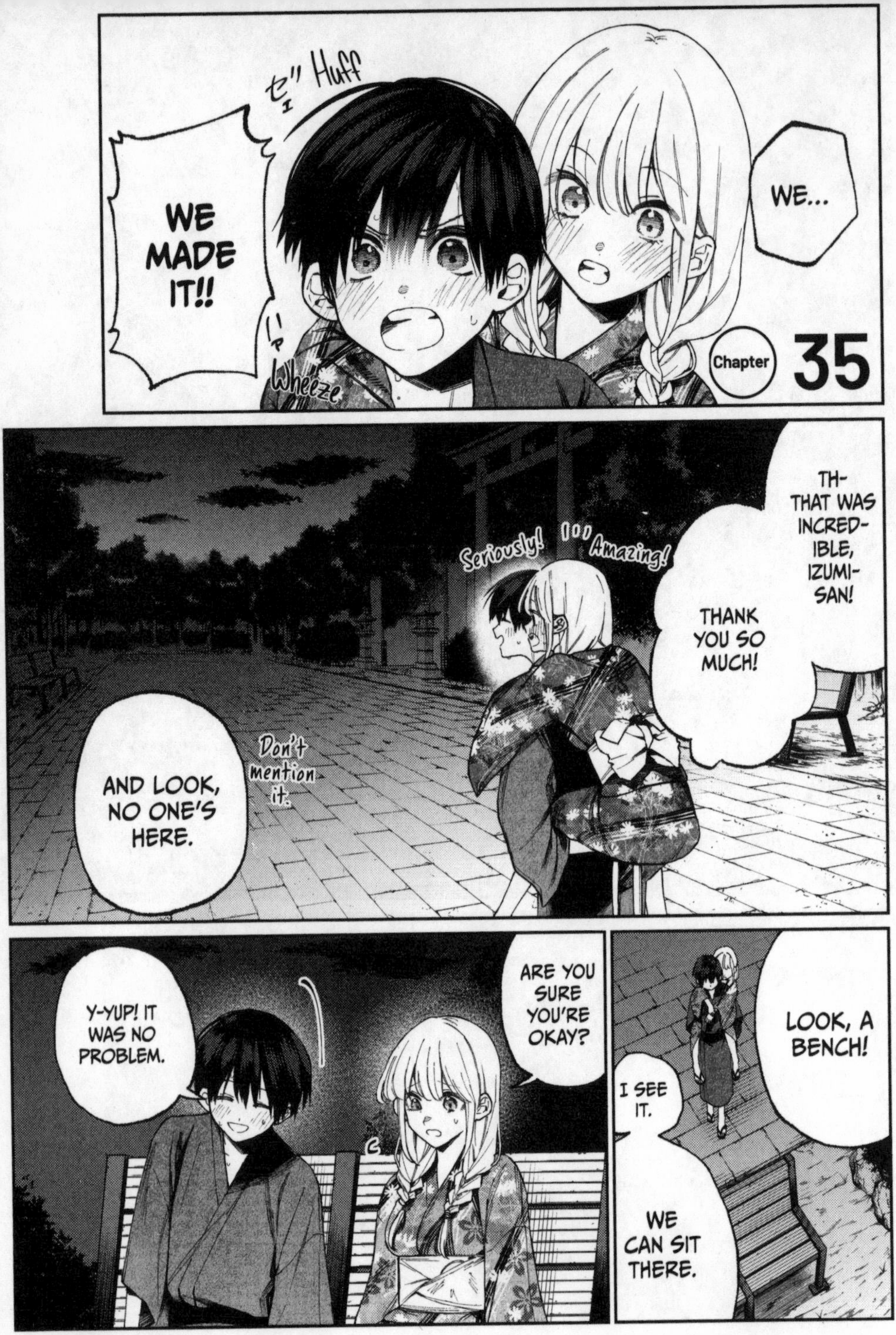
WE...
Huff
WE MADE IT!!
Wheeze
Chapter 35
TH- THAT WAS INCRED- IBLE, IZUMI- SAN!
THANK YOU SO MUCH!
Amazing!
Seriously!
Don't mention it.
AND LOOK, NO ONE'S HERE.
LOOK, A BENCH!
I SEE IT.
WE CAN SIT THERE.
ARE YOU SURE YOU'RE OKAY?
Y-YUP! IT WAS NO PROBLEM.

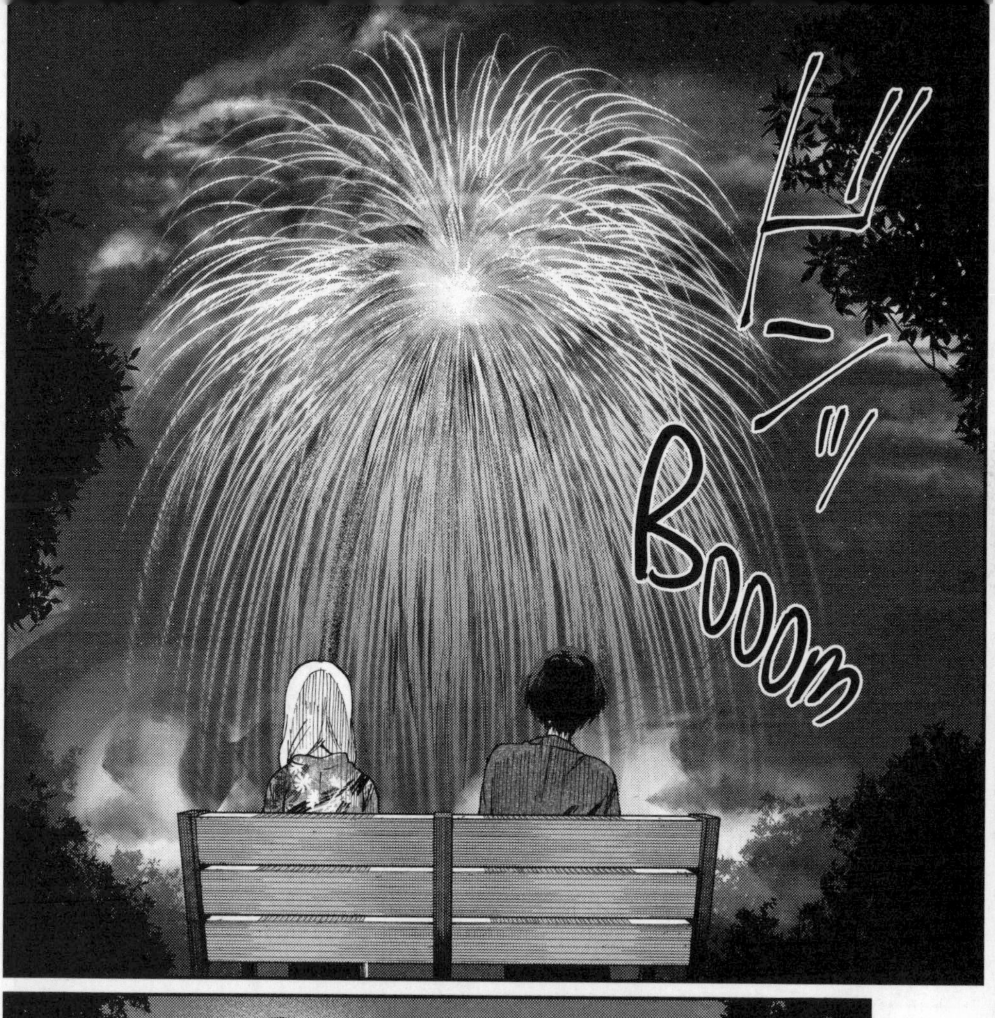
BOOOM
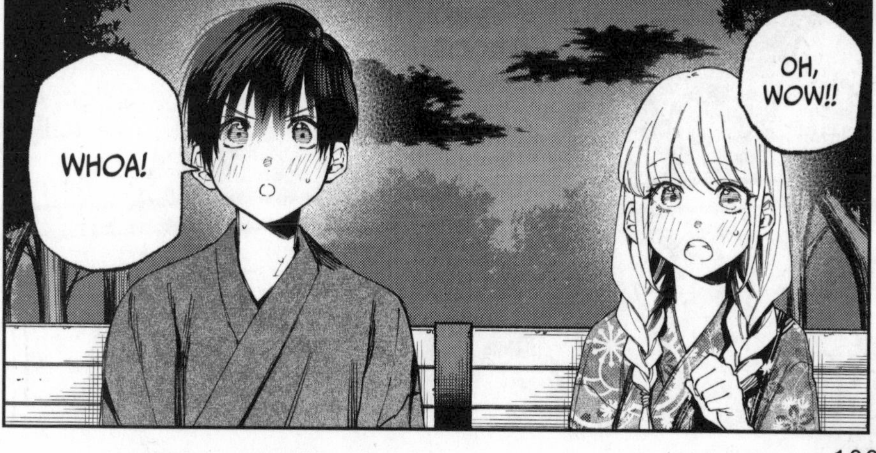
OH, WOW!!
WHOA!

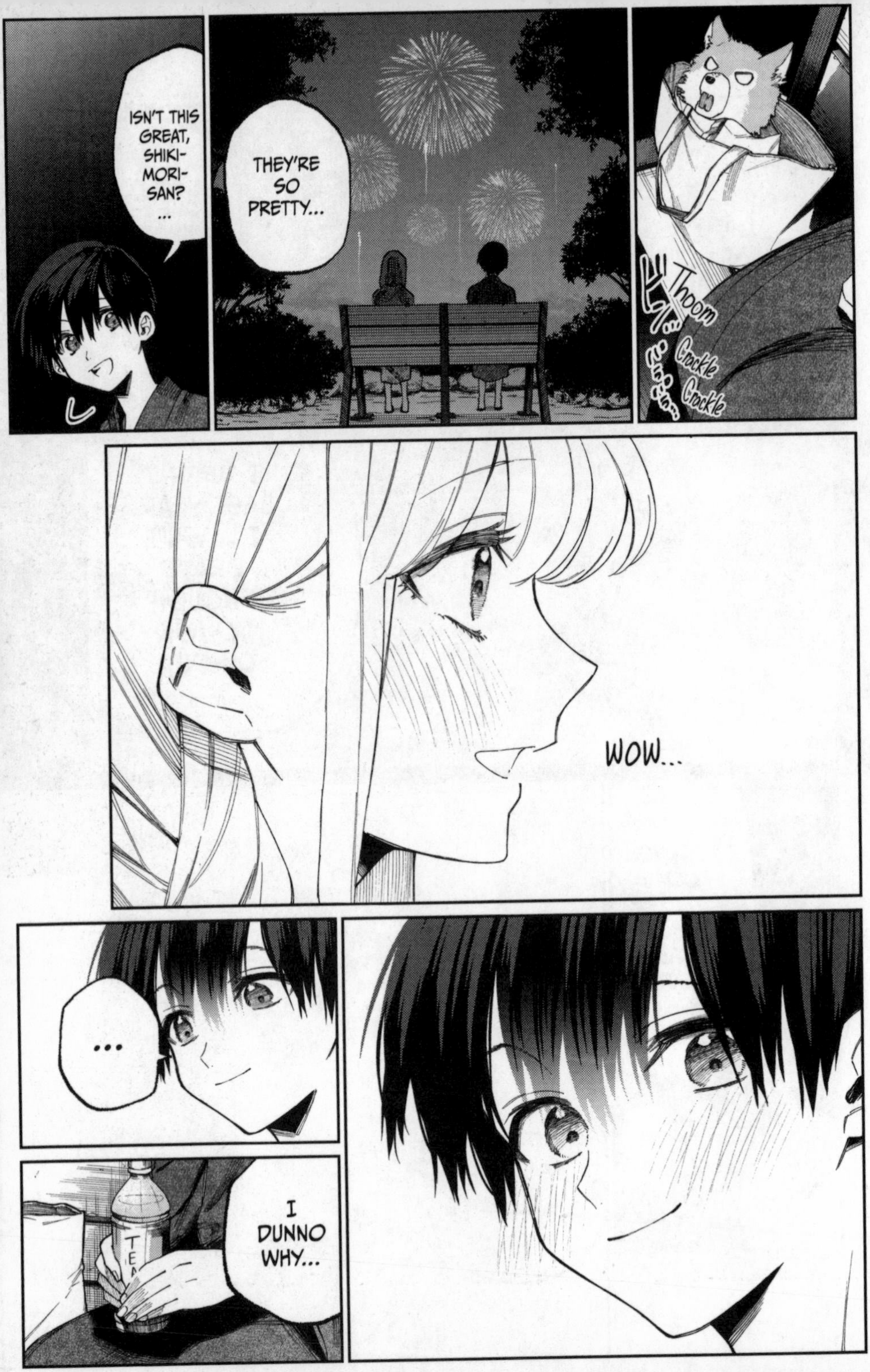
Thoom
Crackle
Crackle
THEY'RE SO PRETTY...
ISN'T THIS GREAT, SHIKIMORI-SAN? ...
WOW...
...
I DUNNO WHY...
TEA

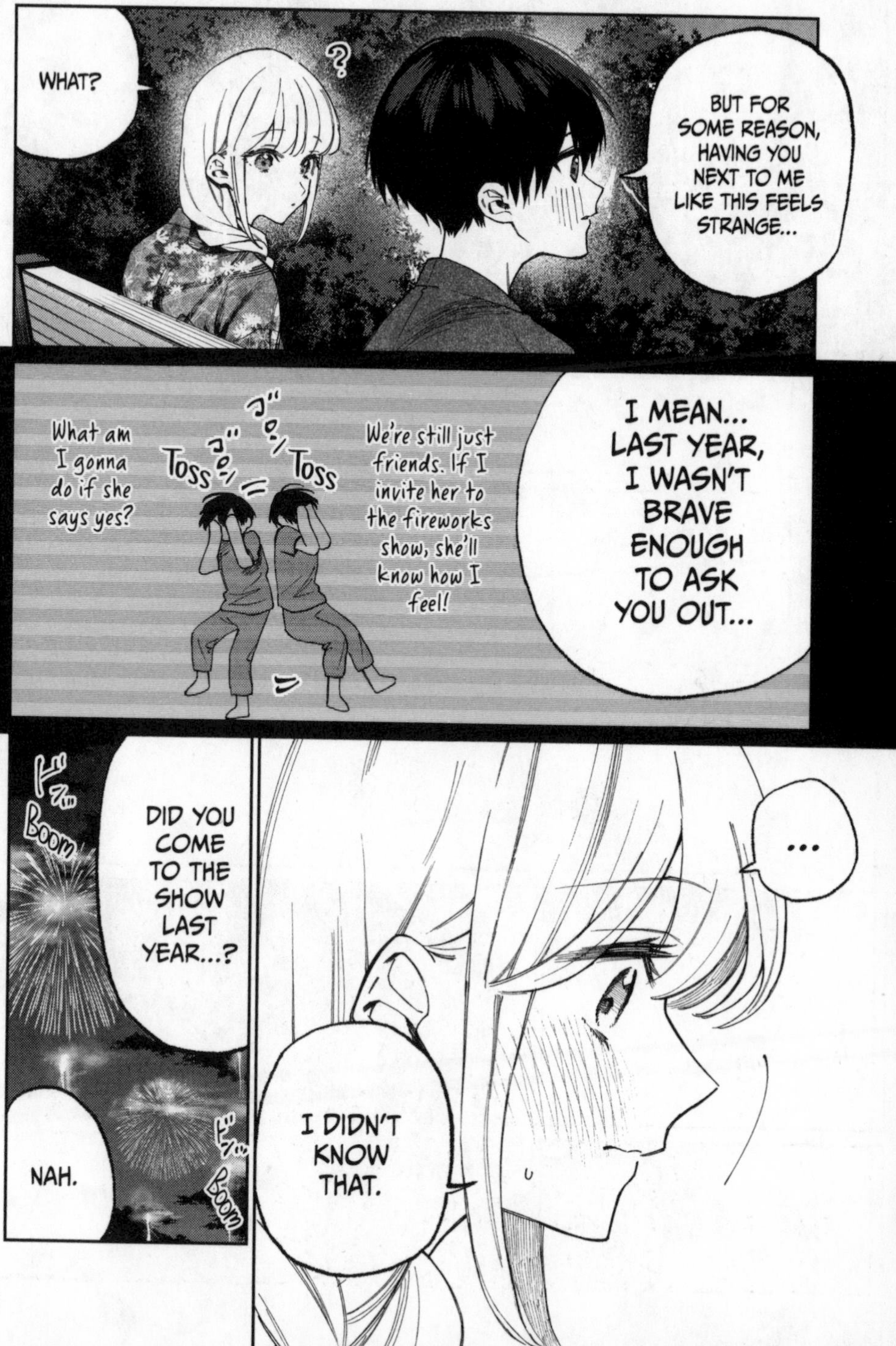
BUT FOR SOME REASON, HAVING YOU NEXT TO ME LIKE THIS FEELS STRANGE...
WHAT?
I MEAN... LAST YEAR, I WASN'T BRAVE ENOUGH TO ASK YOU OUT...
We're still just friends. If I invite her to the fireworks show, she'll know how I feel!
Toss
Toss
What am I gonna do if she says yes?
...
I DIDN'T KNOW THAT.
Boom
DID YOU COME TO THE SHOW LAST YEAR...?
NAH.
Boom

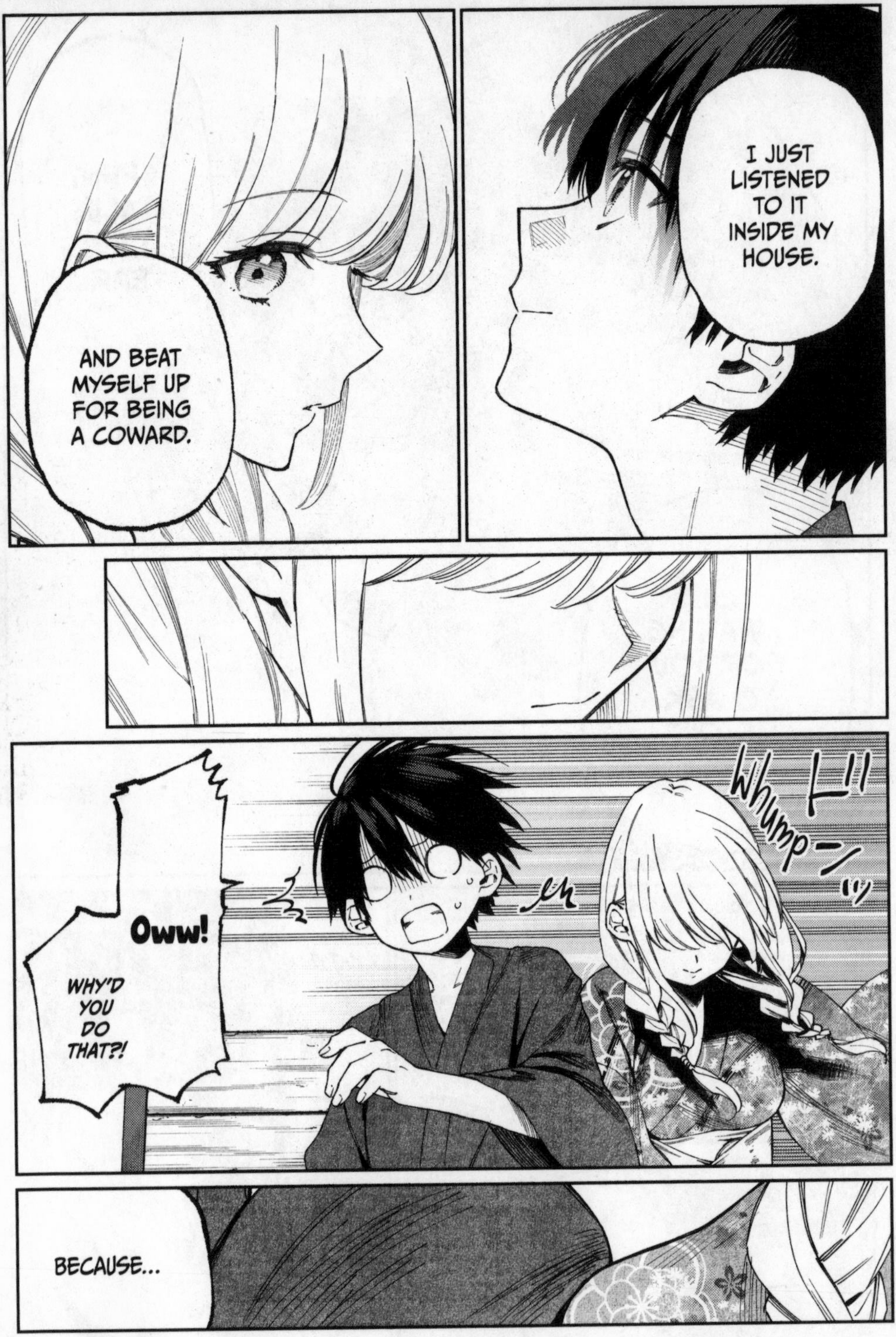
I JUST LISTENED TO IT INSIDE MY HOUSE.
AND BEAT MYSELF UP FOR BEING A COWARD.
Whump
Oww!
WHY'D YOU DO THAT?!
BECAUSE...

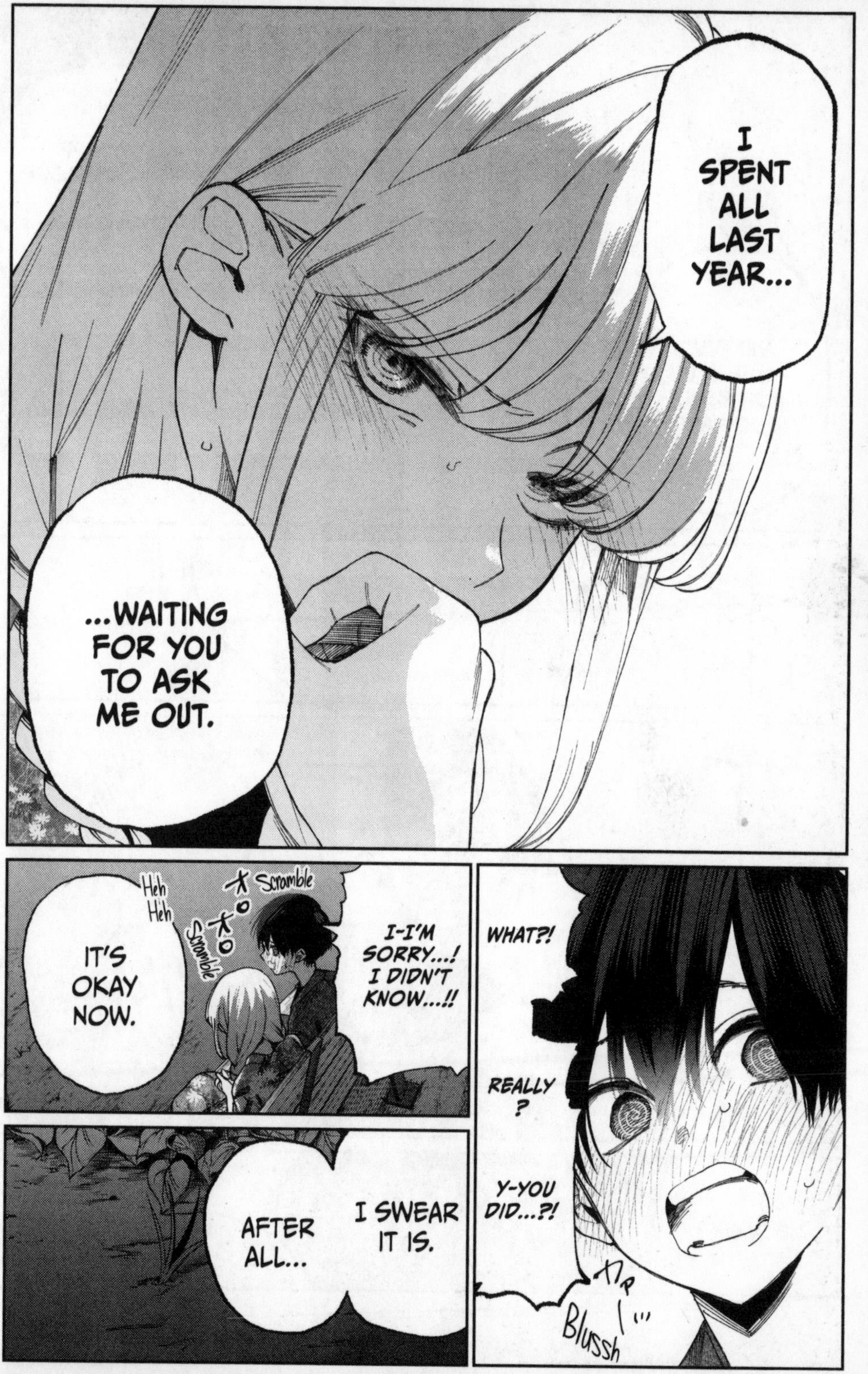
I SPENT ALL LAST YEAR...
...WAITING FOR YOU TO ASK ME OUT.
WHAT?!
REALLY?
Y-YOU DID...?!
Blussh
I-I'M SORRY...! I DIDN'T KNOW...!!
Scramble
Scramble
Heh Heh
IT'S OKAY NOW.
I SWEAR IT IS.
AFTER ALL...

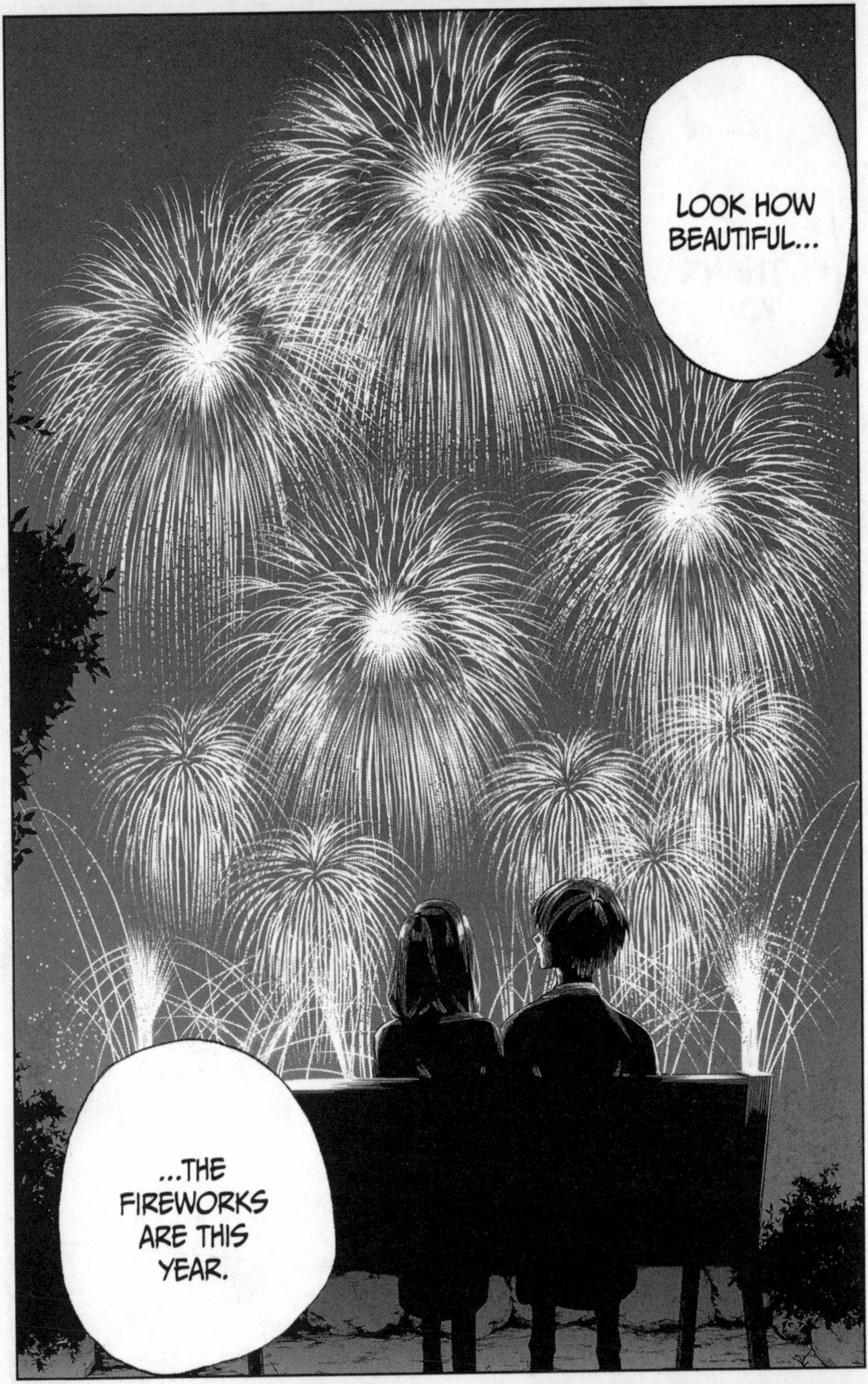
LOOK HOW BEAUTIFUL...
...THE FIREWORKS ARE THIS YEAR.

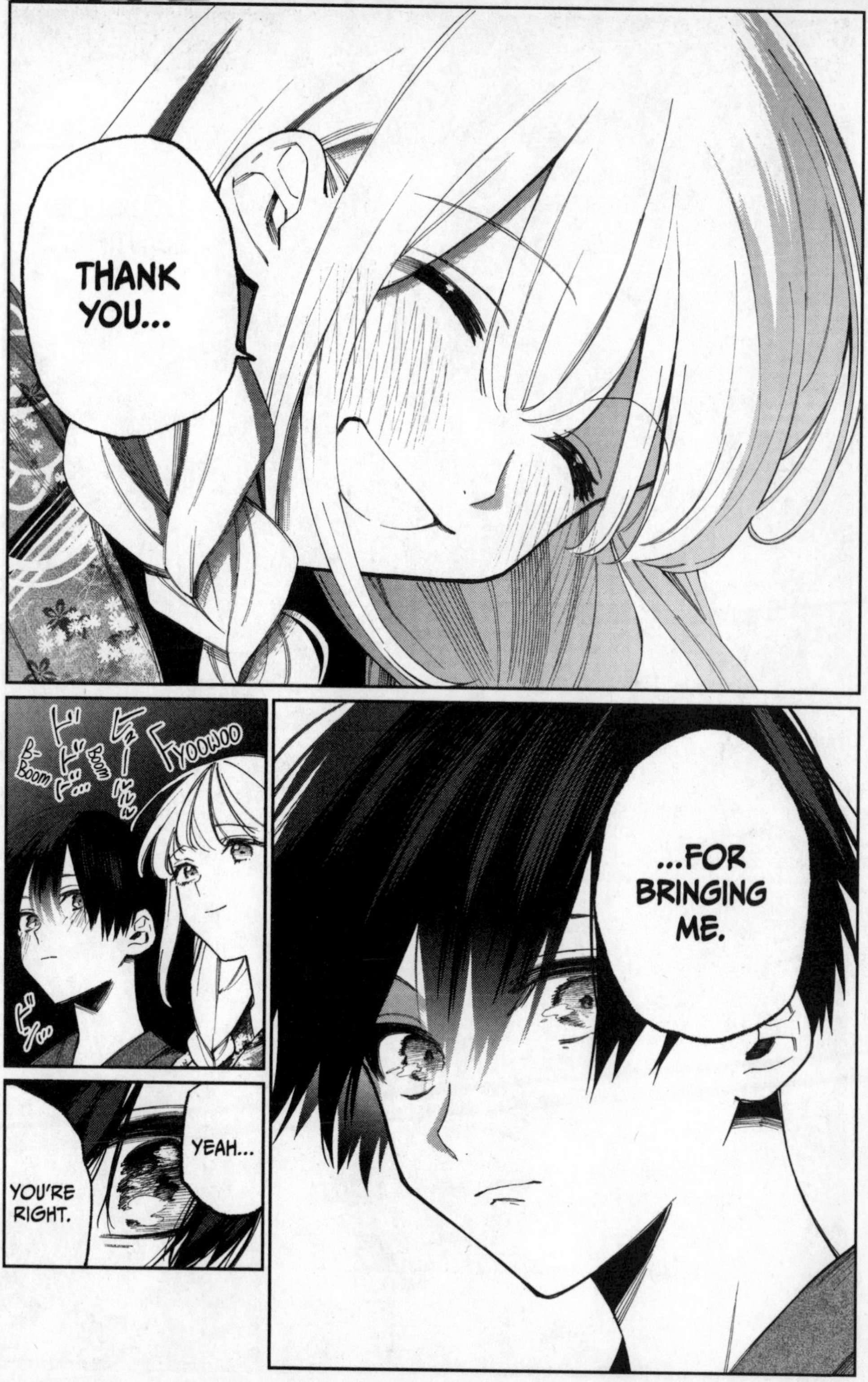
THANK YOU...
...FOR BRINGING ME.
Fyoowoo
Boom
B-Boom
YEAH...
YOU'RE RIGHT.

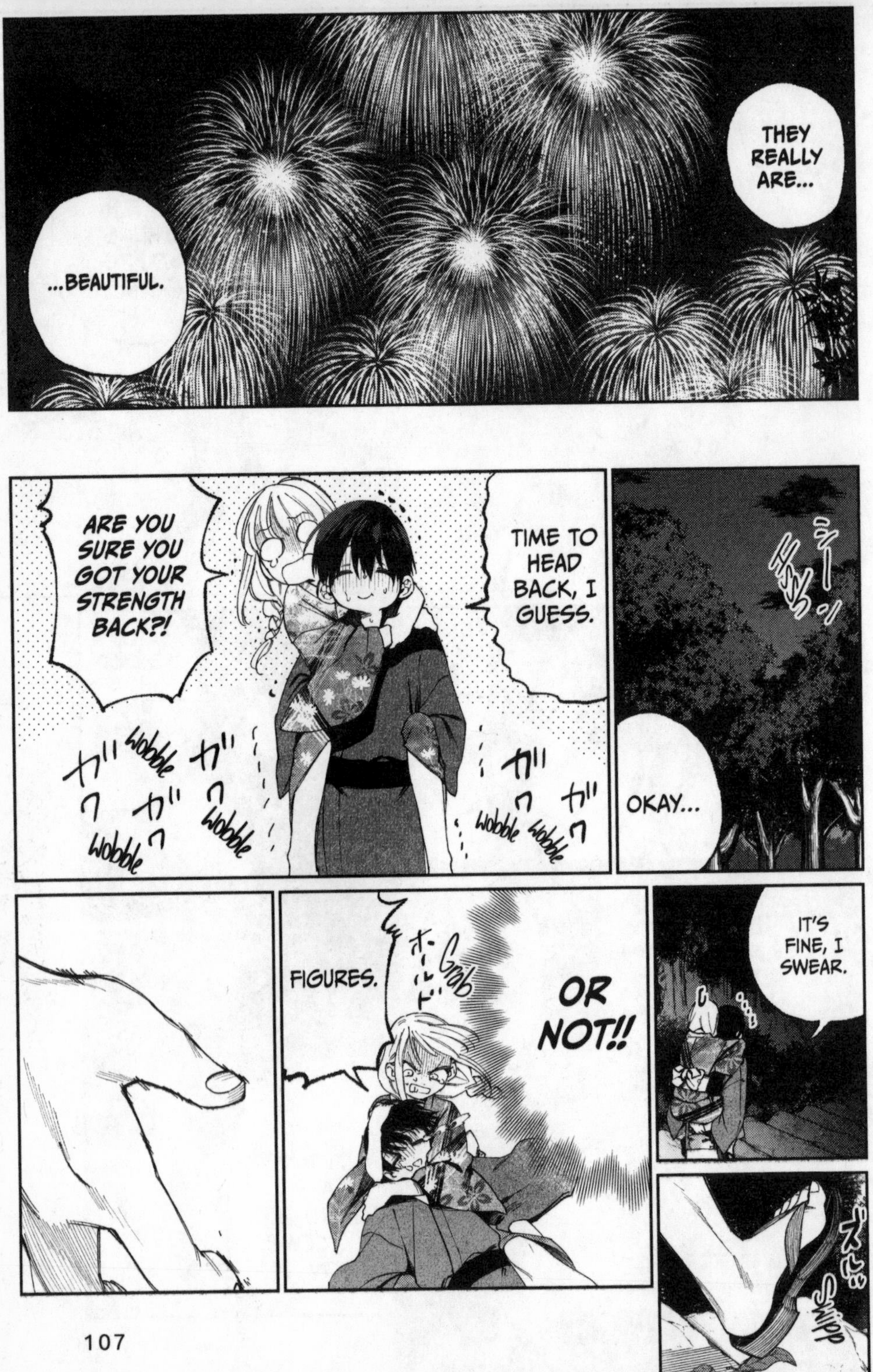
THEY REALLY ARE...
...BEAUTIFUL.
OKAY...
TIME TO HEAD BACK, I GUESS.
wobble
wobble
wobble
wobble
wobble
ARE YOU SURE YOU GOT YOUR STRENGTH BACK?!
IT'S FINE, I SWEAR.
SWIPP
OR NOT!!
Grab
FIGURES.

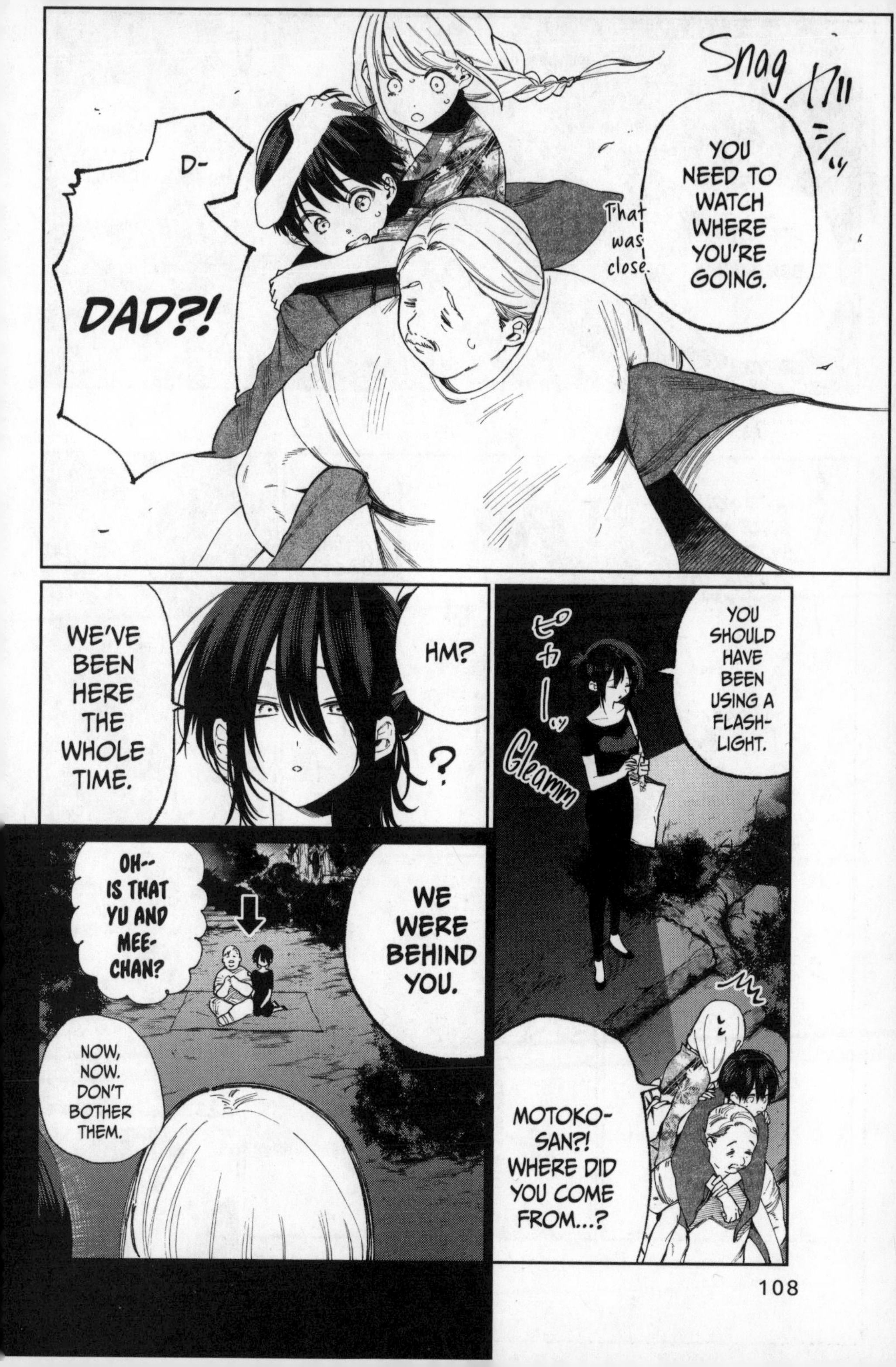
Snag
YOU NEED TO WATCH WHERE YOU'RE GOING.
That was close.
D-
DAD?!
YOU SHOULD HAVE BEEN USING A FLASH-LIGHT.
Gleamm
MOTOKO-SAN?! WHERE DID YOU COME FROM...?
HM?
?
WE'VE BEEN HERE THE WHOLE TIME.
WE WERE BEHIND YOU.
OH-- IS THAT YU AND MEE-CHAN?
NOW, NOW. DON'T BOTHER THEM.

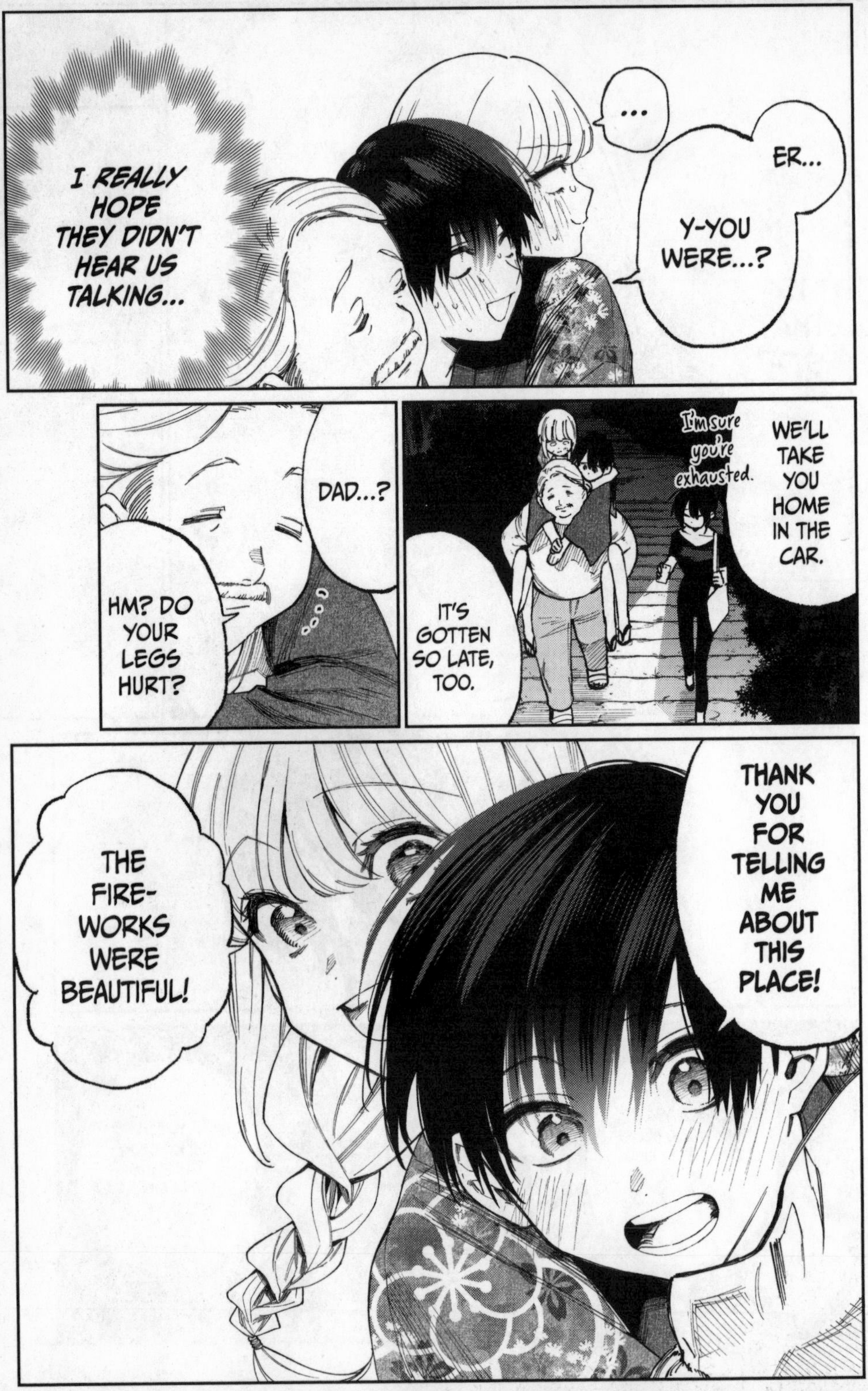
...
ER... Y-YOU WERE...?
I REALLY HOPE THEY DIDN'T HEAR US TALKING...
WE'LL TAKE YOU HOME IN THE CAR.
I'm sure you're exhausted.
IT'S GOTTEN SO LATE, TOO.
DAD...?
HM? DO YOUR LEGS HURT?
THANK YOU FOR TELLING ME ABOUT THIS PLACE!
THE FIRE-WORKS WERE BEAUTIFUL!

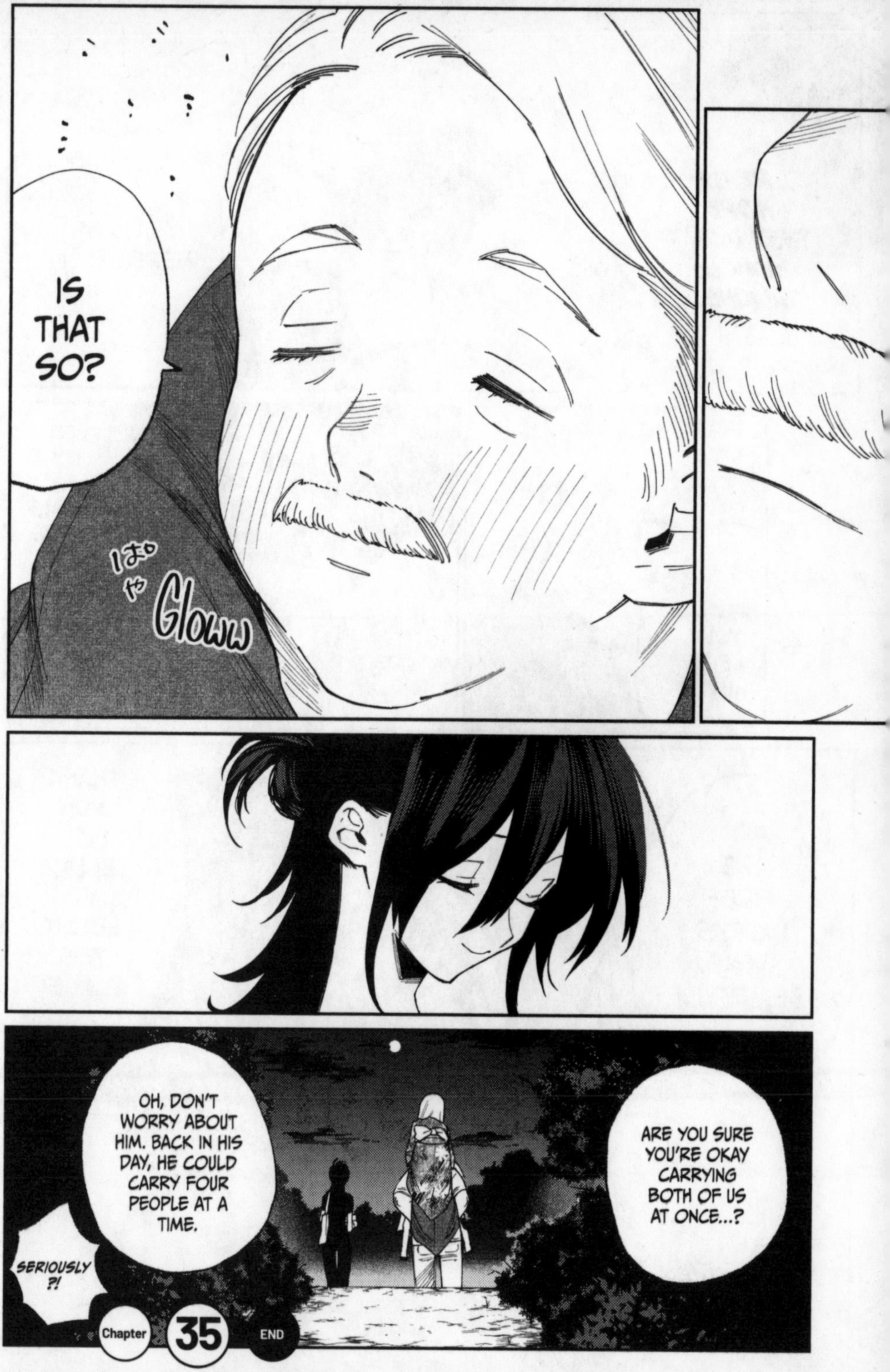
IS THAT SO?
ぱや
Gloww
ARE YOU SURE YOU'RE OKAY CARRYING BOTH OF US AT ONCE...?
OH, DON'T WORRY ABOUT HIM. BACK IN HIS DAY, HE COULD CARRY FOUR PEOPLE AT A TIME.
SERIOUSLY?!
Chapter 35 END

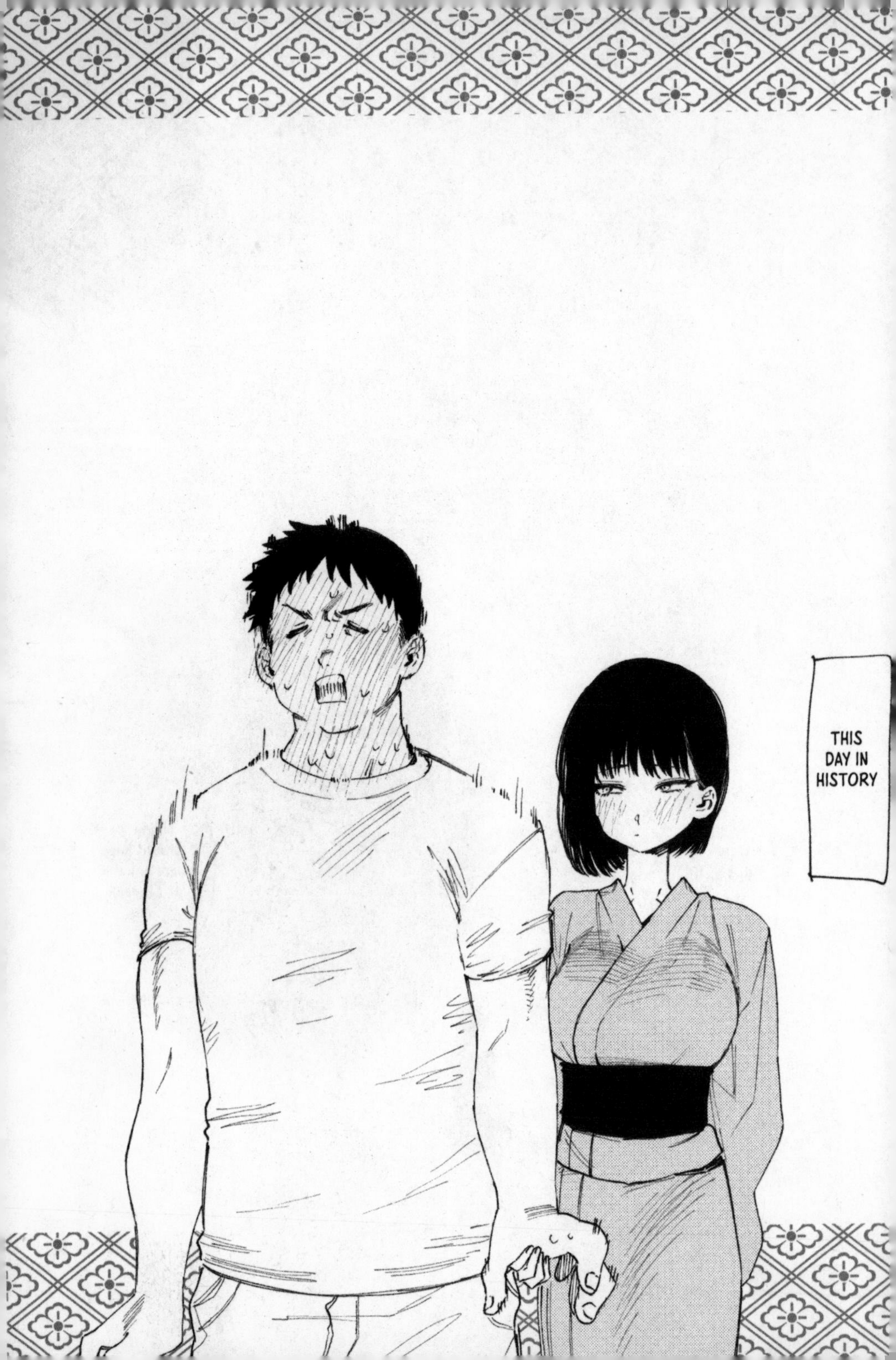
THIS DAY IN HISTORY

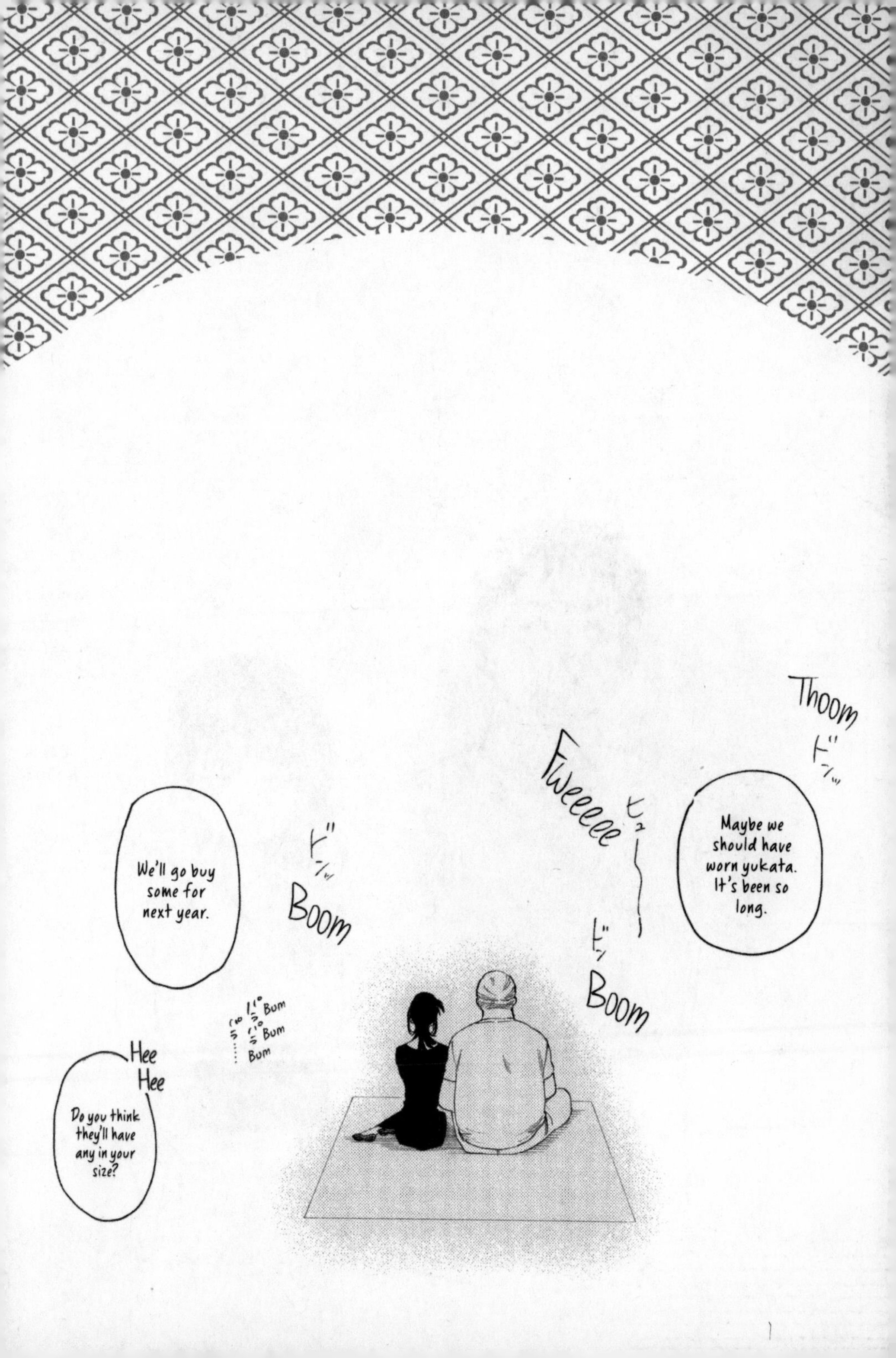

Thoom
Maybe we should have worn yukata. It's been so long.
Fweeeeee
Boom
Boom
We'll go buy some for next year.
Bum Bum Bum
Hee Hee
Do you think they'll have any in your size?

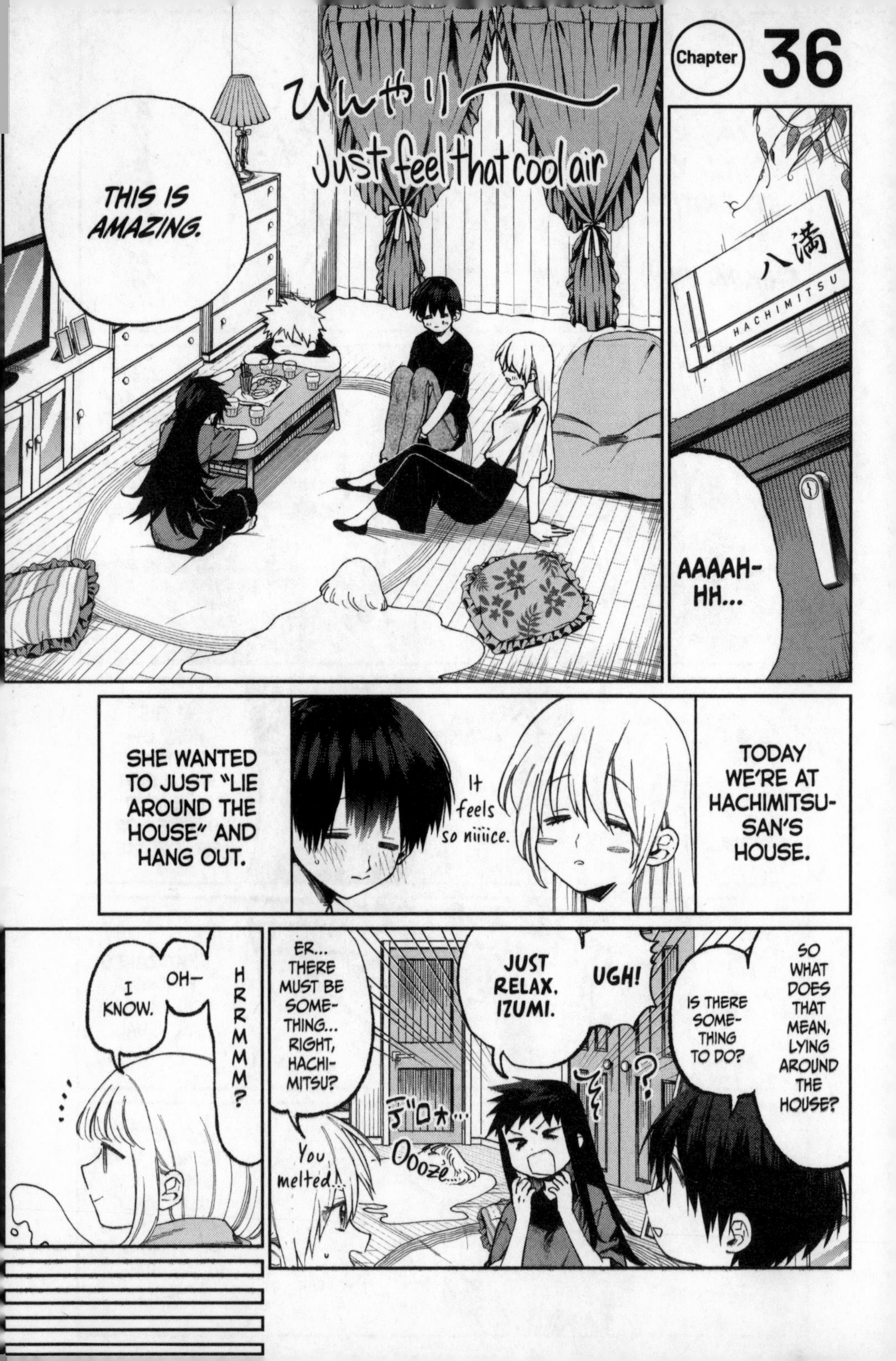
Chapter 36
八満
HACHIMITSU
AAAAH-HH...
ひんやり——
Just feel that cool air
THIS IS AMAZING.
TODAY WE'RE AT HACHIMITSU-SAN'S HOUSE.
It feels so niiiice.
SHE WANTED TO JUST "LIE AROUND THE HOUSE" AND HANG OUT.
SO WHAT DOES THAT MEAN, LYING AROUND THE HOUSE?
IS THERE SOME-THING TO DO?
UGH!
?
JUST RELAX, IZUMI.
ER... THERE MUST BE SOME-THING... RIGHT, HACHI-MITSU?
ドロォ…
Oooze...
You melted...
HRRMMMM?
OH— I KNOW.
...

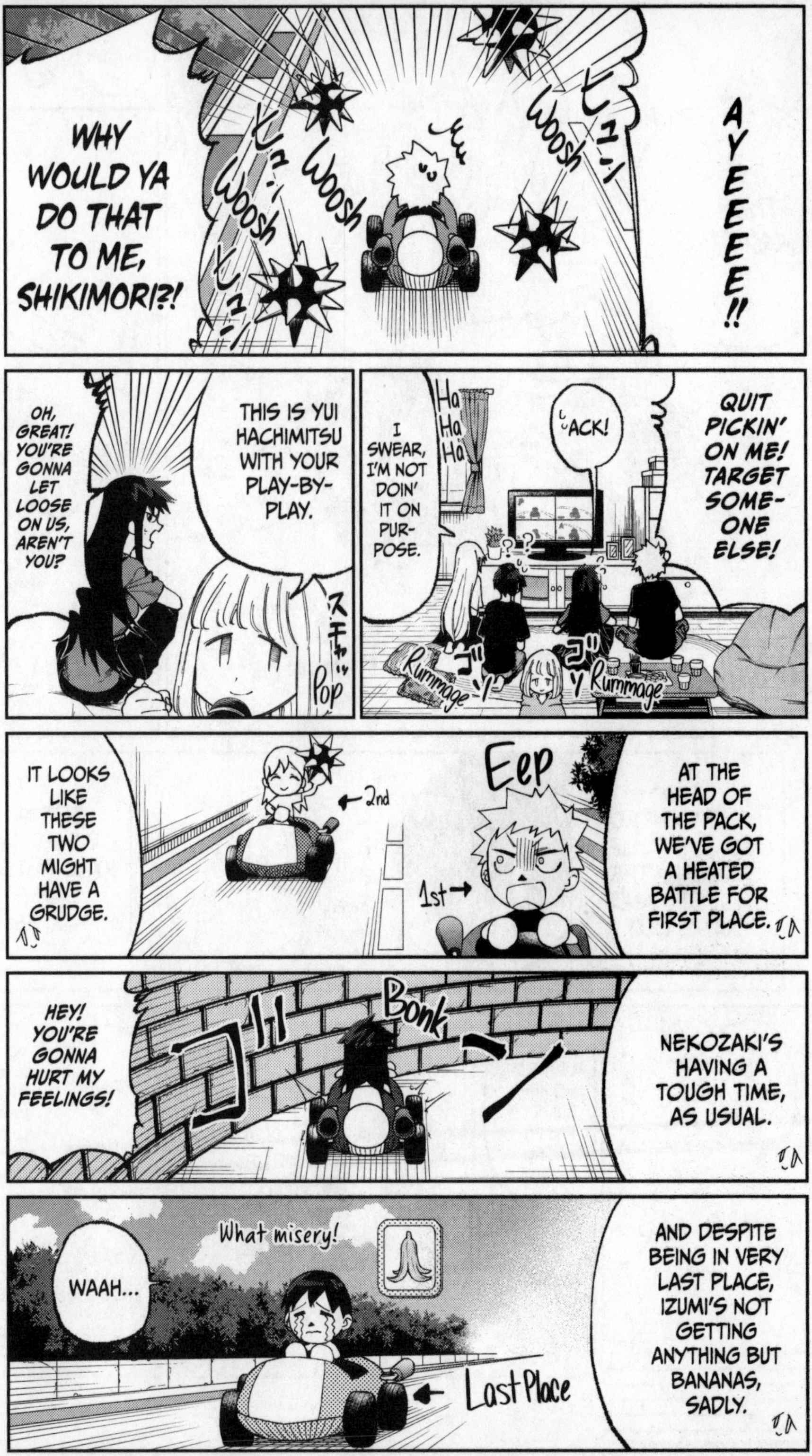
AYEEEEE!!
Woosh
Woosh
Woosh
WHY WOULD YA DO THAT TO ME, SHIKIMORI?!
QUIT PICKIN' ON ME! TARGET SOMEONE ELSE!
ACK!
I SWEAR, I'M NOT DOIN' IT ON PURPOSE.
Ha Ha Ha
Rummage
Rummage
THIS IS YUI HACHIMITSU WITH YOUR PLAY-BY-PLAY.
Pop
OH, GREAT! YOU'RE GONNA LET LOOSE ON US, AREN'T YOU?
AT THE HEAD OF THE PACK, WE'VE GOT A HEATED BATTLE FOR FIRST PLACE.
Eep
1st
2nd
IT LOOKS LIKE THESE TWO MIGHT HAVE A GRUDGE.
NEKOZAKI'S HAVING A TOUGH TIME, AS USUAL.
Bonk
HEY! YOU'RE GONNA HURT MY FEELINGS!
AND DESPITE BEING IN VERY LAST PLACE, IZUMI'S NOT GETTING ANYTHING BUT BANANAS, SADLY.
Last Place
What misery!
WAAH...

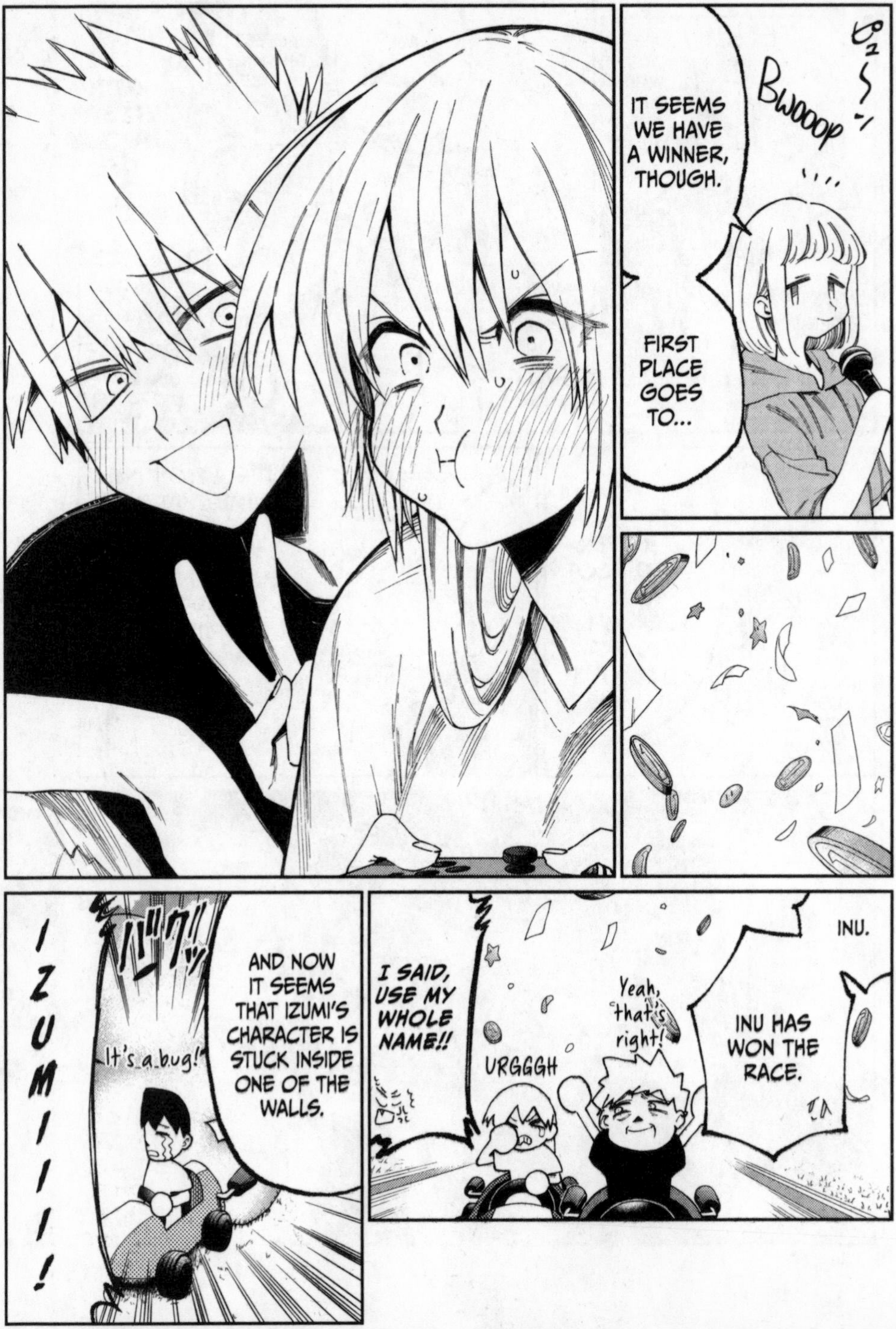
ぴュ～
BWOOOP
IT SEEMS WE HAVE A WINNER, THOUGH.
FIRST PLACE GOES TO...
INU.
INU HAS WON THE RACE.
Yeah, that's right!
URGGGH
I SAID, USE MY WHOLE NAME!!
AND NOW IT SEEMS THAT IZUMI'S CHARACTER IS STUCK INSIDE ONE OF THE WALLS.
バグッ
It's a bug!
IZUMIIII!

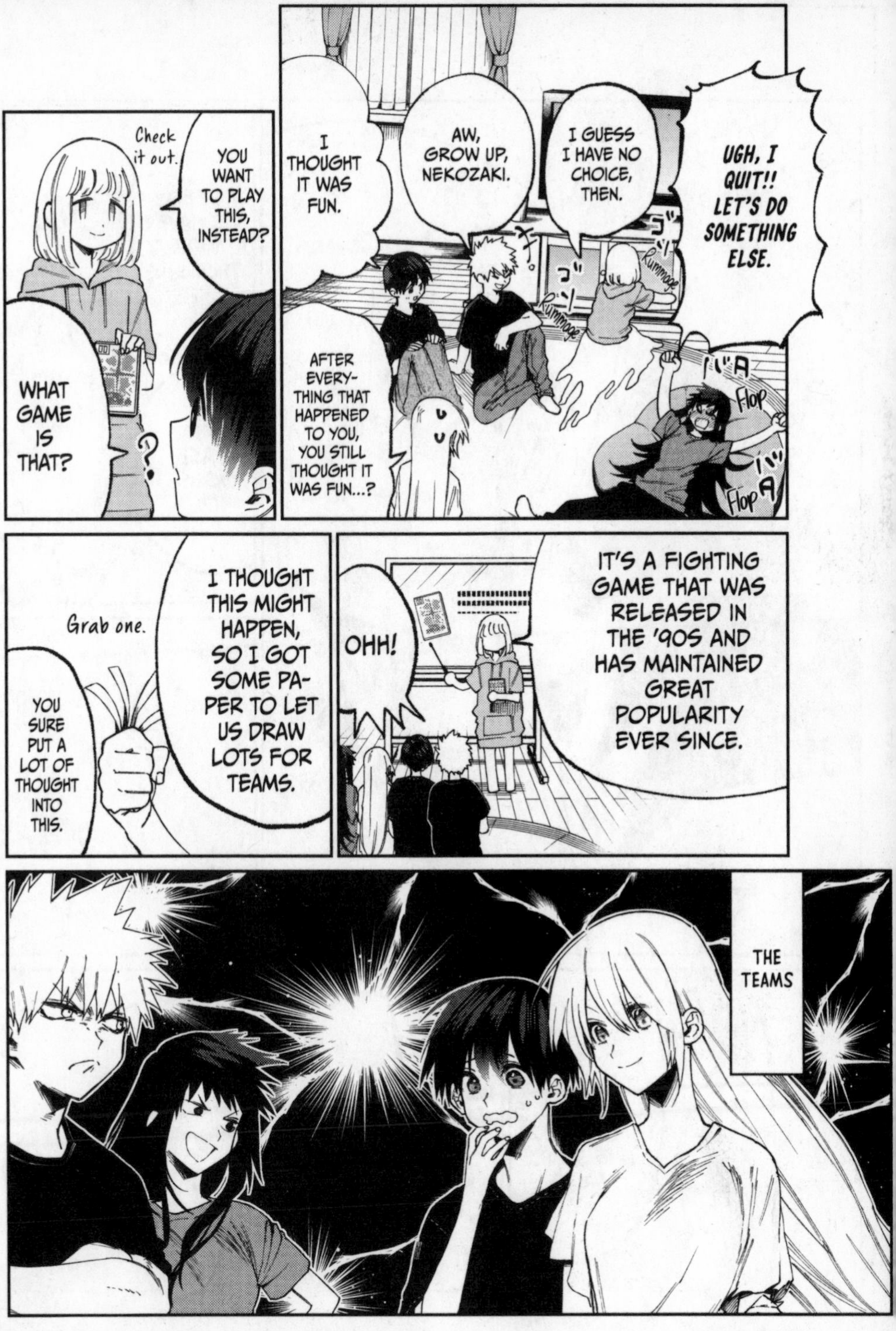
UGH, I QUIT!! LET'S DO SOMETHING ELSE.
Flop
Flop
I GUESS I HAVE NO CHOICE, THEN.
Rummage
Rummage
AW, GROW UP, NEKOZAKI.
I THOUGHT IT WAS FUN.
AFTER EVERY-THING THAT HAPPENED TO YOU, YOU STILL THOUGHT IT WAS FUN...?
YOU WANT TO PLAY THIS, INSTEAD?
Check it out.
WHAT GAME IS THAT?
IT'S A FIGHTING GAME THAT WAS RELEASED IN THE '90S AND HAS MAINTAINED GREAT POPULARITY EVER SINCE.
OHH!
I THOUGHT THIS MIGHT HAPPEN, SO I GOT SOME PA-PER TO LET US DRAW LOTS FOR TEAMS.
Grab one.
YOU SURE PUT A LOT OF THOUGHT INTO THIS.
THE TEAMS

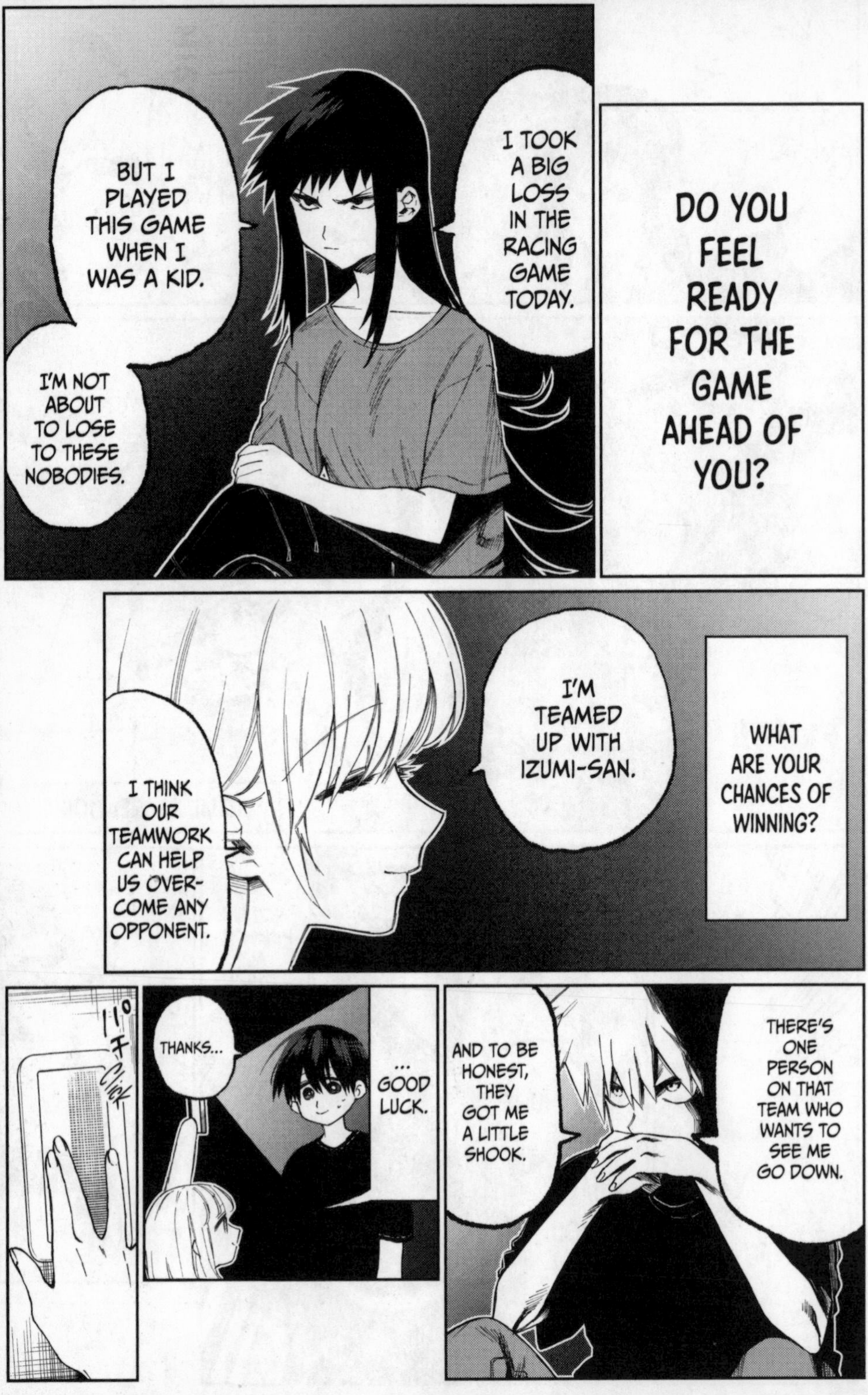

DO YOU FEEL READY FOR THE GAME AHEAD OF YOU?
I TOOK A BIG LOSS IN THE RACING GAME TODAY.
BUT I PLAYED THIS GAME WHEN I WAS A KID.
I'M NOT ABOUT TO LOSE TO THESE NOBODIES.
WHAT ARE YOUR CHANCES OF WINNING?
I'M TEAMED UP WITH IZUMI-SAN.
I THINK OUR TEAMWORK CAN HELP US OVERCOME ANY OPPONENT.
THERE'S ONE PERSON ON THAT TEAM WHO WANTS TO SEE ME GO DOWN.
AND TO BE HONEST, THEY GOT ME A LITTLE SHOOK.
... GOOD LUCK.
THANKS...
Click

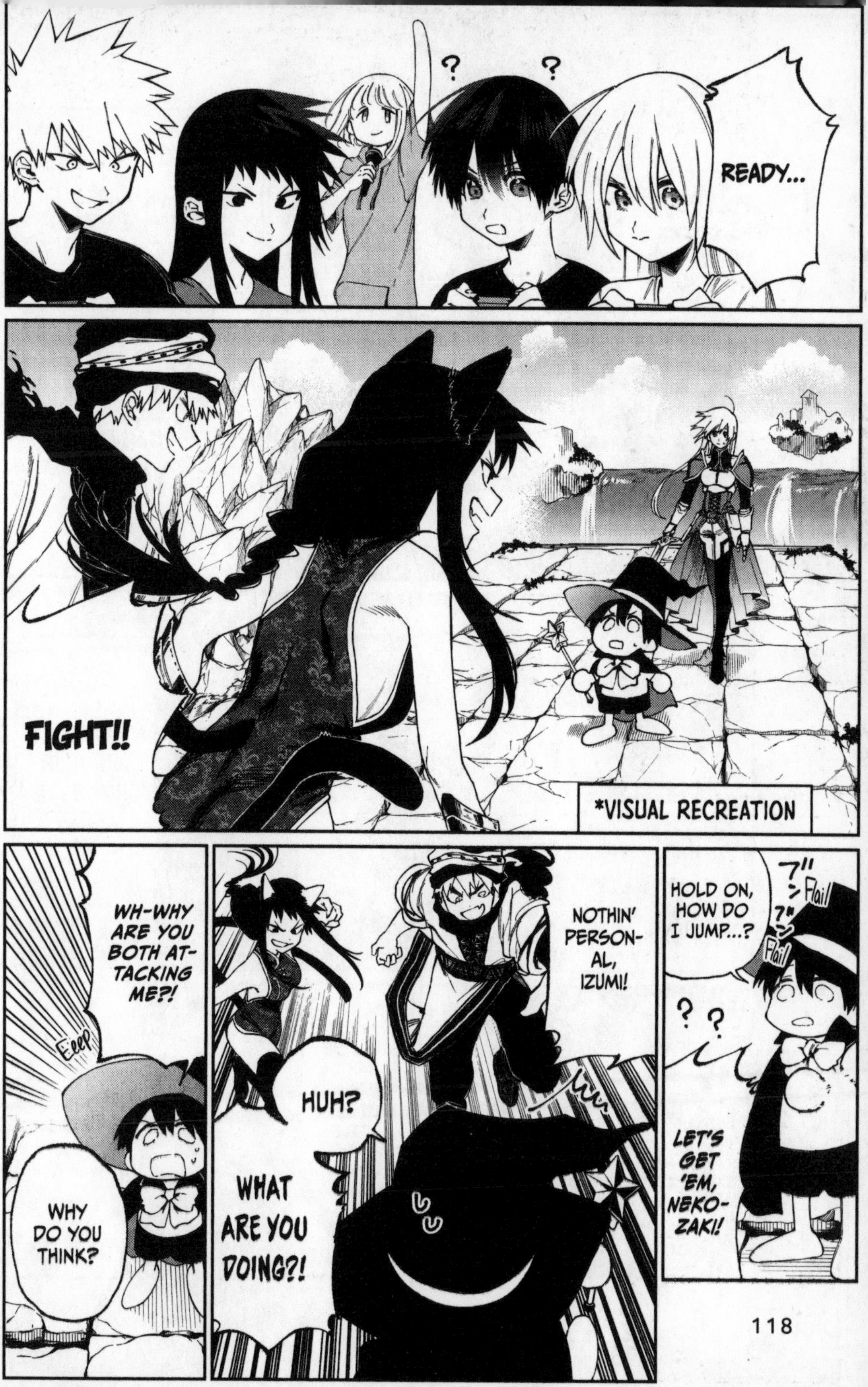

READY...
FIGHT!!
*VISUAL RECREATION
HOLD ON, HOW DO I JUMP...?
ブン Flail
ブン Flail
LET'S GET 'EM, NEKOZAKI!
NOTHIN' PERSON-AL, IZUMI!
HUH?
WHAT ARE YOU DOING?!
WH-WHY ARE YOU BOTH AT-TACKING ME?!
Eeep
WHY DO YOU THINK?

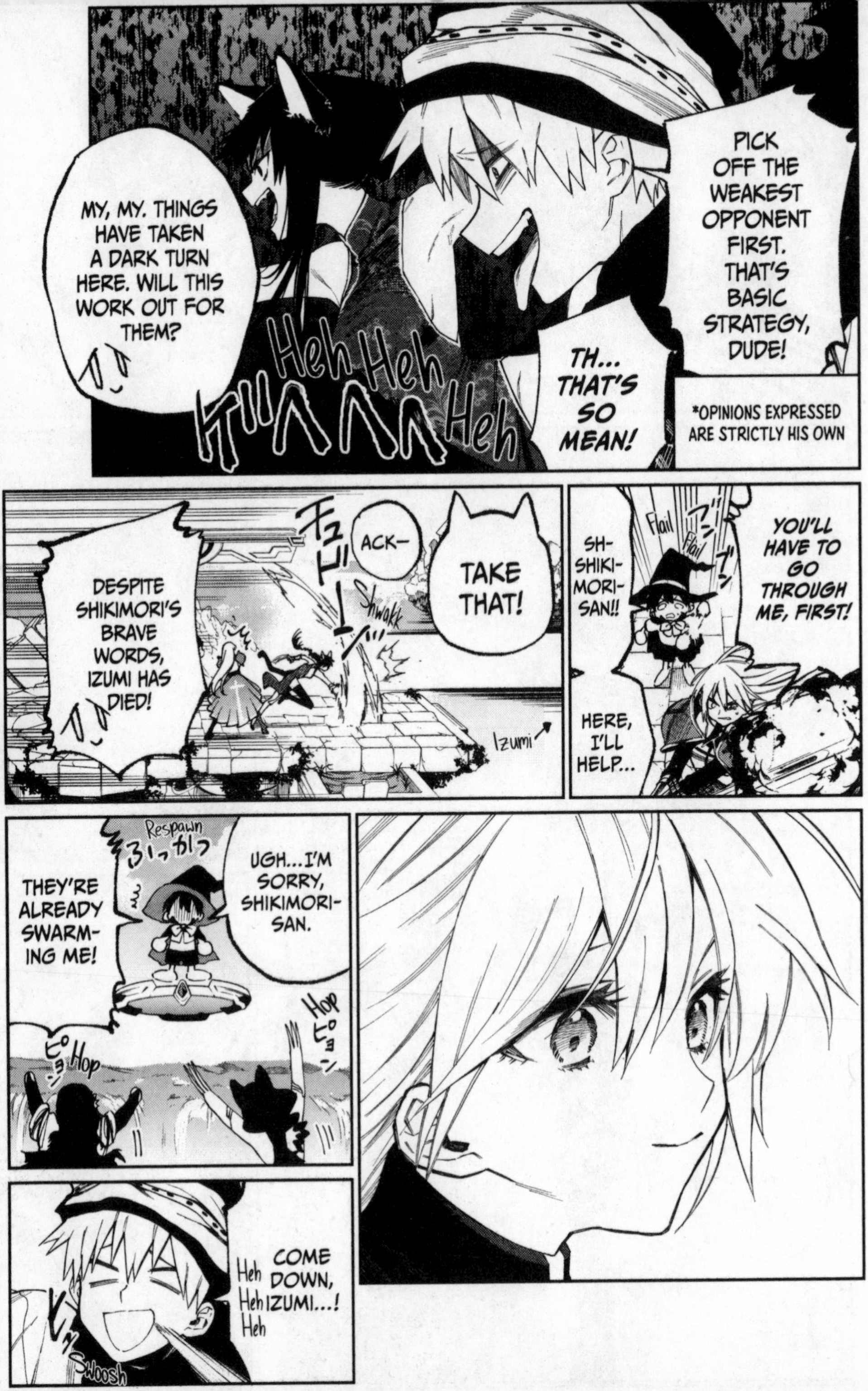
PICK OFF THE WEAKEST OPPONENT FIRST. THAT'S BASIC STRATEGY, DUDE!
*OPINIONS EXPRESSED ARE STRICTLY HIS OWN
TH... THAT'S SO MEAN!
Heh Heh Heh
MY, MY. THINGS HAVE TAKEN A DARK TURN HERE. WILL THIS WORK OUT FOR THEM?
YOU'LL HAVE TO GO THROUGH ME, FIRST!
Flail Flail
SH-SHIKIMORI-SAN!!
HERE, I'LL HELP...
TAKE THAT!
ACK—
Shwakk
Izumi
DESPITE SHIKIMORI'S BRAVE WORDS, IZUMI HAS DIED!
UGH...I'M SORRY, SHIKIMORI-SAN.
Respawn
THEY'RE ALREADY SWARMING ME!
Hop
Hop
COME DOWN, IZUMI...!
Heh Heh Heh
Swoosh

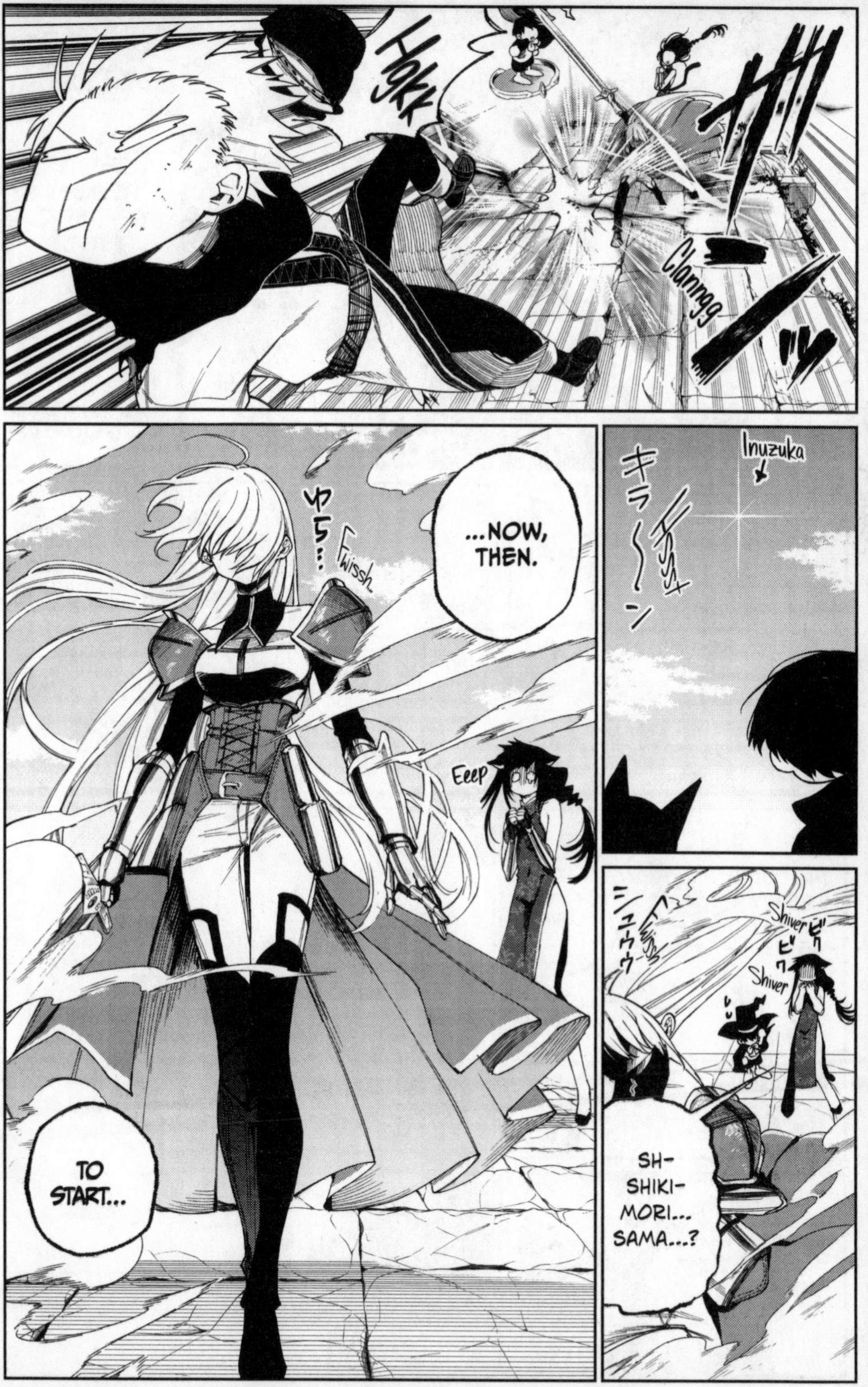
HONK
Clanngg
Inuzuka
キラ～ン
Fssst
シュウウ
Fwissh
Shiver
ビク
ビク
Shiver
SH-SHIKI-MORI... SAMA...?
...NOW, THEN.
ゆら…
Fwissh
Eeep
TO START...

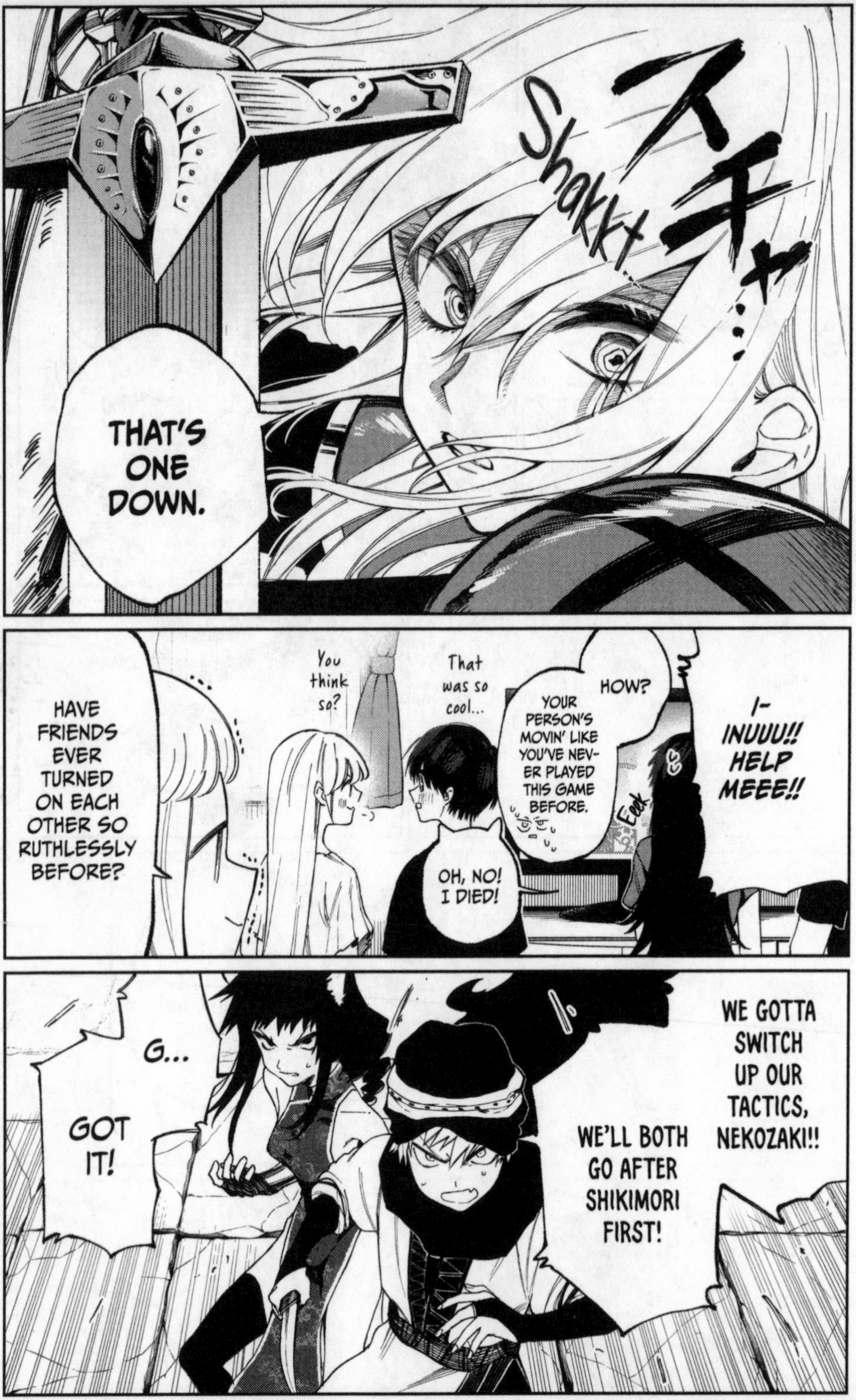
Shakkt
THAT'S ONE DOWN.
I- INUUU!! HELP MEEE!!
Eeek
HOW?
YOUR PERSON'S MOVIN' LIKE YOU'VE NEVER PLAYED THIS GAME BEFORE.
That was so cool...
You think so?
OH, NO! I DIED!
HAVE FRIENDS EVER TURNED ON EACH OTHER SO RUTHLESSLY BEFORE?
WE GOTTA SWITCH UP OUR TACTICS, NEKOZAKI!!
WE'LL BOTH GO AFTER SHIKIMORI FIRST!
G...
GOT IT!

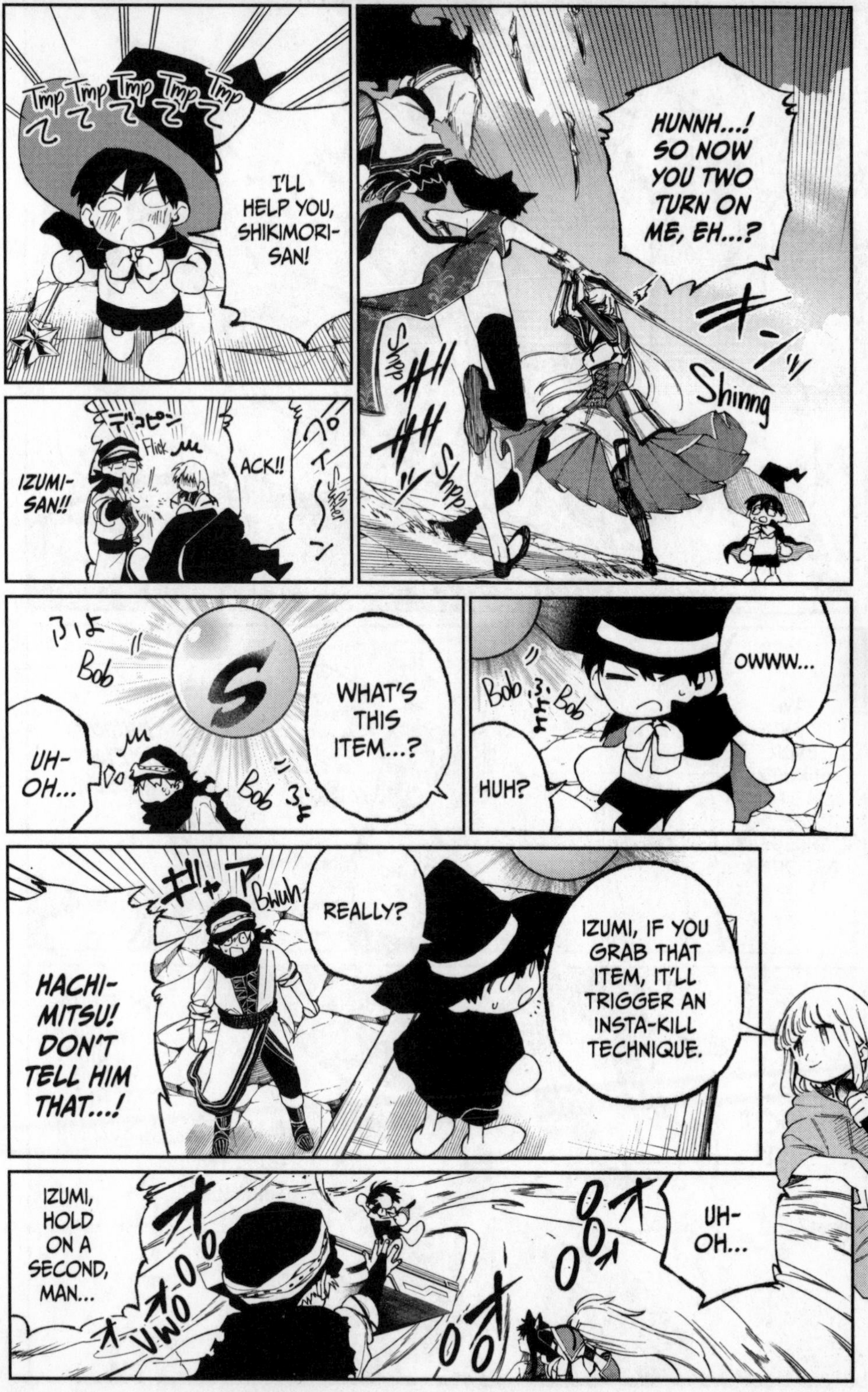
HUNNH...! SO NOW YOU TWO TURN ON ME, EH...?
Shinng
Shpp
Shpp
Tmp Tmp Tmp Tmp Tmp
I'LL HELP YOU, SHIKIMORI-SAN!
ACK!!
Flick
IZUMI-SAN!!
Suffer
OWWW...
Bob Bob
HUH?
WHAT'S THIS ITEM...?
Bob
Bob
UH-OH...
IZUMI, IF YOU GRAB THAT ITEM, IT'LL TRIGGER AN INSTA-KILL TECHNIQUE.
REALLY?
Bwuh
HACHIMITSU! DON'T TELL HIM THAT...!
UH-OH...
IZUMI, HOLD ON A SECOND, MAN...
VWOO

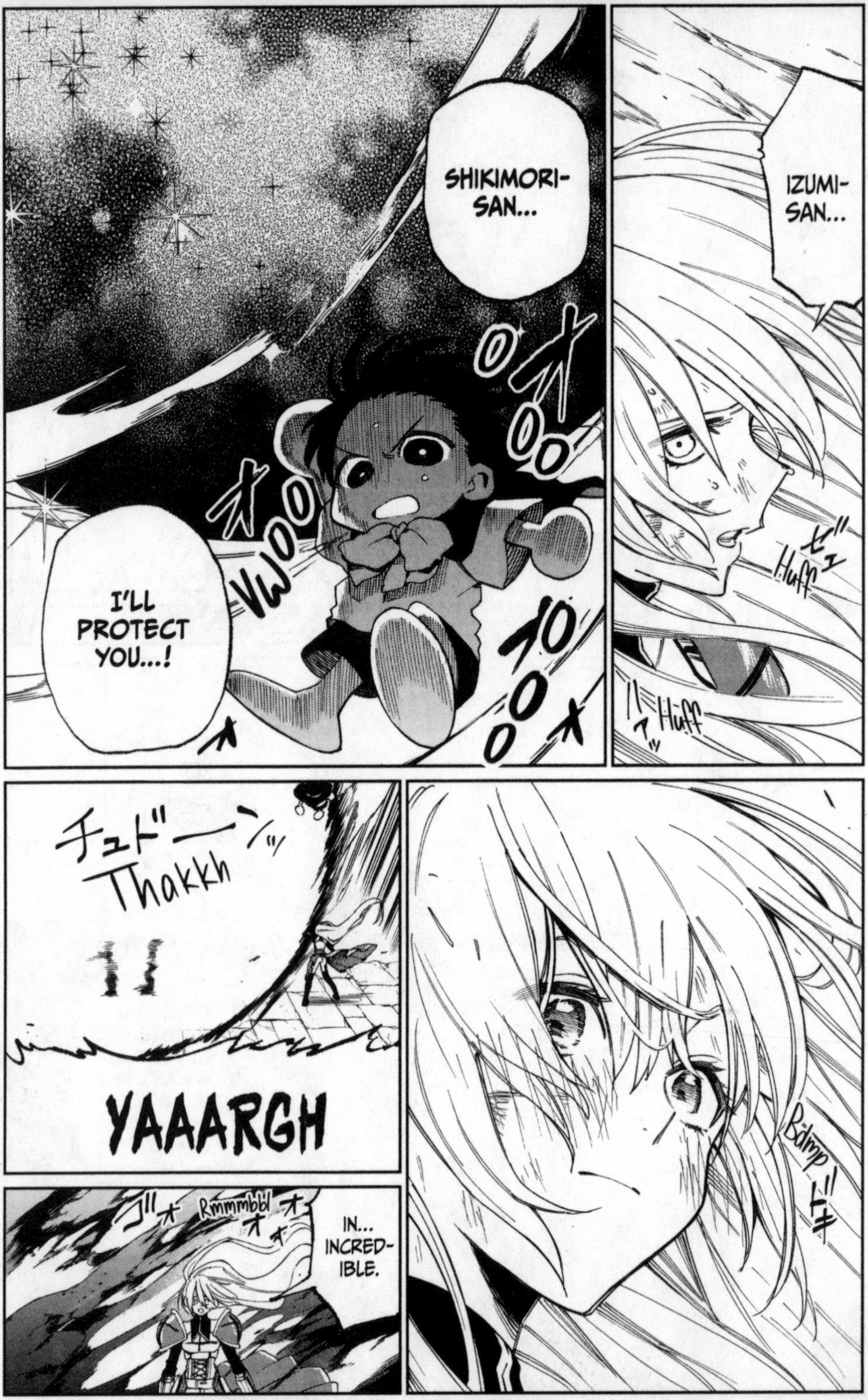

IZUMI-SAN...
ゼェ Huff
ハァッ Huff
SHIKIMORI-SAN...
VWOOOO
I'LL PROTECT YOU...!
Bdmp ドキ
チュドーンッ Thakkh
YAAARGH
Rmmmbbl
IN... INCREDIBLE.

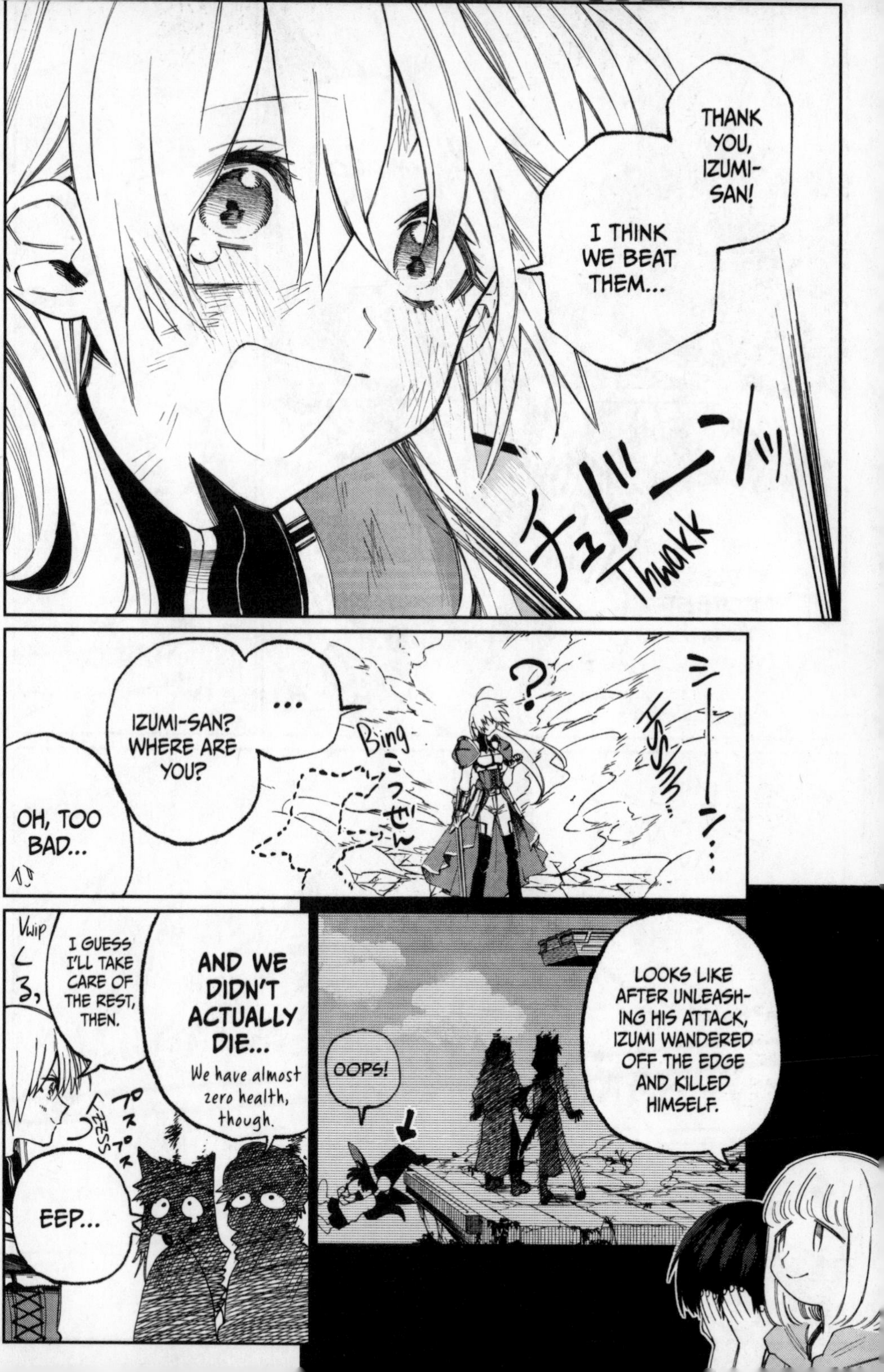
THANK YOU, IZUMI-SAN!
I THINK WE BEAT THEM...
チュドーンッ
Thwakk
?
シーン...
Hsssh...
...
Bing
こつぜん
IZUMI-SAN? WHERE ARE YOU?
OH, TOO BAD...
LOOKS LIKE AFTER UNLEASHING HIS ATTACK, IZUMI WANDERED OFF THE EDGE AND KILLED HIMSELF.
OOPS!
AND WE DIDN'T ACTUALLY DIE...
We have almost zero health, though.
I GUESS I'LL TAKE CARE OF THE REST, THEN.
Vwip
くる,
EEP...

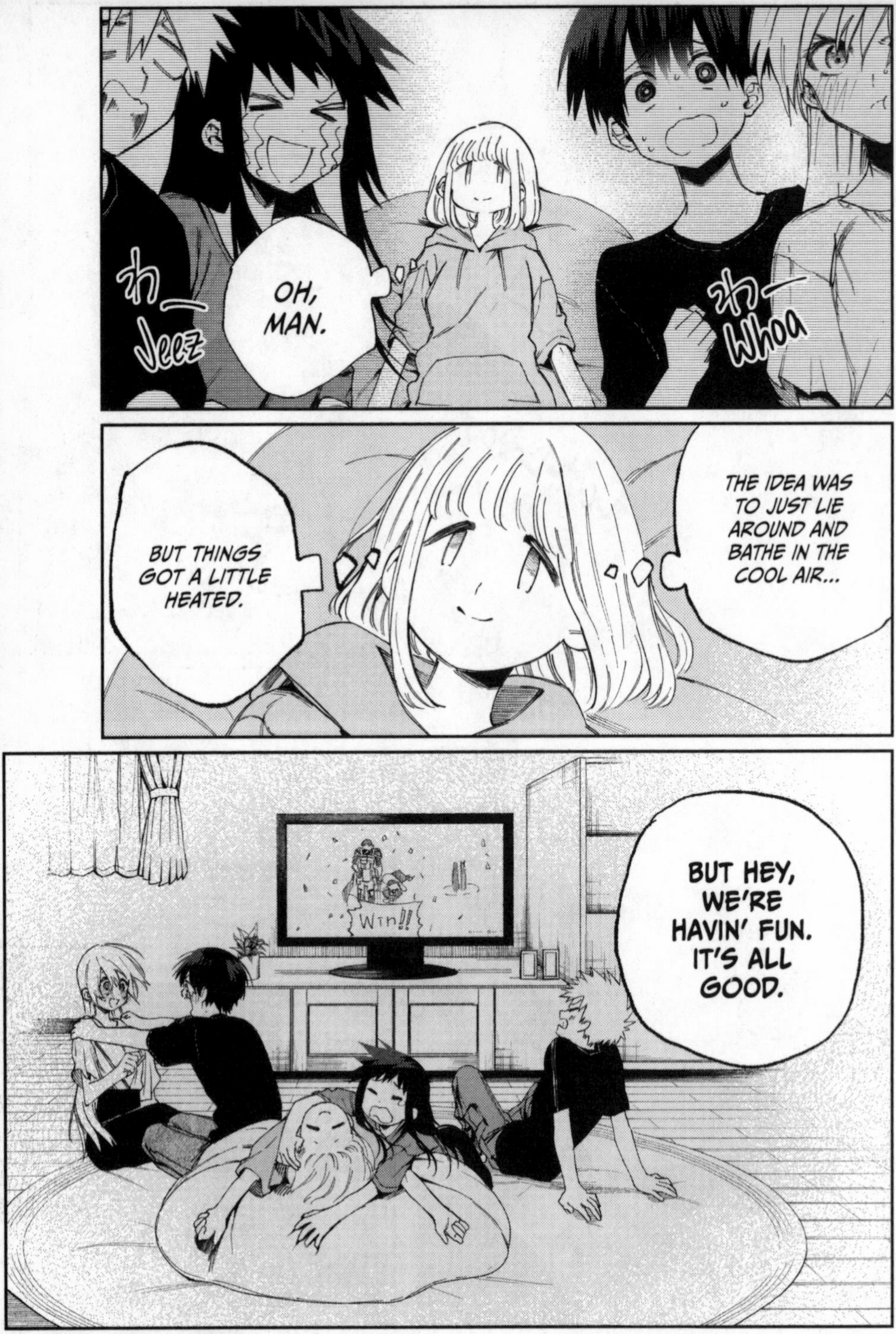
わー Whoa
OH, MAN.
わー Jeez
THE IDEA WAS TO JUST LIE AROUND AND BATHE IN THE COOL AIR...
BUT THINGS GOT A LITTLE HEATED.
BUT HEY, WE'RE HAVIN' FUN. IT'S ALL GOOD.
Win!!

Chapter 36 END

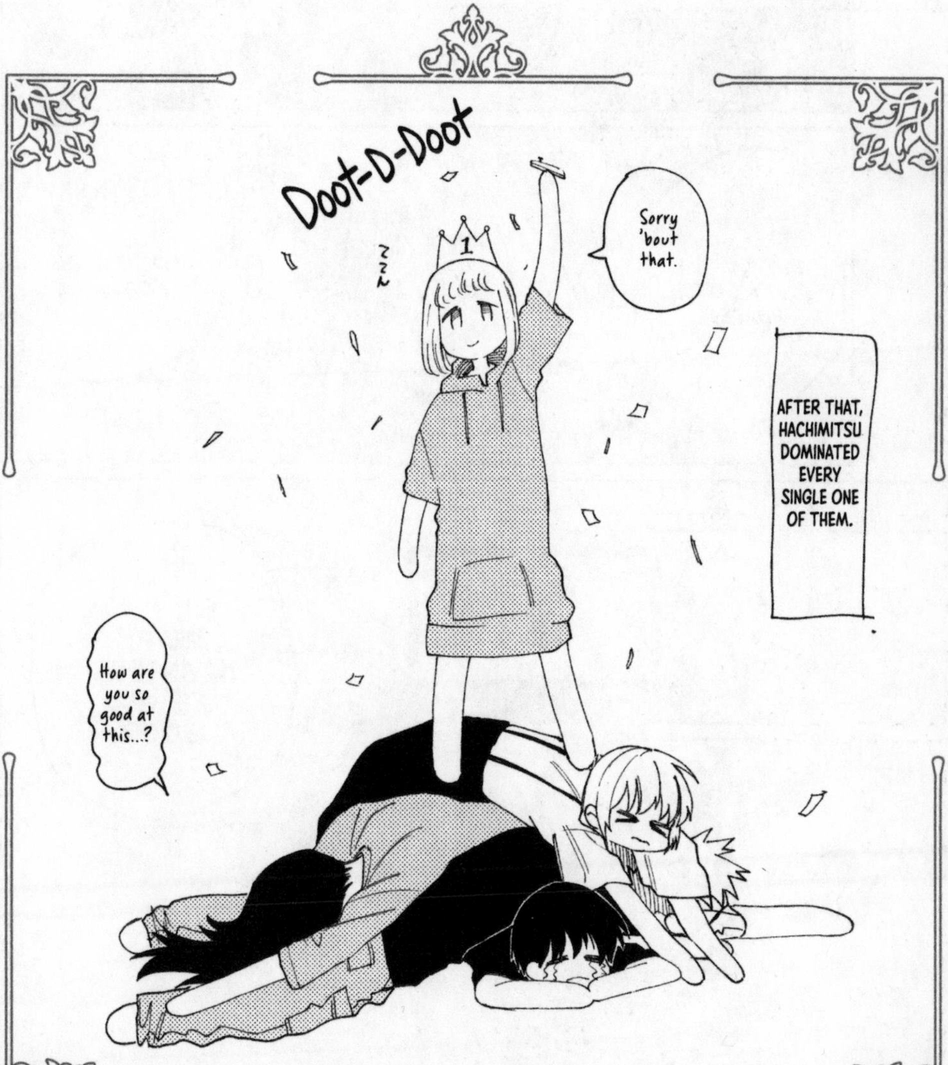

Sorry 'bout that.
Doot-D-Doot
AFTER THAT, HACHIMITSU DOMINATED EVERY SINGLE ONE OF THEM.
How are you so good at this...?

YUI HACHIMITSU

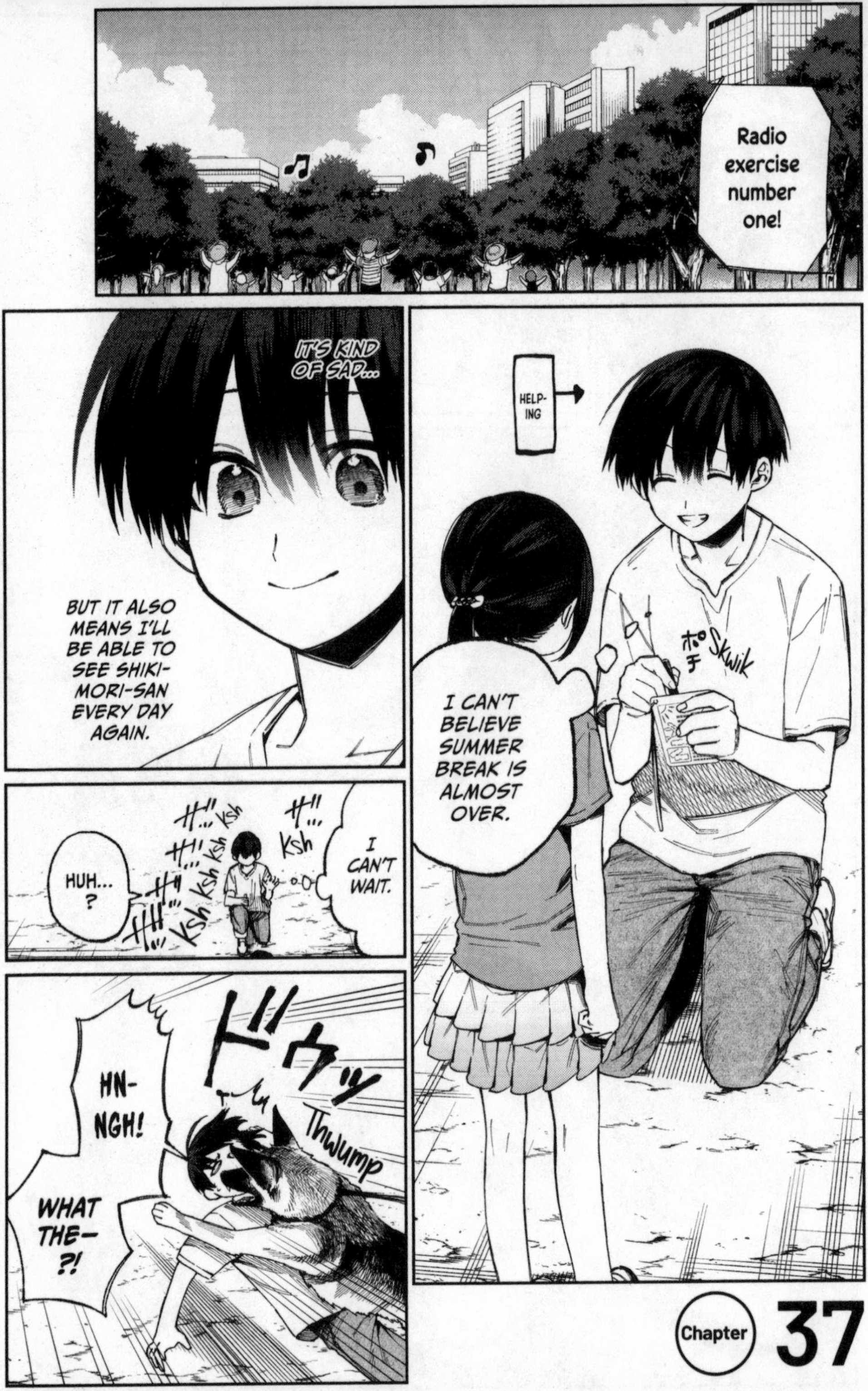
Radio exercise number one!
Skwik
HELPING
I CAN'T BELIEVE SUMMER BREAK IS ALMOST OVER.
IT'S KIND OF SAD...
BUT IT ALSO MEANS I'LL BE ABLE TO SEE SHIKIMORI-SAN EVERY DAY AGAIN.
I CAN'T WAIT.
Ksh Ksh Ksh Ksh Ksh
HUH...?
Thwump
HN-NGH!
WHAT THE—?!

Chapter 37

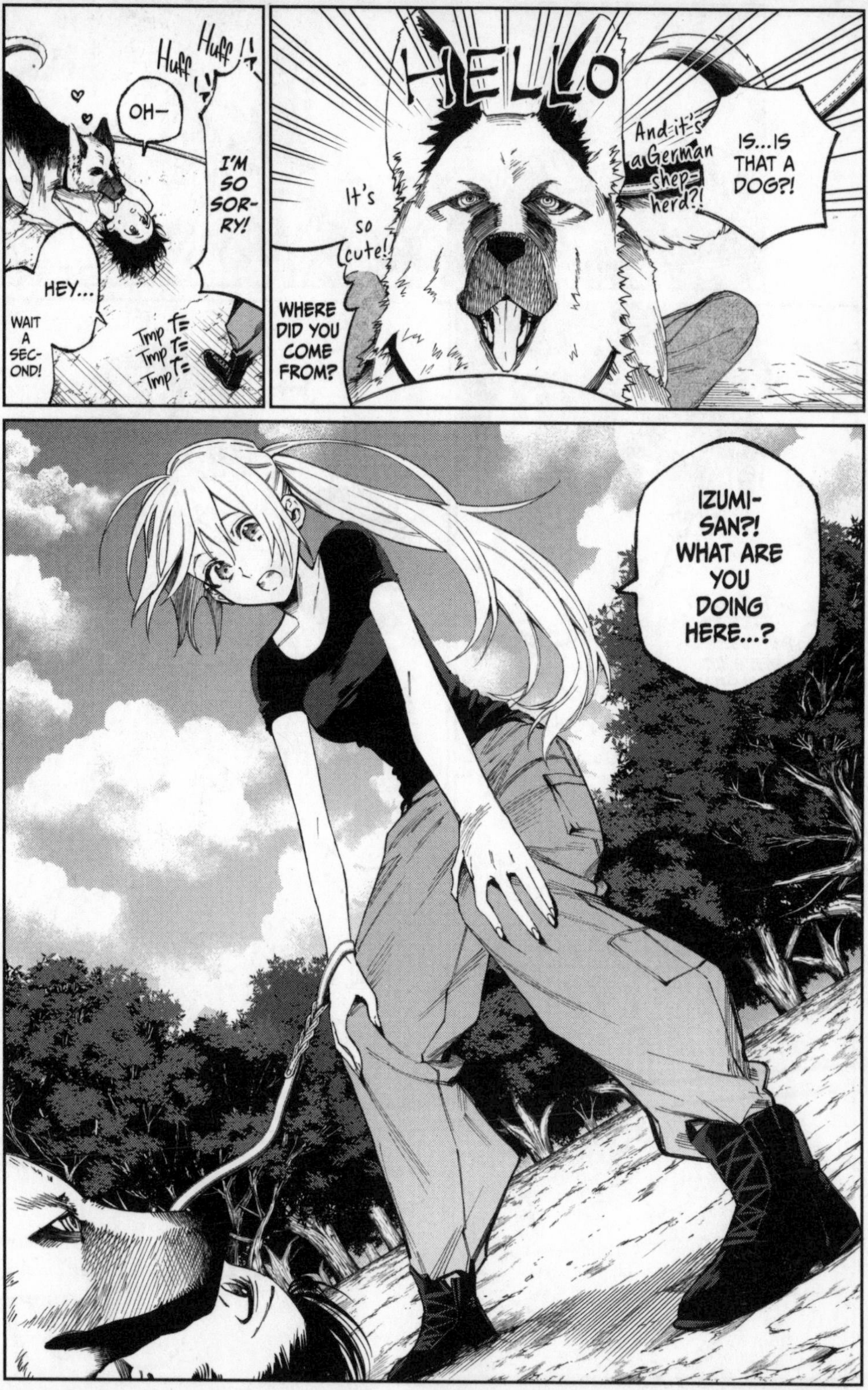
HELLO
IS...IS THAT A DOG?!
And it's a German shep-herd?!
It's so cute!
WHERE DID YOU COME FROM?
Huff Huff
OH—
I'M SO SOR-RY!
HEY...
WAIT A SEC-OND!
Tmp Tmp Tmp
IZUMI-SAN?! WHAT ARE YOU DOING HERE...?

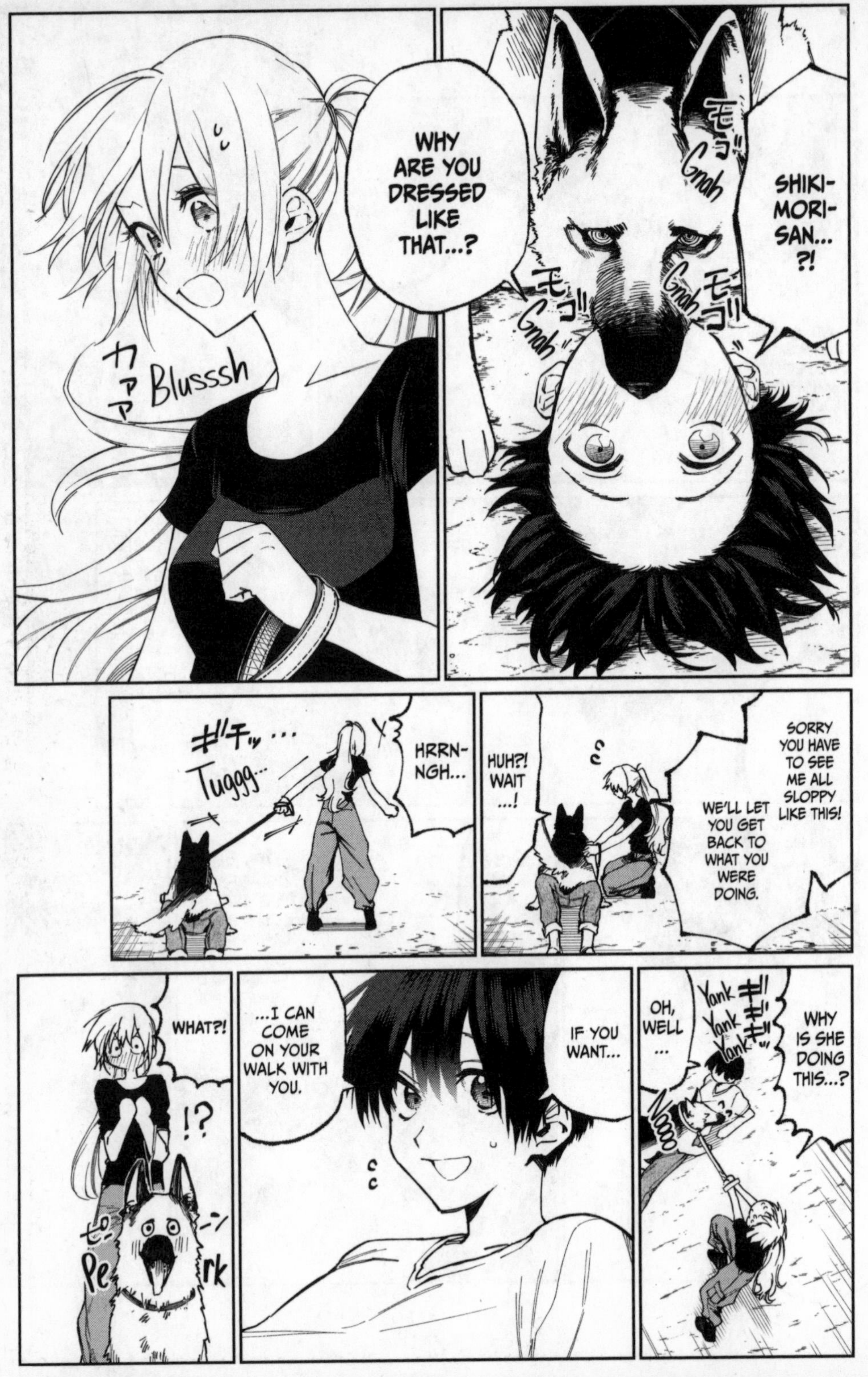

SHIKI-MORI-SAN...?!
モゴ Gnah
モゴ Gnah
モゴ Gnah
WHY ARE YOU DRESSED LIKE THAT...?
カァァ Blusssh
SORRY YOU HAVE TO SEE ME ALL SLOPPY LIKE THIS!
WE'LL LET YOU GET BACK TO WHAT YOU WERE DOING.
HUH?! WAIT ...!
HRRN-NGH...
ギチッ... Tuggg...
WHY IS SHE DOING THIS...?
OH, WELL ...
Yank Yank Yank
Nooo
IF YOU WANT...
...I CAN COME ON YOUR WALK WITH YOU.
WHAT?!
!?
Perk

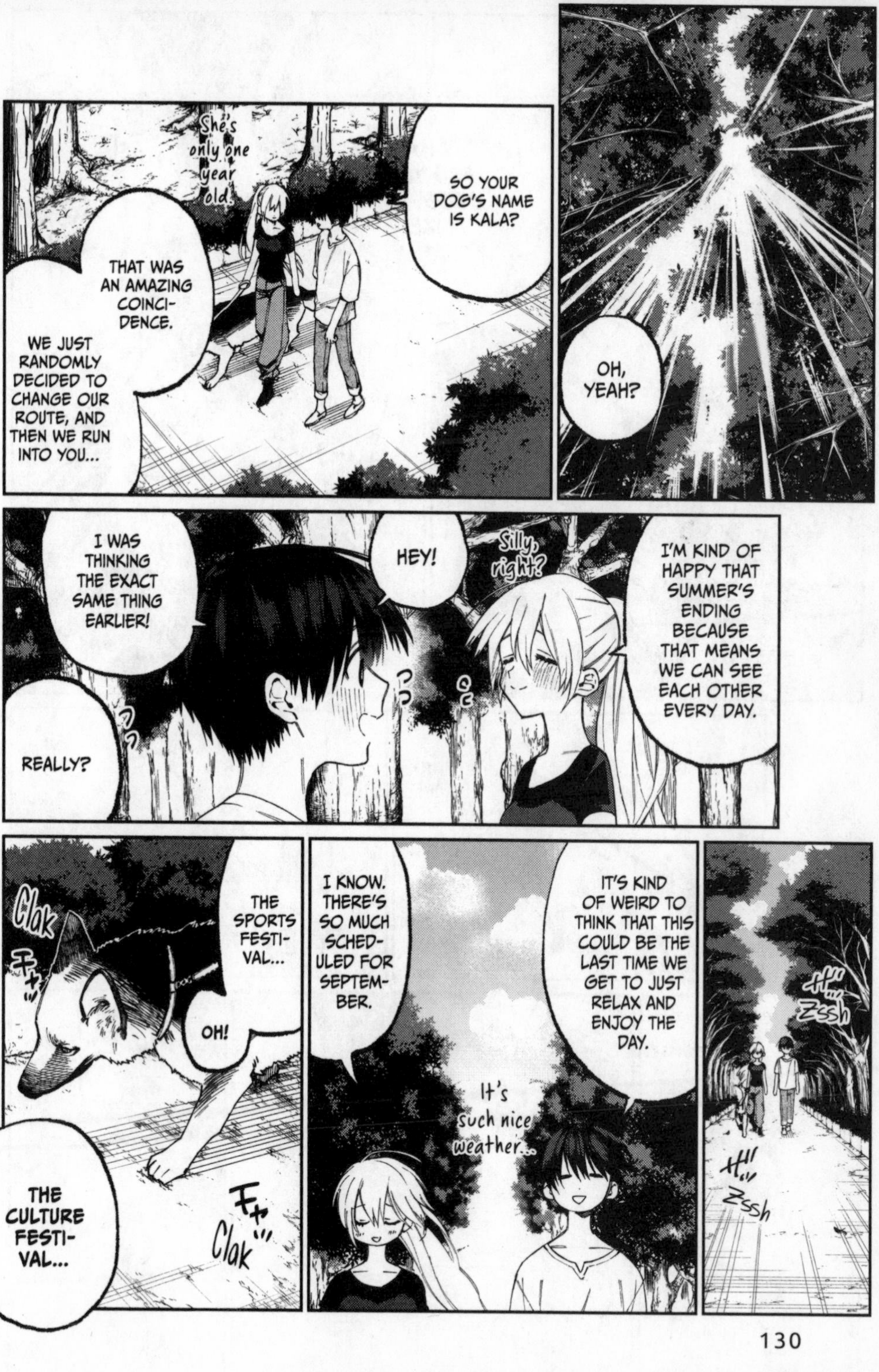
OH, YEAH?
SO YOUR DOG'S NAME IS KALA?
She's only one year old.
THAT WAS AN AMAZING COINCI- DENCE.
WE JUST RANDOMLY DECIDED TO CHANGE OUR ROUTE, AND THEN WE RUN INTO YOU...
I'M KIND OF HAPPY THAT SUMMER'S ENDING BECAUSE THAT MEANS WE CAN SEE EACH OTHER EVERY DAY.
Silly, right?
HEY!
I WAS THINKING THE EXACT SAME THING EARLIER!
REALLY?
Zssh
Zssh
IT'S KIND OF WEIRD TO THINK THAT THIS COULD BE THE LAST TIME WE GET TO JUST RELAX AND ENJOY THE DAY.
It's such nice weather...
I KNOW. THERE'S SO MUCH SCHED- ULED FOR SEPTEM- BER.
THE SPORTS FESTI- VAL...
OH!
Clak
THE CULTURE FESTI- VAL...
Clak

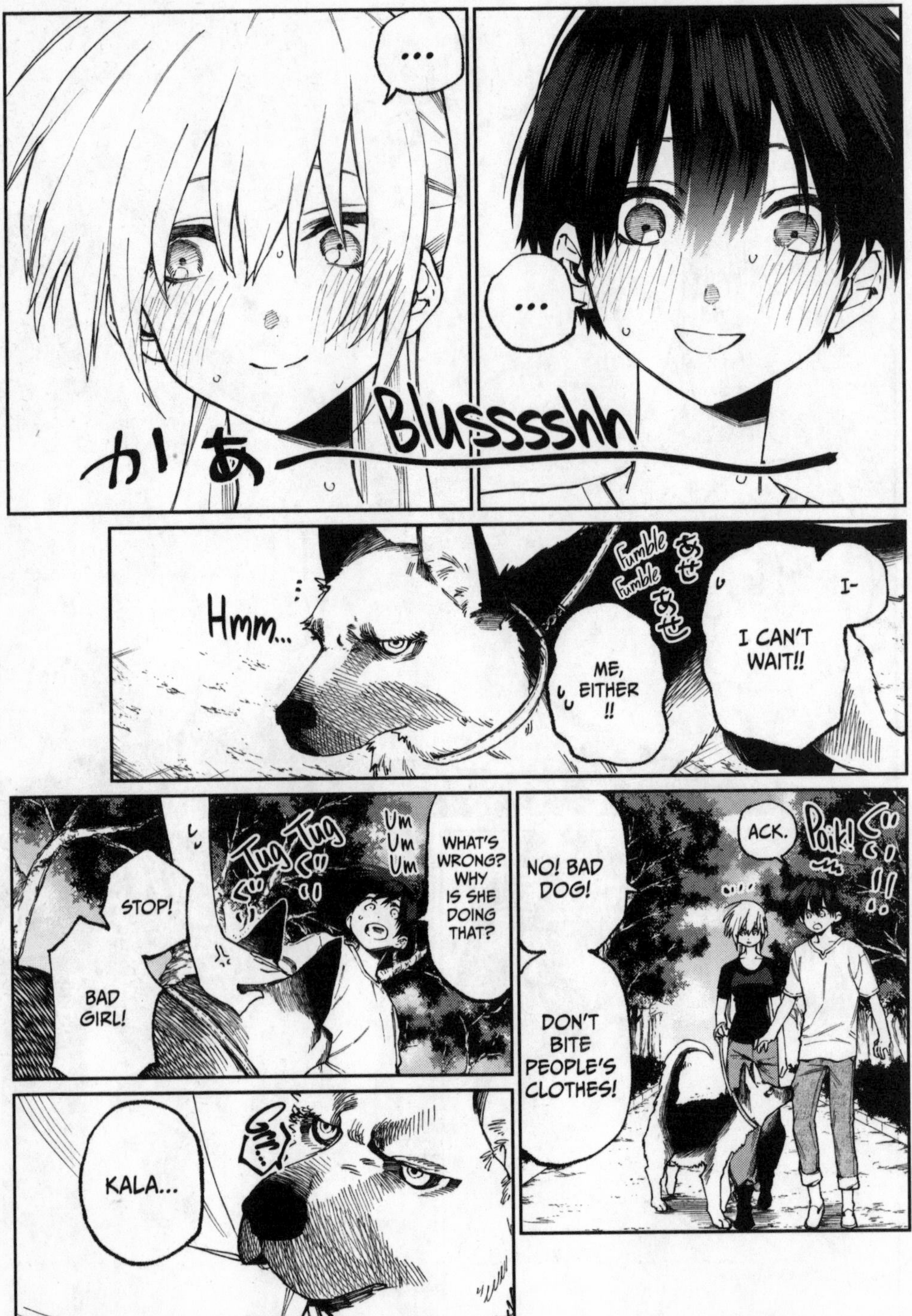
...
...
かあ
Blussssshh
I-
I CAN'T WAIT!!
Fumble Fumble
あせあせ
ME, EITHER!!
Hmm...
Poik!
ACK.
...
NO! BAD DOG!
DON'T BITE PEOPLE'S CLOTHES!
WHAT'S WRONG? WHY IS SHE DOING THAT?
Um Um Um
Tug Tug
STOP!
BAD GIRL!
Grr...
KALA...

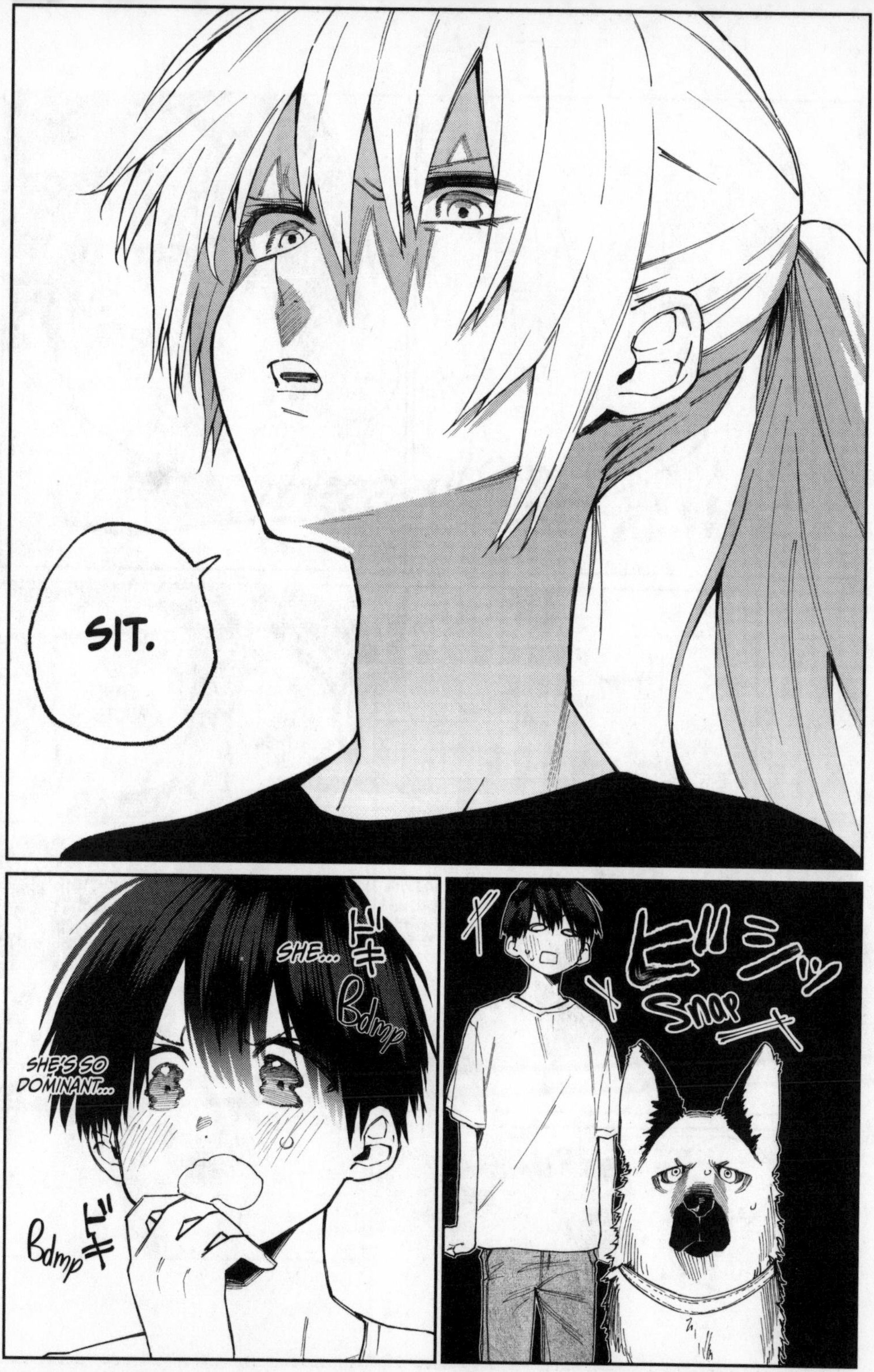
SIT.
Snap
ドキ
Bdmp
SHE...
SHE'S SO DOMINANT...
ドキ
Bdmp

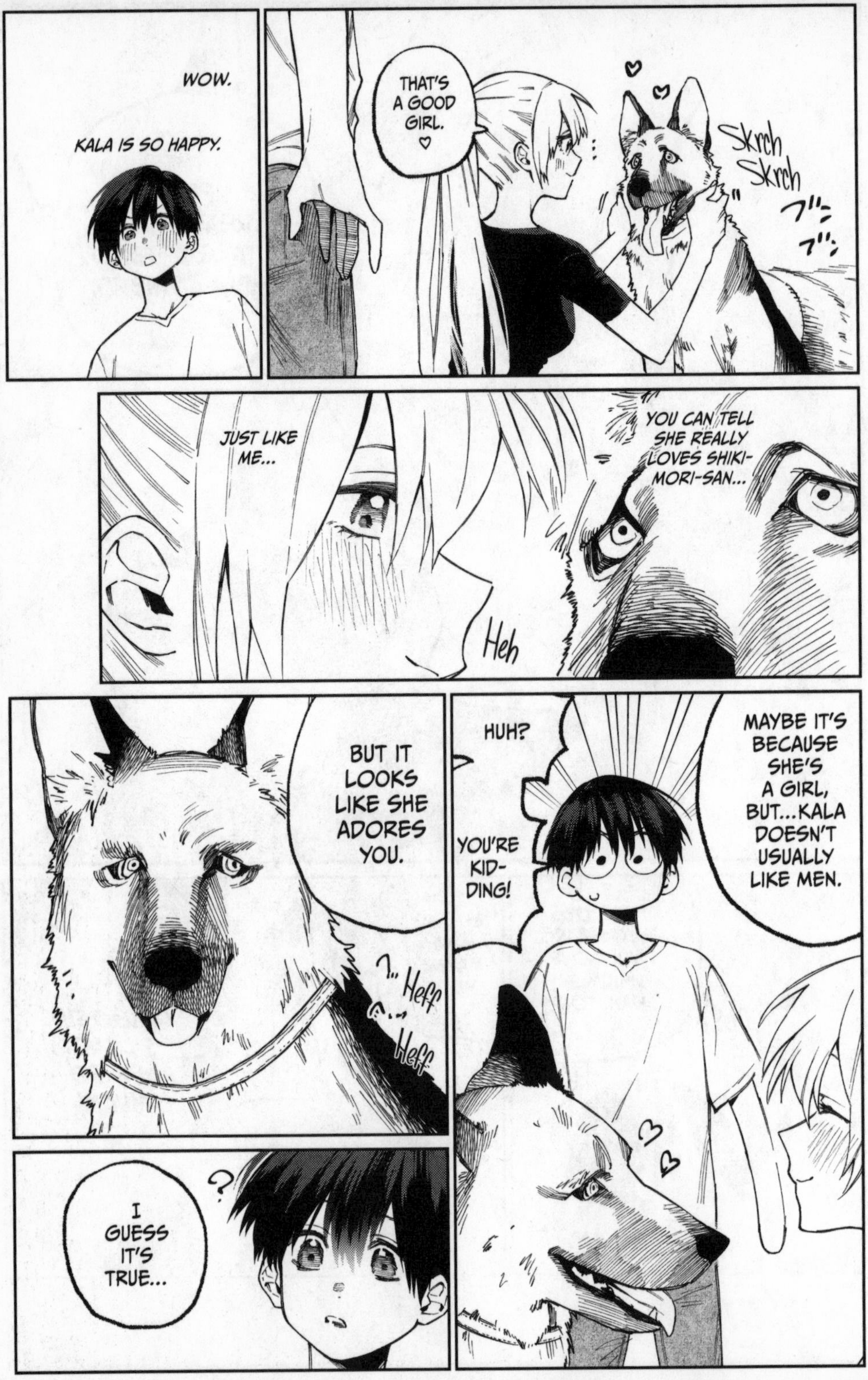

THAT'S A GOOD GIRL. ♡
Skrch Skrch
ブン
ブン
WOW.
KALA IS SO HAPPY.
YOU CAN TELL SHE REALLY LOVES SHIKI-MORI-SAN...
Heh
JUST LIKE ME...
MAYBE IT'S BECAUSE SHE'S A GIRL, BUT...KALA DOESN'T USUALLY LIKE MEN.
HUH?
YOU'RE KID-DING!
BUT IT LOOKS LIKE SHE ADORES YOU.
Heff
Heff
I GUESS IT'S TRUE...

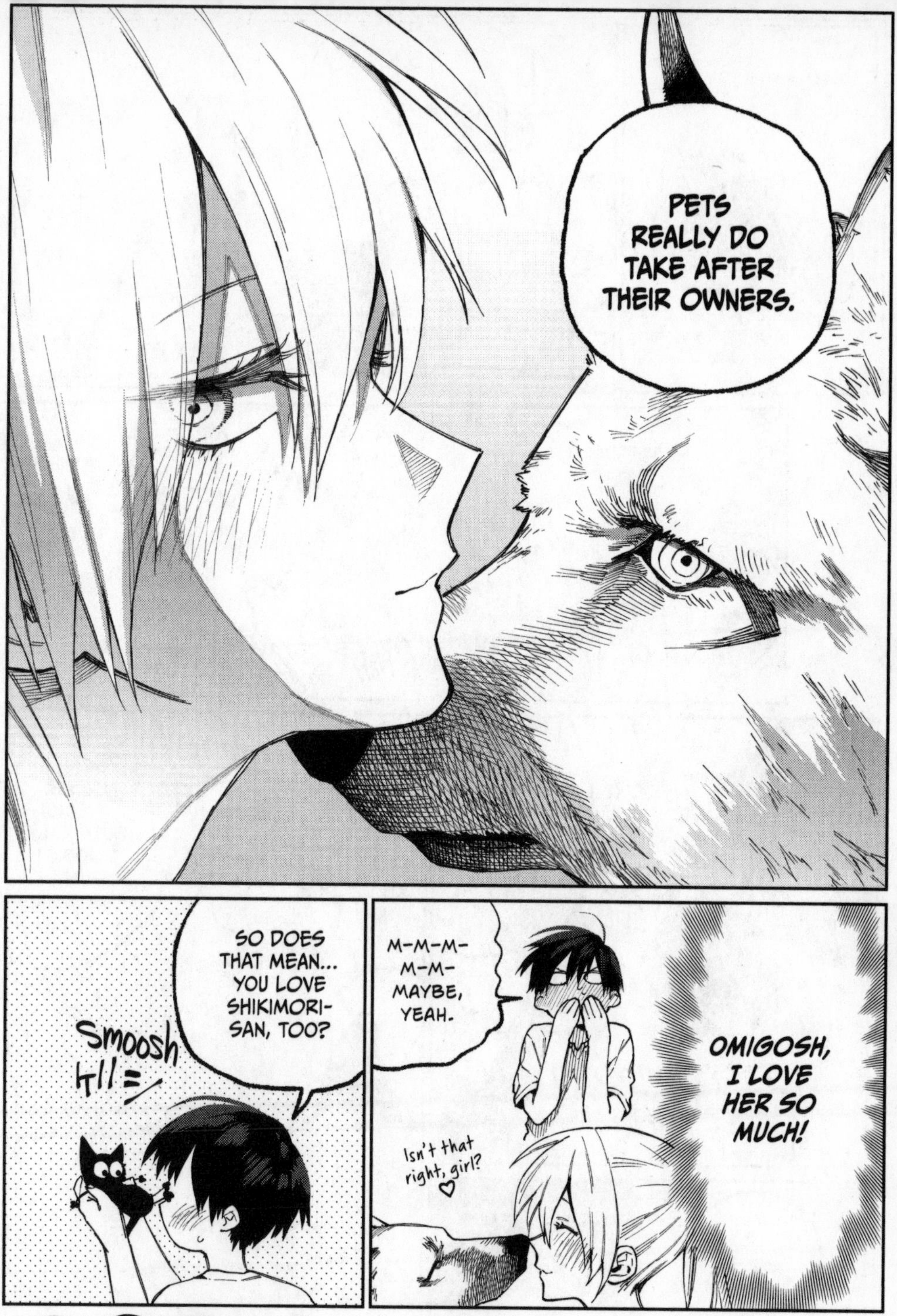
PETS REALLY DO TAKE AFTER THEIR OWNERS.
OMIGOSH, I LOVE HER SO MUCH!
M-M-M-M-M-MAYBE, YEAH.
Isn't that right, girl? ♡
SO DOES THAT MEAN... YOU LOVE SHIKIMORI-SAN, TOO?
Smoosh

Chapter 37 END

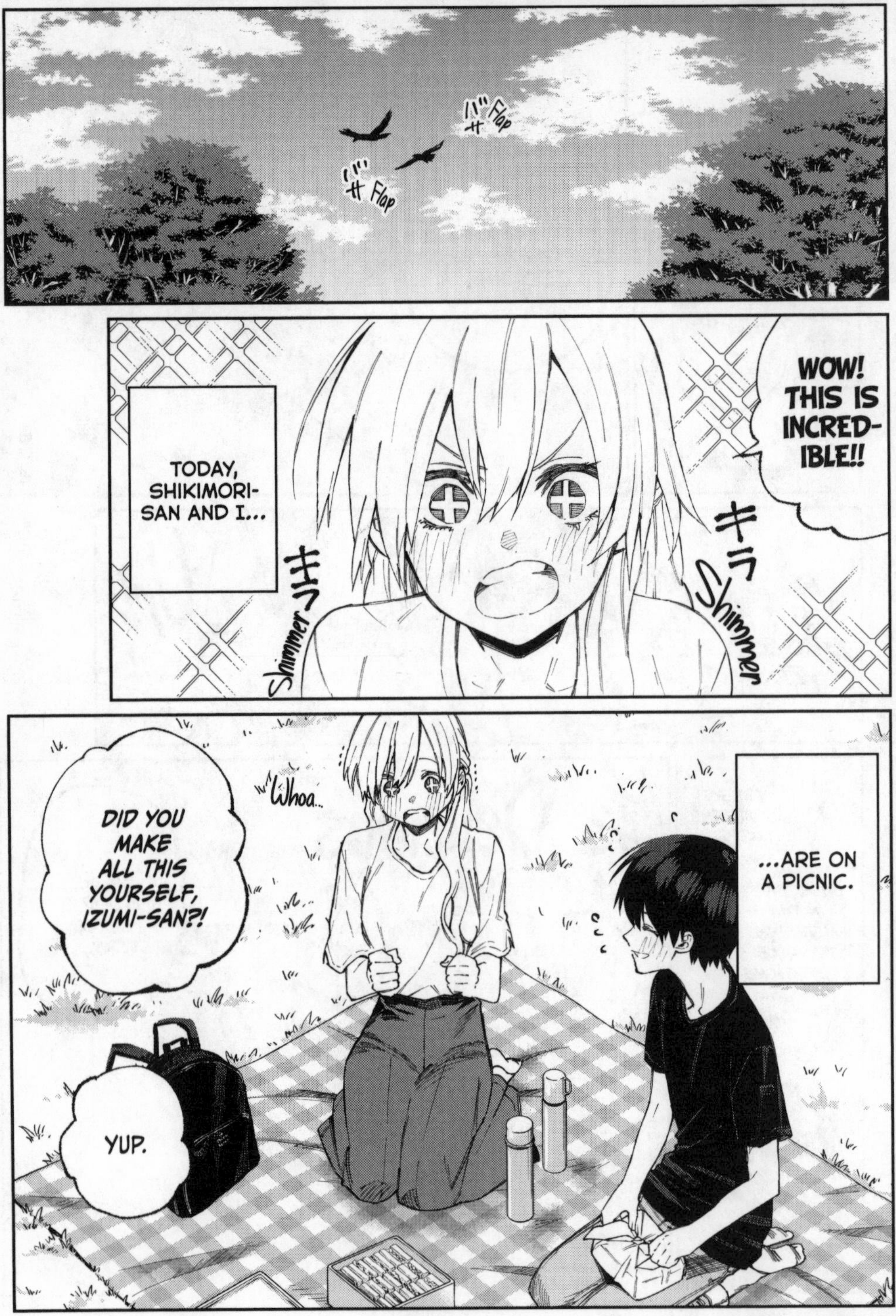
バサ Flap
バサ Flap
WOW! THIS IS INCREDIBLE!!
キラ Shimmer
キラ Shimmer
TODAY, SHIKIMORI-SAN AND I...
...ARE ON A PICNIC.
Whoa..
DID YOU MAKE ALL THIS YOURSELF, IZUMI-SAN?!
YUP.

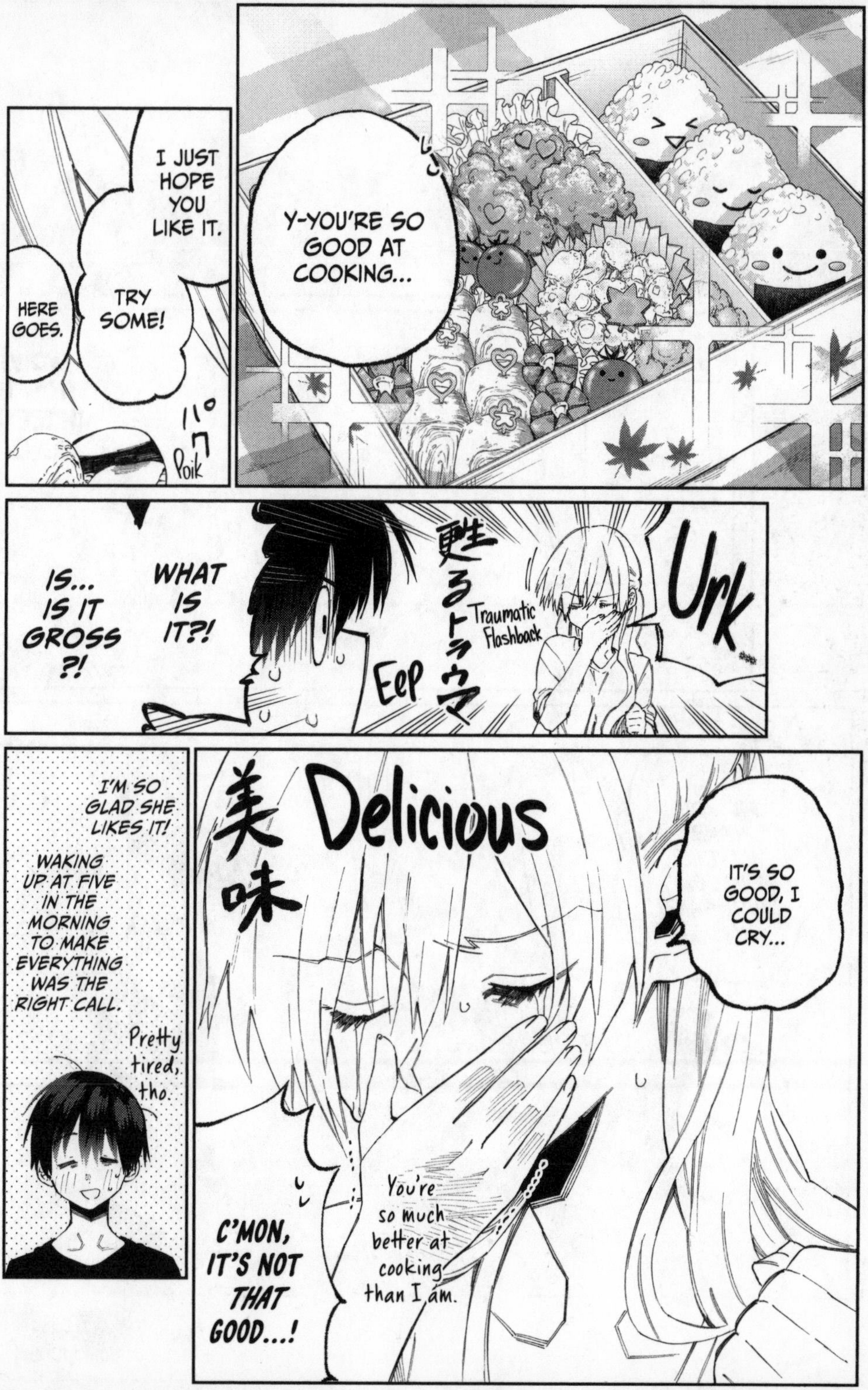
Y-YOU'RE SO GOOD AT COOKING...
I JUST HOPE YOU LIKE IT.
TRY SOME!
HERE GOES.
パク
Poik
Urk
甦るトラウマ
Traumatic Flashback
Eep
WHAT IS IT?!
IS... IS IT GROSS ?!
美味
Delicious
IT'S SO GOOD, I COULD CRY...
You're so much better at cooking than I am.
C'MON, IT'S NOT THAT GOOD...!
I'M SO GLAD SHE LIKES IT!
WAKING UP AT FIVE IN THE MORNING TO MAKE EVERYTHING WAS THE RIGHT CALL.
Pretty tired, tho.

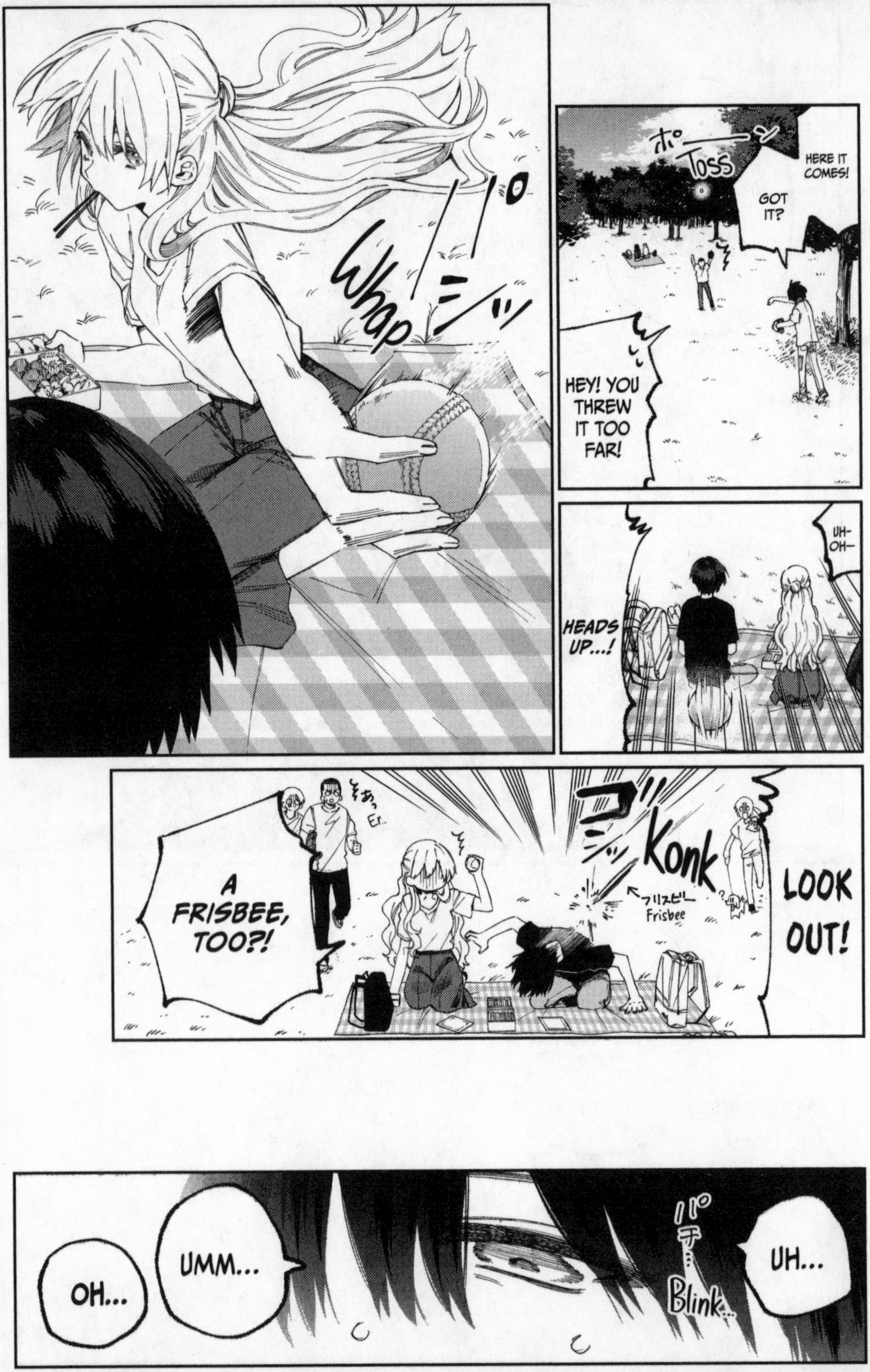
ポーーン
Toss
HERE IT COMES!
GOT IT?
HEY! YOU THREW IT TOO FAR!
UH-OH-
HEADS UP...!
Whap
LOOK OUT!
Konk
フリスビー
Frisbee
Er..
A FRISBEE, TOO?!
UH...
Blink...
UMM...
OH...

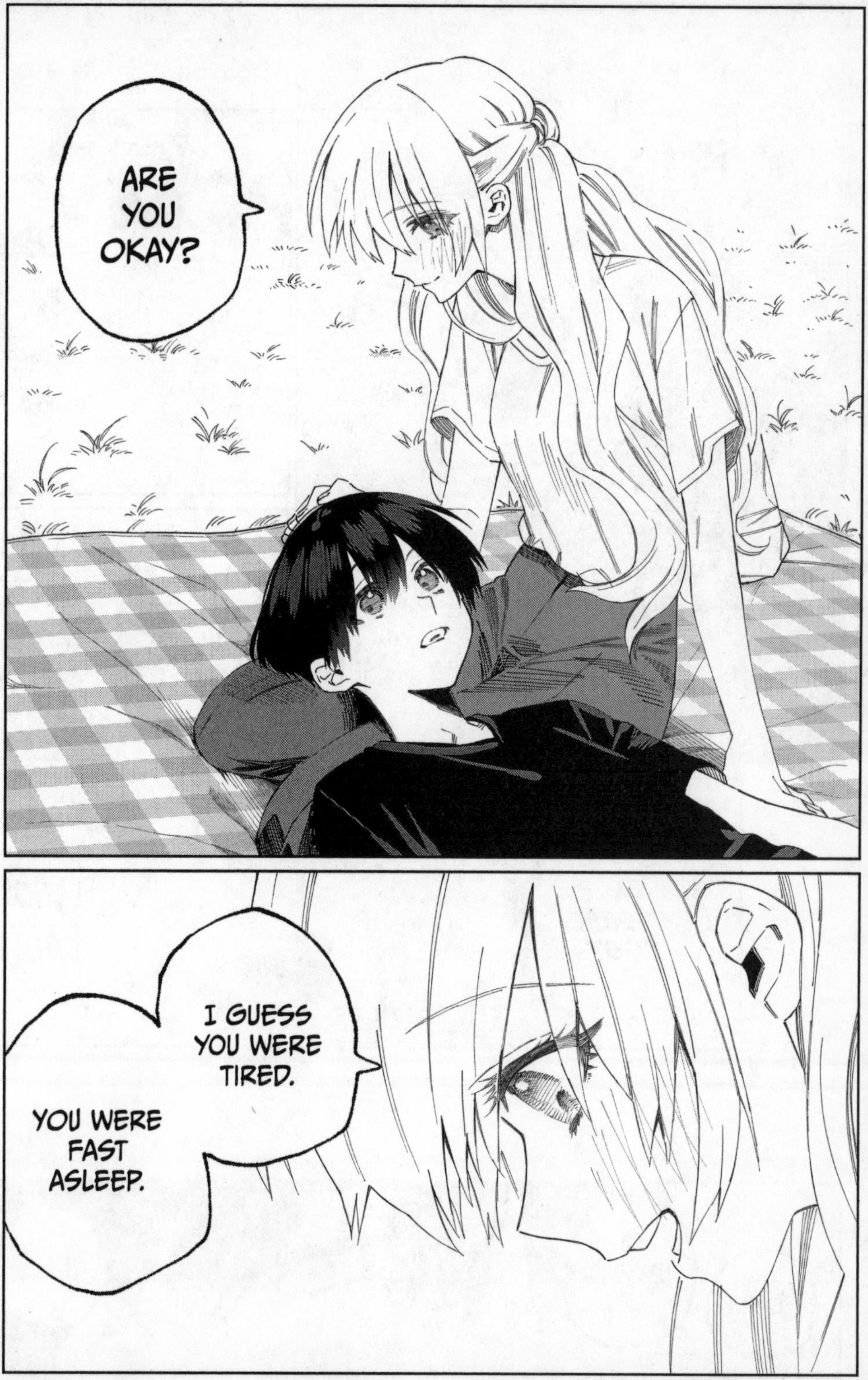
ARE YOU OKAY?
I GUESS YOU WERE TIRED.
YOU WERE FAST ASLEEP.

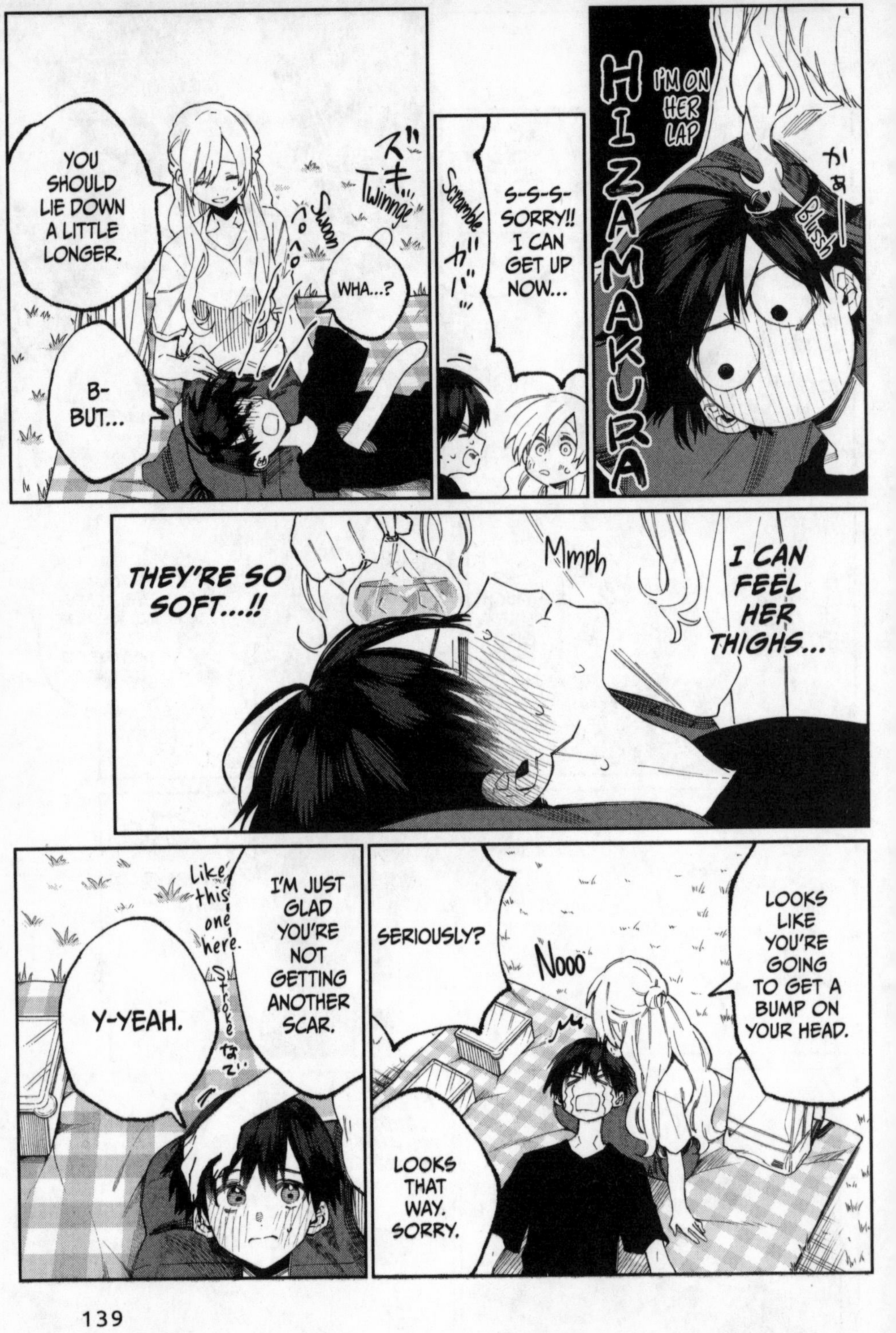

I'M ON HER LAP
HIZAMAKURA
かぁー
Blush
S-S-S-SORRY!! I CAN GET UP NOW...
Scramble
ガバ
ズキ
Twinnge
Swoon
WHA...?
YOU SHOULD LIE DOWN A LITTLE LONGER.
B-BUT...
I CAN FEEL HER THIGHS...
Mmph
THEY'RE SO SOFT...!!
LOOKS LIKE YOU'RE GOING TO GET A BUMP ON YOUR HEAD.
SERIOUSLY?
Nooo
LOOKS THAT WAY. SORRY.
I'M JUST GLAD YOU'RE NOT GETTING ANOTHER SCAR.
Like this one here.
Stroke
なで
Y-YEAH.

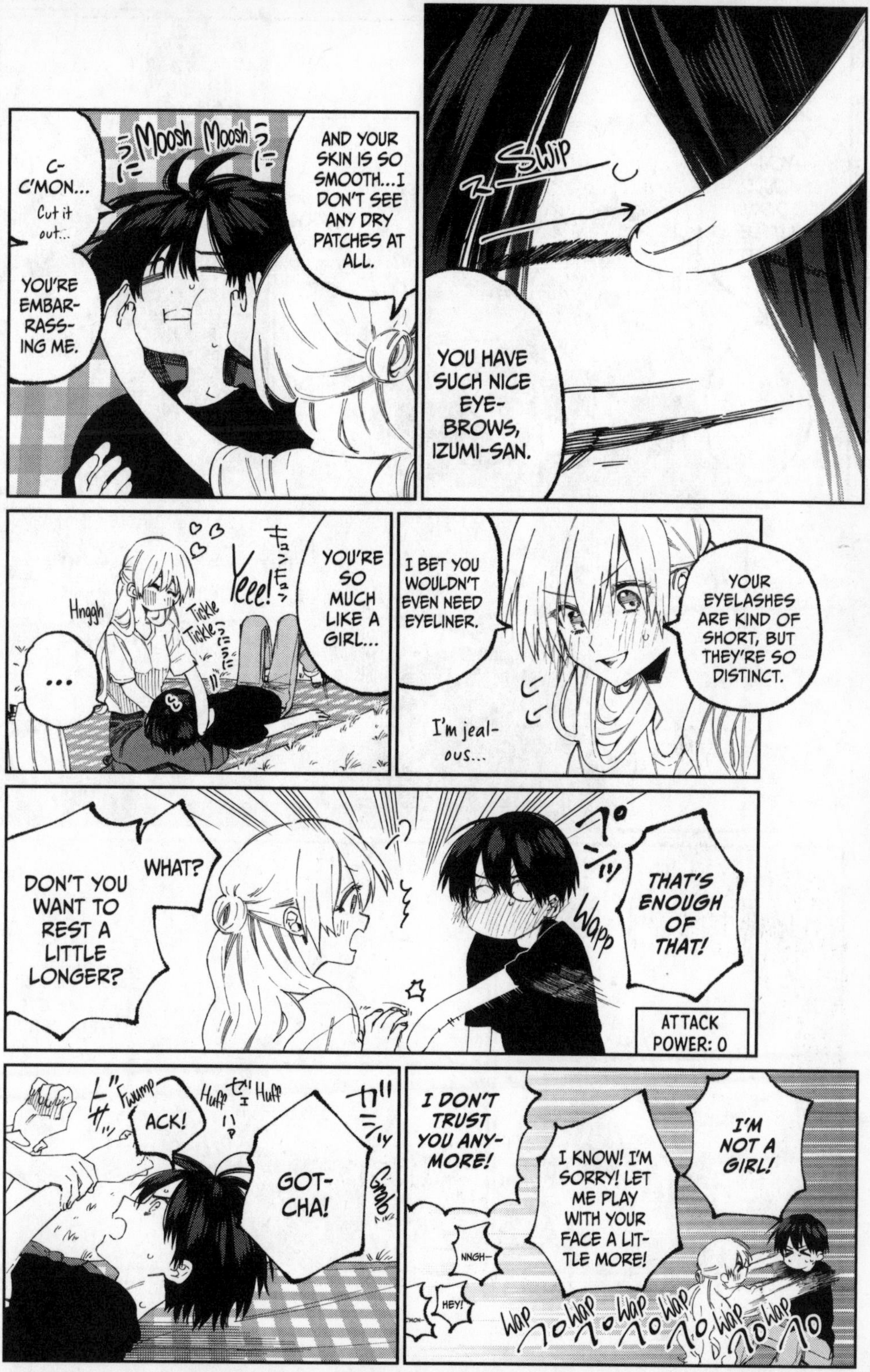
Swip
YOU HAVE SUCH NICE EYE-BROWS, IZUMI-SAN.
AND YOUR SKIN IS SO SMOOTH...I DON'T SEE ANY DRY PATCHES AT ALL.
Moosh Moosh
C-C'MON...
Cut it out...
YOU'RE EMBAR-RASS-ING ME.
YOUR EYELASHES ARE KIND OF SHORT, BUT THEY'RE SO DISTINCT.
I BET YOU WOULDN'T EVEN NEED EYELINER.
I'm jeal-ous...
YOU'RE SO MUCH LIKE A GIRL...
Yeee!
Tickle Tickle
Hnggh
...
THAT'S ENOUGH OF THAT!
Wapp
ATTACK POWER: 0
WHAT?
DON'T YOU WANT TO REST A LITTLE LONGER?
I'M NOT A GIRL!
I KNOW! I'M SORRY! LET ME PLAY WITH YOUR FACE A LIT-TLE MORE!
I DON'T TRUST YOU ANY-MORE!
NNGH—
HEY!
Wap Wap Wap Wap Wap Wap
GOT-CHA!
Huff Huff
ACK!
Fwump

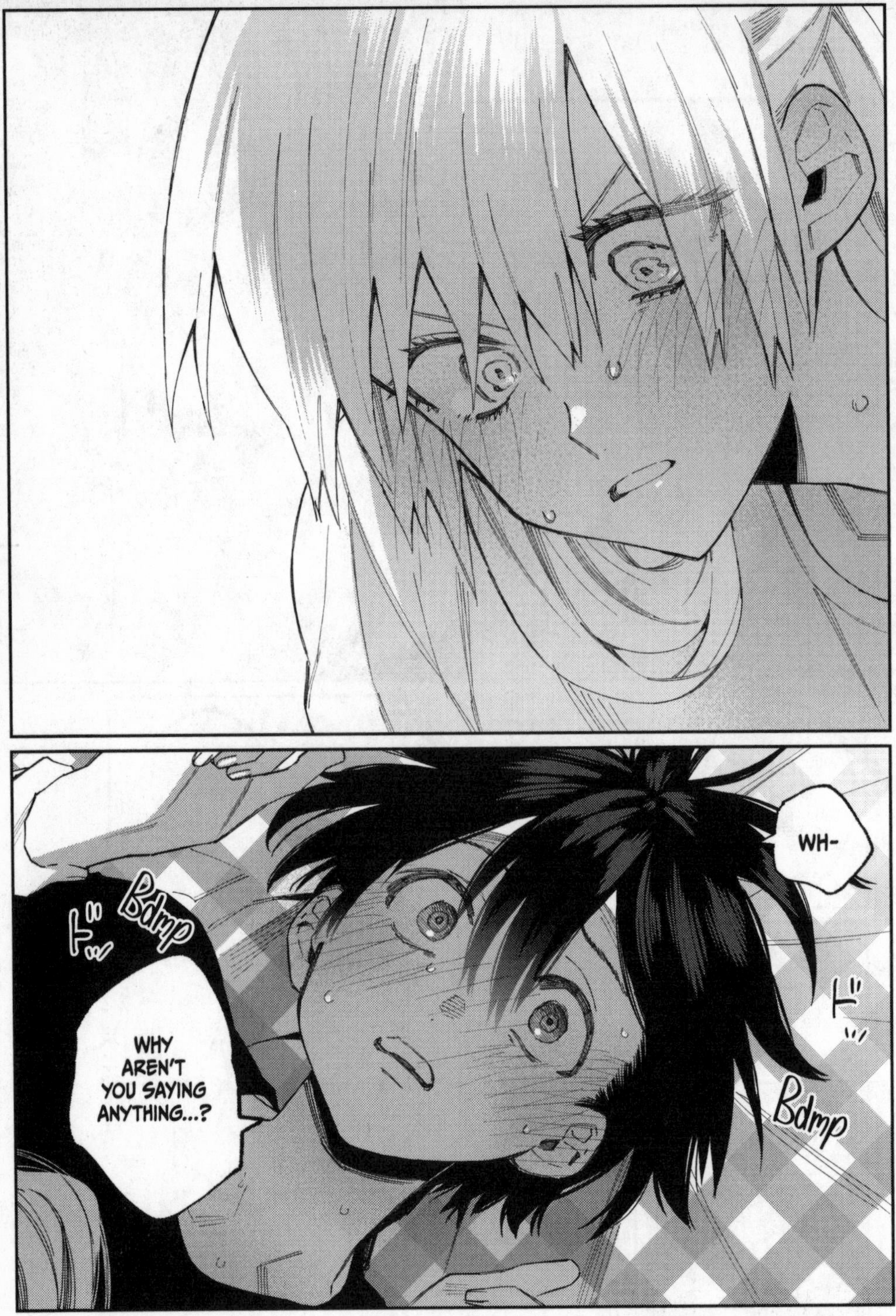
WH-
ドッ
Bdmp
ドッ
Bdmp
WHY AREN'T YOU SAYING ANYTHING...?

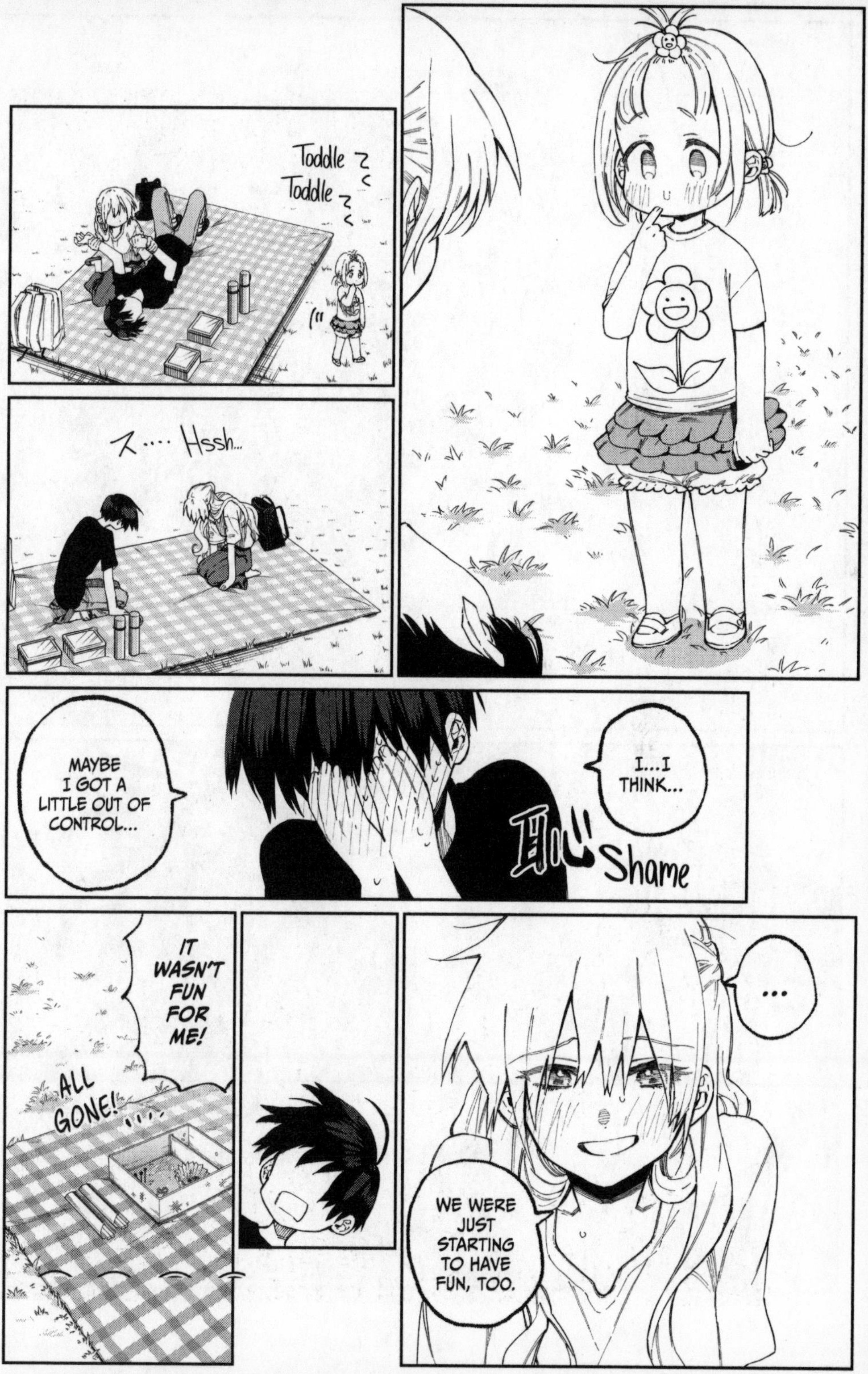
Toddle てく
Toddle てく
ス.... Hssh...
I...I THINK...
恥 Shame
MAYBE I GOT A LITTLE OUT OF CONTROL...
...
WE WERE JUST STARTING TO HAVE FUN, TOO.
IT WASN'T FUN FOR ME!
ALL GONE!

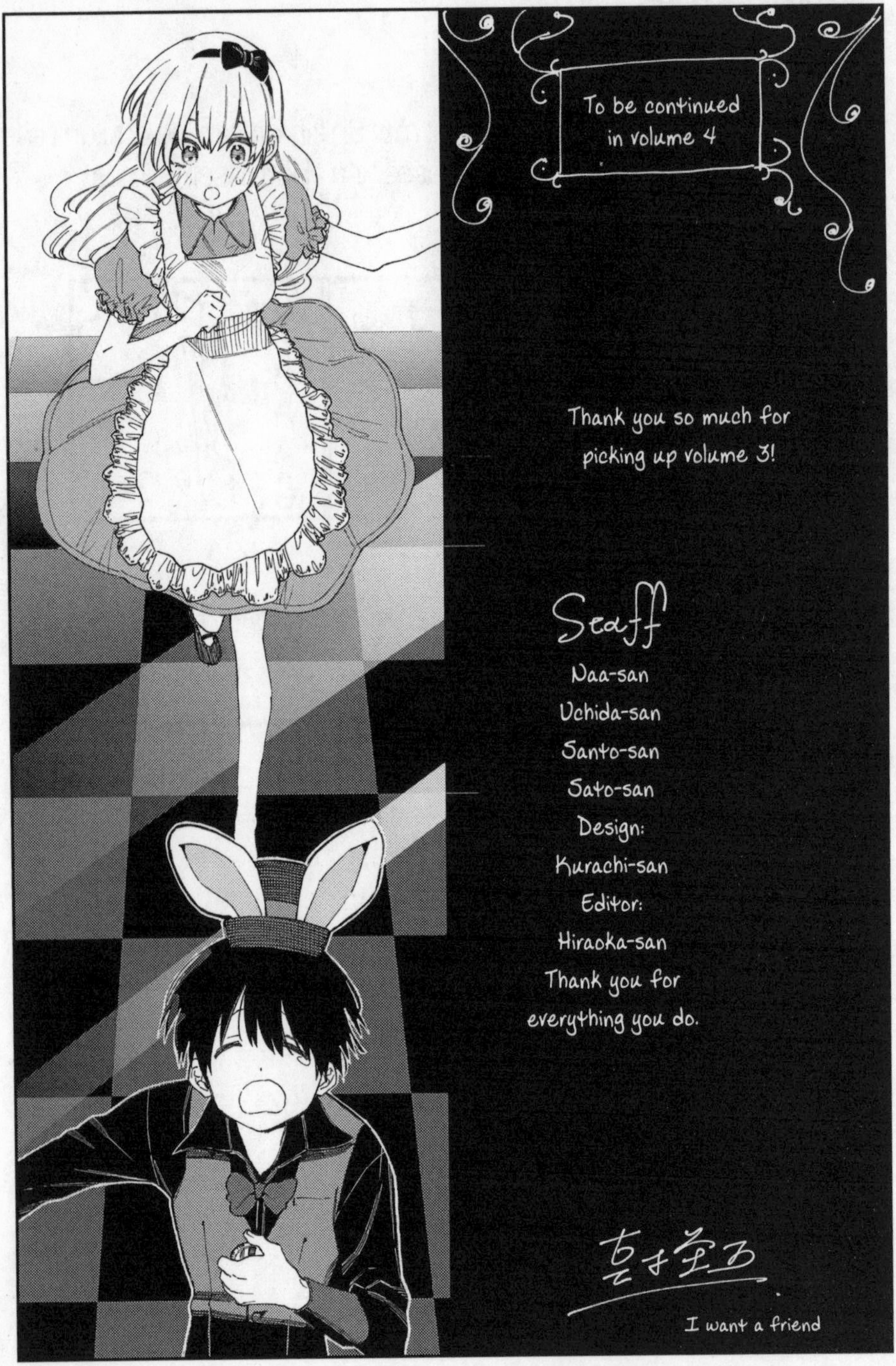
To be continued in volume 4
Thank you so much for picking up volume 3!
Staff
Naa-san
Uchida-san
Santo-san
Sato-san
Design:
Kurachi-san
Editor:
Hiraoka-san
Thank you for everything you do.
I want a friend

TRANSLATOR'S NOTES

Ijumi, page 18

Izumi was so nervous when he first met Shikimori-san, he couldn't even say his own name right. She still teases him about it sometimes. (See volume 1, chapter 14.)

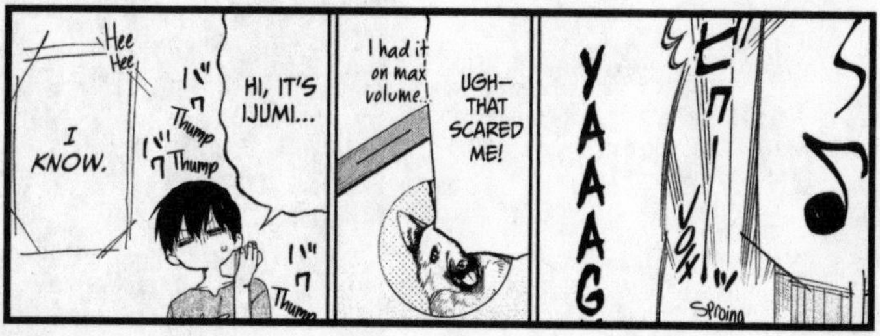
YAAAG
Sproing
UGH— THAT SCARED ME!
I had it on max volume..!
HI, IT'S IJUMI...
Thump
Thump
Thump
Hee Hee
I KNOW.

"Hey, Neko," page 49

The first part of Nekozaki's name (*neko*) means "cat." Thus the cat ears she winds up with so often!

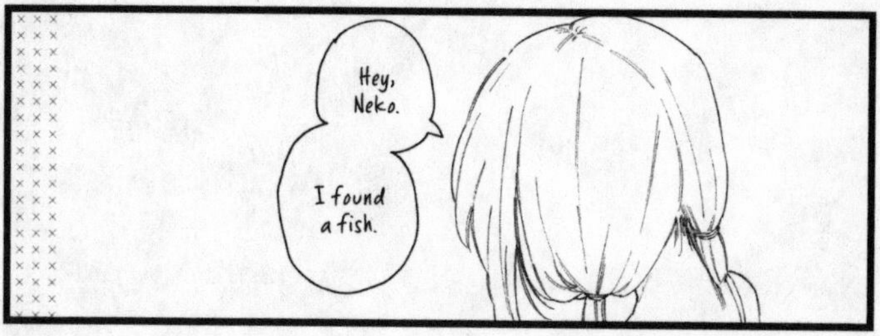
Hey, Neko.
I found a fish.

TRANSLATOR'S NOTES

"I told you to say my whole name," page 52

Inuzuka is a little touchy about his name because "inu" on its own means "dog."

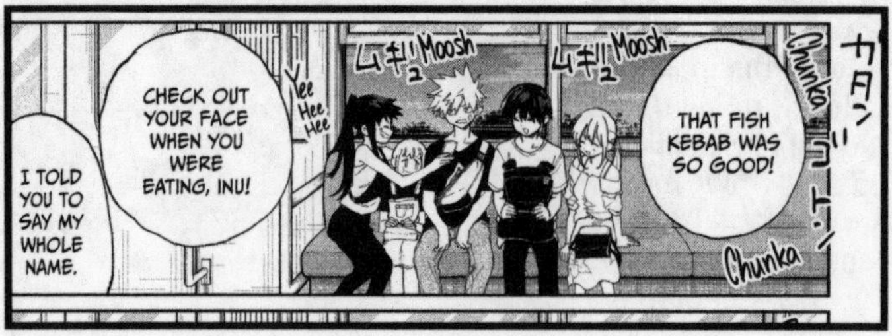
カタン
Chunka
THAT FISH KEBAB WAS SO GOOD!
Chunka
ムギュ Moosh
ムギュ Moosh
Yee Hee Hee
CHECK OUT YOUR FACE WHEN YOU WERE EATING, INU!
I TOLD YOU TO SAY MY WHOLE NAME.

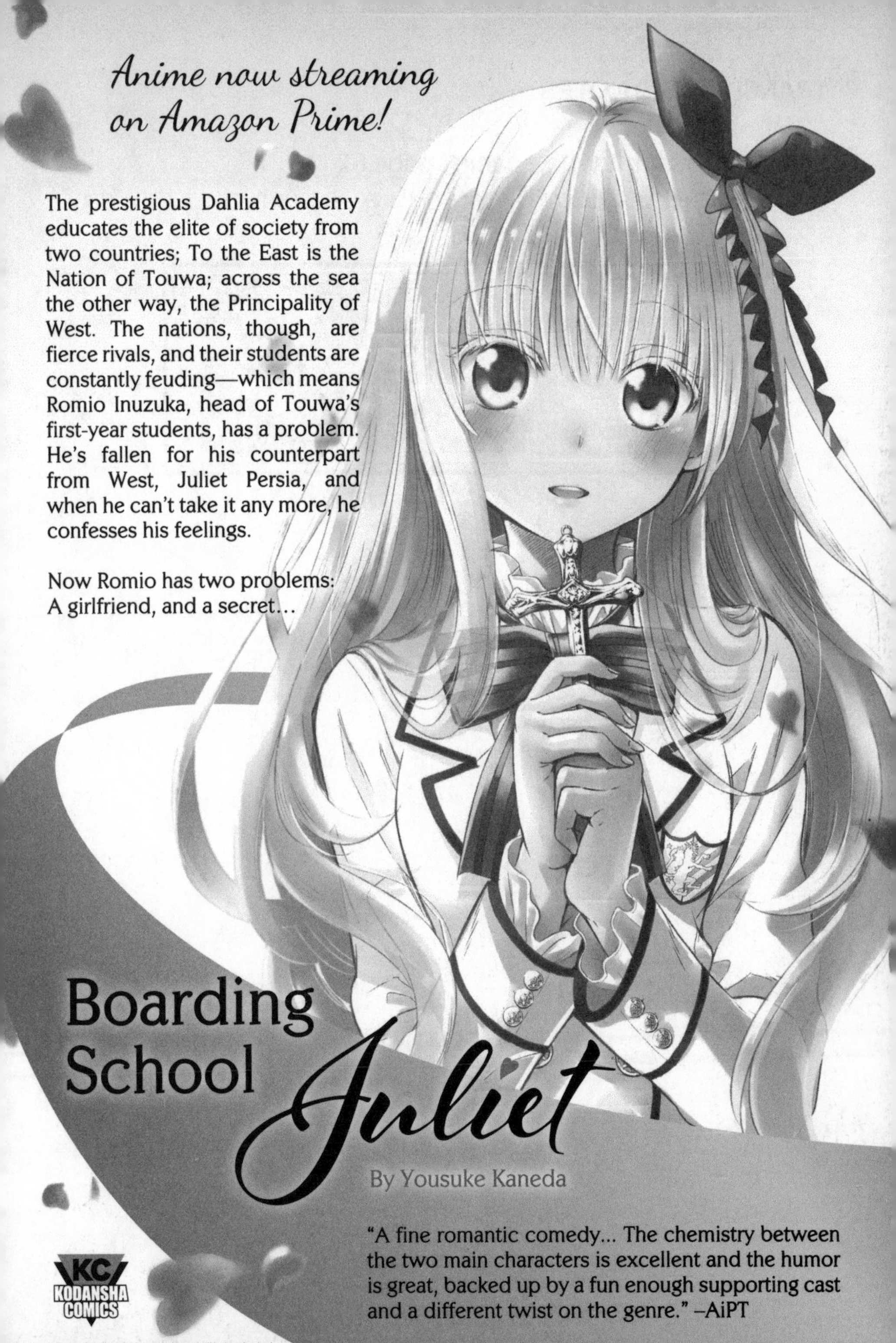
Anime now streaming on Amazon Prime!
The prestigious Dahlia Academy educates the elite of society from two countries; To the East is the Nation of Touwa; across the sea the other way, the Principality of West. The nations, though, are fierce rivals, and their students are constantly feuding—which means Romio Inuzuka, head of Touwa's first-year students, has a problem. He's fallen for his counterpart from West, Juliet Persia, and when he can't take it any more, he confesses his feelings.
Now Romio has two problems: A girlfriend, and a secret…
Boarding School Juliet
By Yousuke Kaneda
"A fine romantic comedy... The chemistry between the two main characters is excellent and the humor is great, backed up by a fun enough supporting cast and a different twist on the genre." –AiPT
KC KODANSHA COMICS

Magus of the Library

Mitsu Izumi

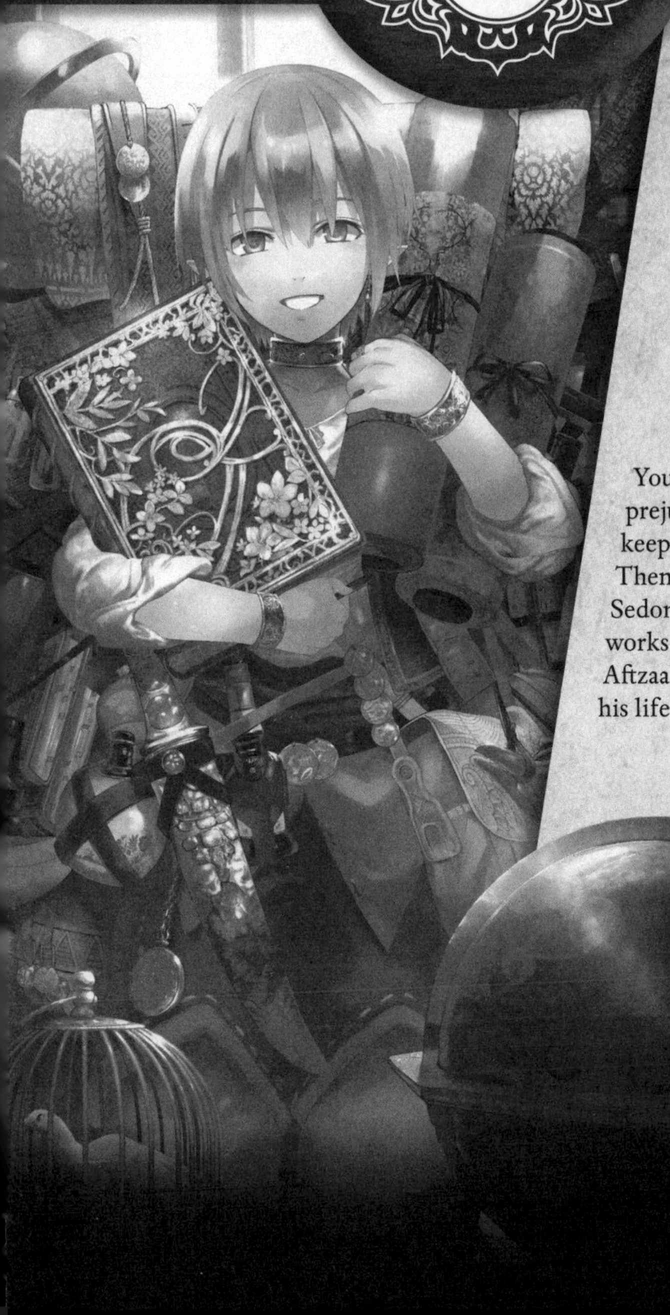

MITSU IZUMI'S STUNNING ARTWORK BRINGS A FANTASTICAL LITERARY ADVENTURE TO LUSH, THRILLING LIFE!

Young Theo adores books, but the prejudice and hatred of his village keeps them ever out of his reach. Then one day, he chances to meet Sedona, a traveling librarian who works for the great library of Aftzaak, City of Books, and his life changes forever...

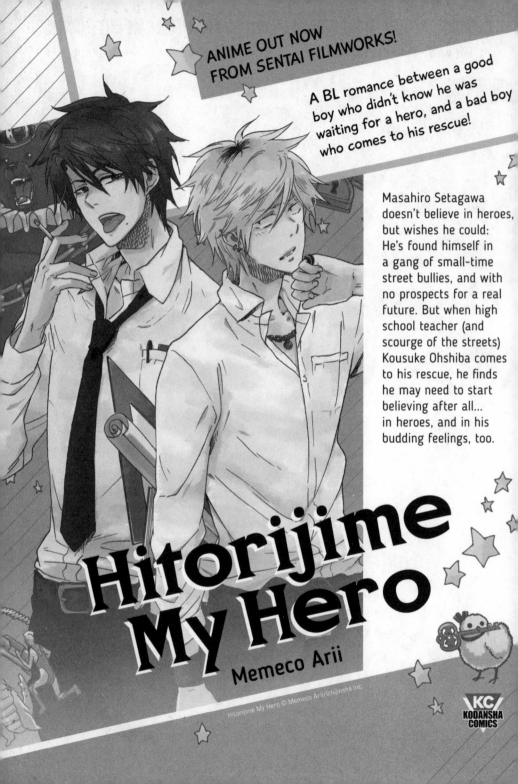

ANIME OUT NOW
FROM SENTAI FILMWORKS!

A BL romance between a good boy who didn't know he was waiting for a hero, and a bad boy who comes to his rescue!

Masahiro Setagawa doesn't believe in heroes, but wishes he could: He's found himself in a gang of small-time street bullies, and with no prospects for a real future. But when high school teacher (and scourge of the streets) Kousuke Ohshiba comes to his rescue, he finds he may need to start believing after all... in heroes, and in his budding feelings, too.

Hitorijime My Hero

Memeco Arii

KC KODANSHA COMICS

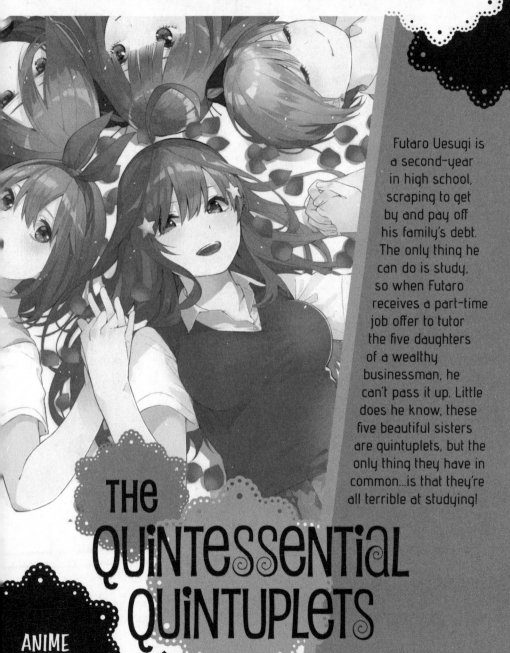

THE HIGH SCHOOL HAREM COMEDY WITH FIVE TIMES THE CUTE GIRLS!

"An entertaining romantic-comedy with a snarky edge to it." —Taykobon

Futaro Uesugi is a second-year in high school, scraping to get by and pay off his family's debt. The only thing he can do is study, so when Futaro receives a part-time job offer to tutor the five daughters of a wealthy businessman, he can't pass it up. Little does he know, these five beautiful sisters are quintuplets, but the only thing they have in common...is that they're all terrible at studying!

THE QUINTESSENTIAL QUINTUPLETS

negi haruba

ANIME OUT NOW!

KC
KODANSHA
COMICS

Yuri Is My Job!

miman

JOIN US FOR AFTERNOON TEA WITH EQUAL PARTS YURI, ROM-COM, AND DRAMA!

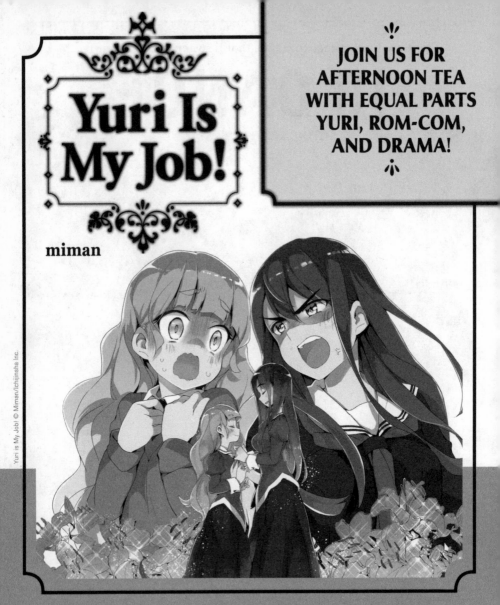

Hime is a picture-perfect high school princess, so when she accidentally injures a café manager named Mai, she's willing to cover some shifts to keep her façade intact. To Hime's surprise, the café is themed after a private school where the all-female staff always puts on their best act for their loyal customers. However, under the guidance of the most graceful girl there, Hime can't help but blush and blunder! Beneath all the frills and laughter, Hime feels tension brewing as she finds out more about her new job and her budding feelings...

KC KODANSHA COMICS

"A quirky, fun comedy series... If you're a yuri fan, or perhaps interested in getting into it but not sure where to start, this book is worth picking up."
— Anime UK News

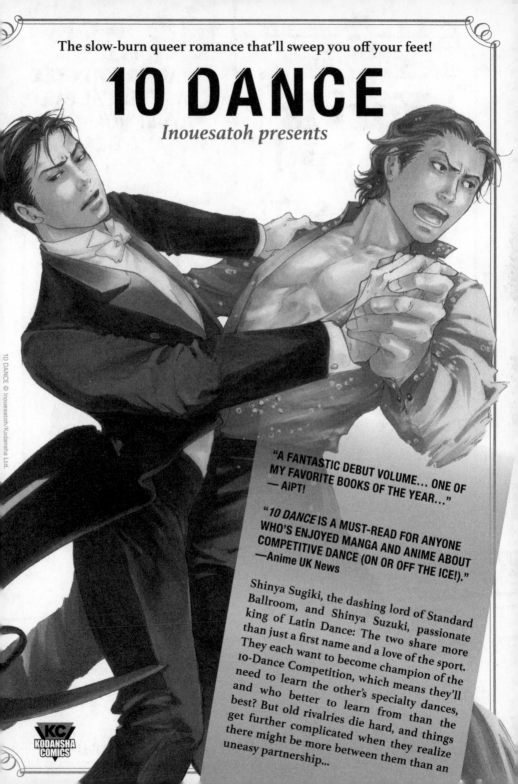

SAINT ☆ YOUNG MEN

A LONG AWAITED ARRIVAL IN PREMIUM 2-IN-1 HARDCOVER

After centuries of hard work, Jesus and Buddha take a break from their heavenly duties to relax among the people of Japan, and their adventures in this lighthearted buddy comedy are sure to bring mirth and merriment to all!

KC KODANSHA COMICS

"Brilliant…the physical comedy and facial expressions will make you literally LOL."
—Sam Humphries
(host of *DC Daily*;
writer, *Green Lanterns*,
Legendary Star-Lord)

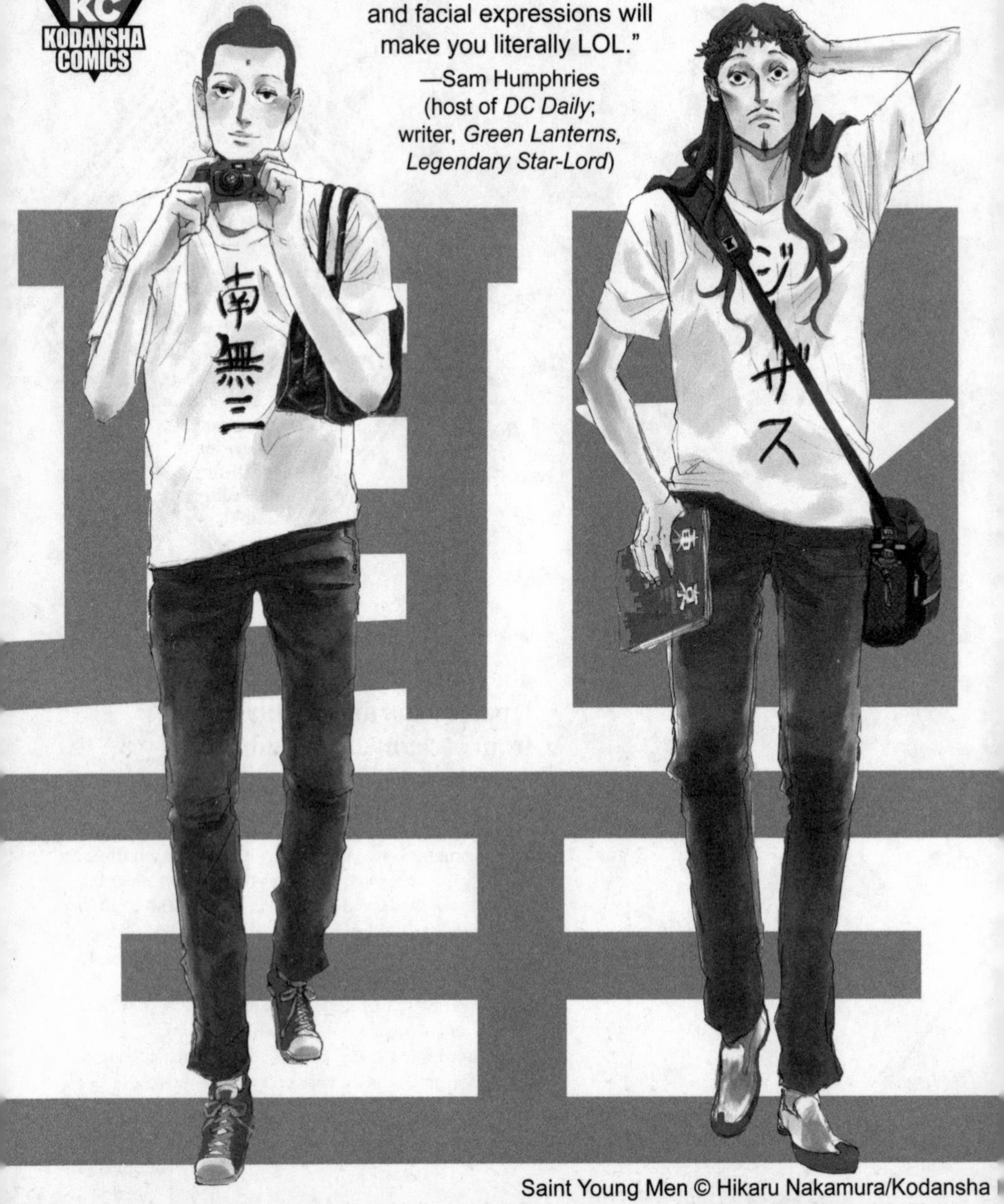
南無三

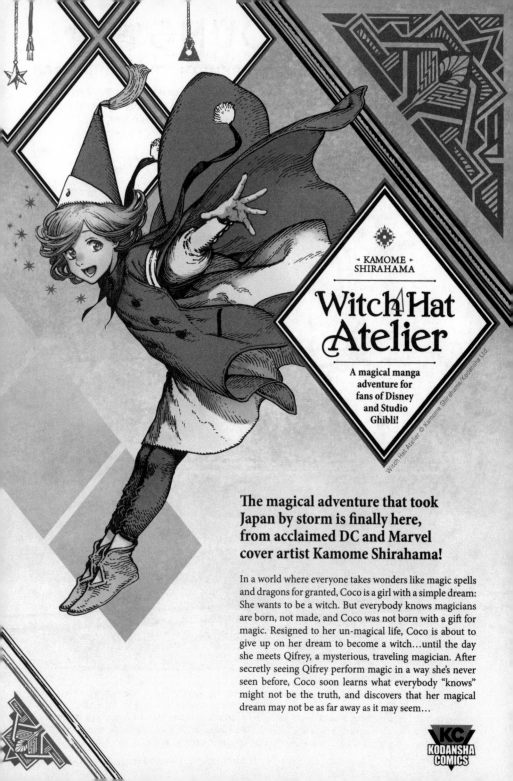

THE WORLD OF CLAMP!

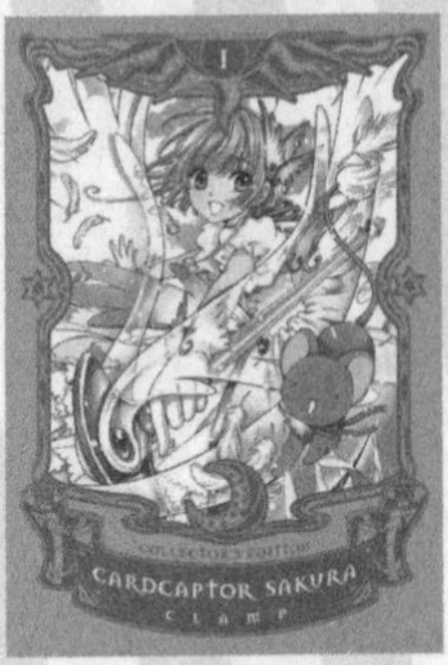
CARDCAPTOR SAKURA
CLAMP
Cardcaptor Sakura
Collector's Edition

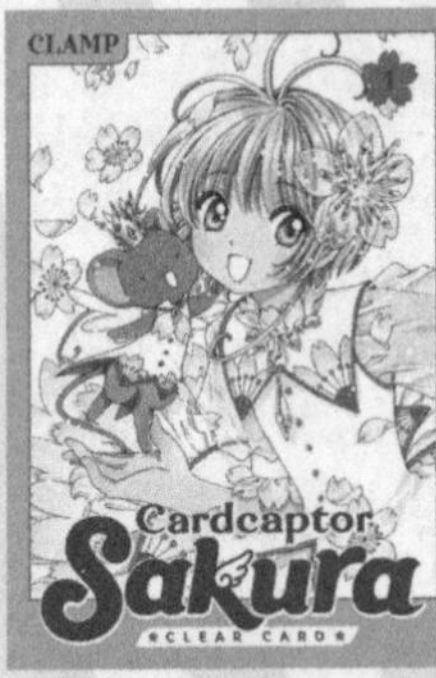
CLAMP
Cardcaptor
Sakura
CLEAR CARD
Cardcaptor Sakura:
Clear Card

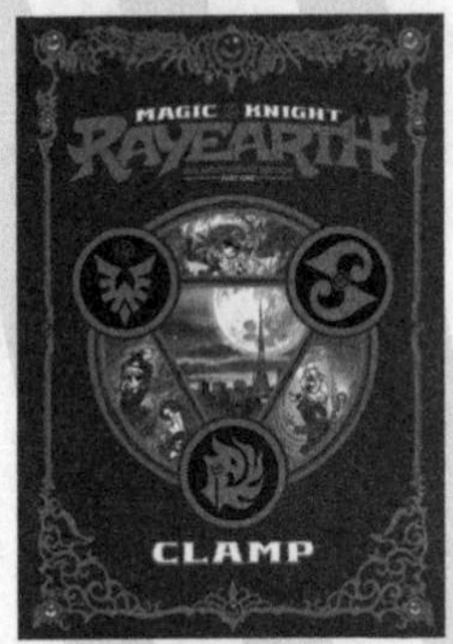
MAGIC KNIGHT
RAYEARTH
CLAMP
Magic Knight Rayearth
25th Anniversary Box Set

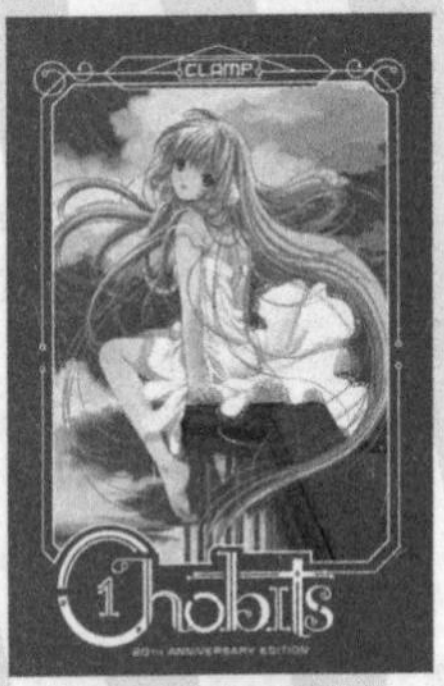
CLAMP
Chobits
Chobits

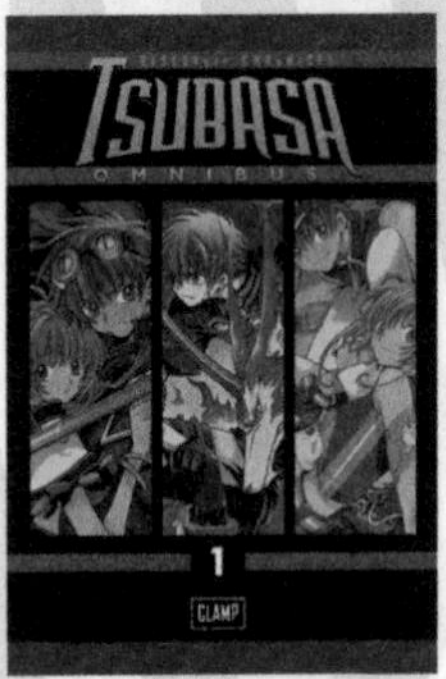
TSUBASA
OMNIBUS
1
CLAMP
TSUBASA Omnibus

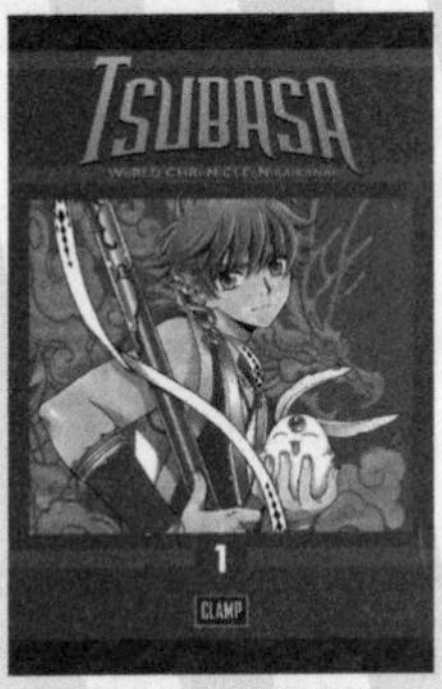
TSUBASA
1
CLAMP
TSUBASA WoRLD CHRoNiCLE

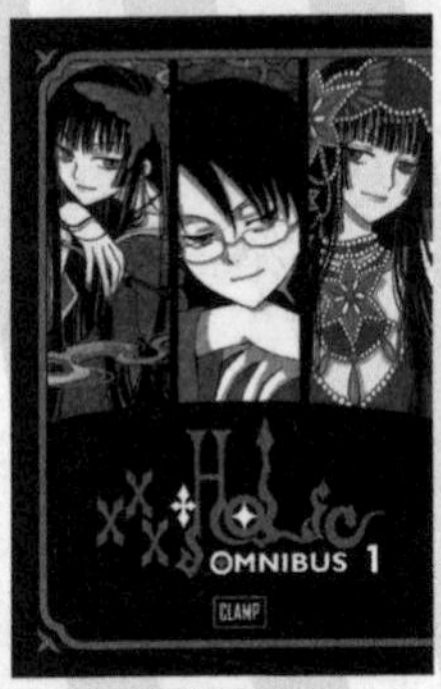
xxxHOLiC
OMNIBUS 1
CLAMP
xxxHOLiC Omnibus

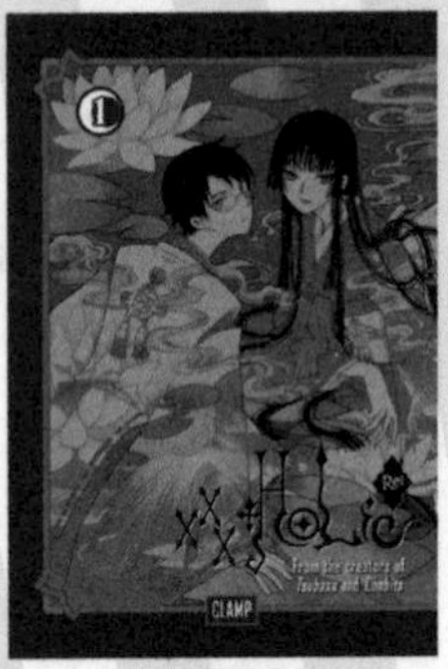
xxxHOLiC
CLAMP
xxxHOLiC Rei

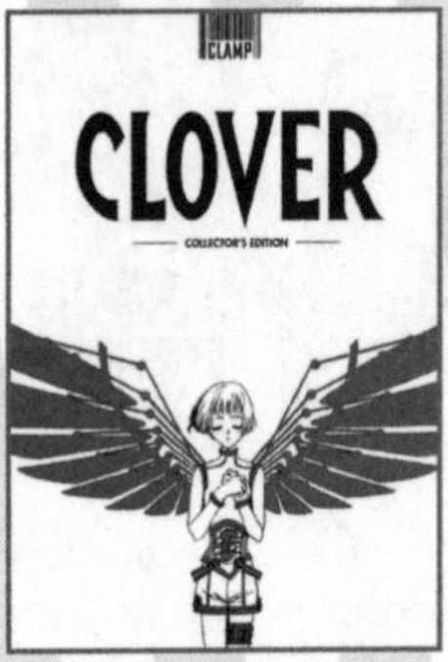
CLAMP
CLOVER
COLLECTOR'S EDITION
CLOVER Collector's Edition

KC KODANSHA COMICS

Kodansha Comics welcomes you to explore the expansive world of CLAMP, the all-female artist collective that has produced some of the most acclaimed manga of the century. Our growing catalog includes icons like *Cardcaptor Sakura* and *Magic Knight Rayearth*, each crafted with CLAMP's one-of-a-kind style and characters!

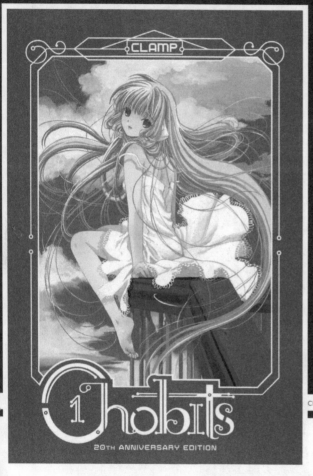

Chobits © CLAMP·ShigatsuTsuitachi CO.,LTD./Kodansha Ltd.

Poor college student Hideki is down on his luck. All he wants is a
good job, a girlfriend, and his very own "persocom"—the latest
and greatest in humanoid computer technology. Hideki's luck
changes one night when he finds Chi—a persocom thrown out in
a pile of trash. But Hideki soon discovers that there's much more
to his cute new persocom than meets the eye.

CARDCAPTOR SAKURA
COLLECTOR'S EDITION
C L A M P

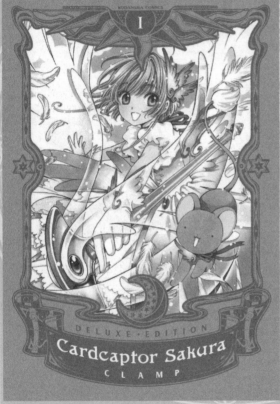

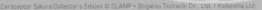

Cardcaptor Sakura Collector's Edition © CLAMP • Shigatsu Tsuitachi Co., Ltd. / Kodansha Ltd.

Ten-year-old Sakura Kinomoto lives a pretty normal life with her older brother, Tōya, and widowed father, Fujitaka—until the day she discovers a strange book in her father's library, and her life takes a magical turn...

- A deluxe large-format hardcover edition of CLAMP's shojo manga classic
- All-new foil-stamped cover art on each volume
- Comes with exclusive collectible art card

KC
KODANSHA
COMICS

The art-deco cyberpunk classic from the creators of *xxxHOLiC* and *Cardcaptor Sakura*!

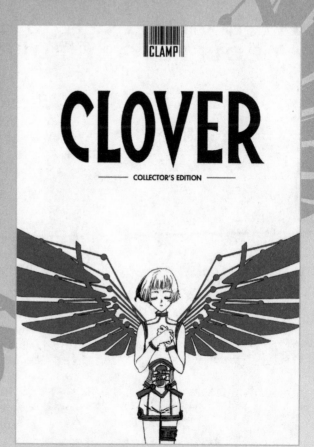

CLOVER © CLAMP ShigatsuTsuitachi CO.,LTD./Kodansha Ltd.

Su was born into a bleak future, where the government keeps tight control over children with magical powers—codenamed "Clovers." With Su being the only "four-leaf" Clover in the world, she has been kept isolated nearly her whole life. Can ex-military agent Kazuhiko deliver her to the happiness she seeks? Experience the complete series in this hardcover edition, which also includes over twenty pages of ravishing color art!

KC KODANSHA COMICS